BEGINNING EARLY, STARTING LATE

(An Autobiography)

UNITY GRANTHAM

Copyright © 2007 Rosa Grantham-Gener
All rights reserved.

ISBN 978-1-84799-393-9
ID 1210239
Printed in Spain

Contents and Dates

Chapter 1	- Beginnings (1903-1914)	1
Chapter 2	- West Keal Hall (1915-1920)	4
Chapter 3	- The Sugar Farm (1920)	15
Chapter 4	- The Governesses (1921-1925)	19
Chapter 5	- A Very Different Scene (1925)	24
Chapter 6	- A Waste of Time (1925-1930)	27
Chapter 7	- Last Days at Keal (1930)	30
Chapter 8	- Back in Africa (1930-1933)	32
Chapter 9	- Dance and Work (1933-1935)	38
Chapter 10	- Paris (1935)	43
Chapter 11	- Amsterdam (1936)	49
Chapter 12	- Hitler's First Move (1936)	52
Chapter 13	- Kissing the Blarney Stone (1936)	54
Chapter 14	- Ballet Russe de Monte Carlo (1936)	57
Chapter 15	- Monte Carlo (1937-1939)	63
Chapter 16	- The Tour and After (1939)	68
Chapter 17	- London and Milan (1938-1939)	72
Chapter 18	- War (1939-1942)	77
Chapter 19	- Back on the Boards Again (1942)	86
Chapter 20	- West Africa (1943)	90
Chapter 21	- Enugu (1943)	100
Chapter 22	- Again in Hospital and East Africa (1943)	104
Chapter 23	- Two Weeks on the Nile (1943)	108
Chapter 24	- Khartoum (1943)	113
Chapter 25	- Working Again in Europe (1944-1945)	116
Chapter 26	- Post-War Germany (1945)	120
Chapter 27	- India (1946)	125
Chapter 28	- Odd Jobs (1947-1948)	130
Chapter 29	- The Last Tour (1949)	135
Chapter 30	- The Little House in Durban (1949)	142
Chapter 31	- Taxi Driver (1950)	146
Chapter 32	- Problems (1950-1952)	151
Chapter 33	- Spain at Last (1952)	154
Chapter 34	- The Middle East (1952-1953)	162
Chapter 35	- Easter Week and the April Fair (1953)	166
Chapter 36	- El Rubio and Bullfighting (1954)	172
Chapter 37	- Disastrous Return (1954-1955)	178
Chapter 38	- Torremolinos (1955)	182
Chapter 39	- An End and a Beginning (1956)	188
Epilogue		191
A Last Comment		195

To the young –

May they pursue what they want in life.

Chapter 1

BEGINNINGS

Miles of green sugar-cane, whispering in the breeze - A bungalow with a tin roof - Verandas encased in mosquito-netting - The smell of cattle and the sickly sweet aroma of the sugar mill.
At night, came the distant sound of drumming and singing, and the smell of wood fires from the round Zulu huts across the valley. People were celebrating with a roasted ox, the birth of a white baby girl.
The whine of mosquitoes, the bark of a jackal, the silent passing of a house snake:
Such was the background of my birth.

My father - an army officer - had been sent to South Africa to fight in the Boer War. He fell in love with the country and returned at the turn of the century; hoping I think, to make a fortune and one day go back to England and save the family estate in Lincolnshire. He did not make a fortune (he didn't have time) but he founded a family in South Africa which is now in its fifth generation.
At first, he tried his luck prospecting for gold and other adventurous activities on the Rand with no success.
My mother sailed from England to join him and they were married in Durban on the twentieth of May, 1903.
My brother Jim and sister Barbara were born in Heidelberg in the Transvaal, where for a time my parents ran a hotel – this was never to be mentioned to the family at home, not being considered a suitable occupation for a gentleman. During this time both my parents nearly died of typhoid fever. My mother told me how the doctor sat on her bed and repeated over and over again: "Don't die Mrs. Grantham, don't allow yourself to die, think of your children and your husband, don't die Mrs. Grantham…….." She said that she only wanted to let herself drift away, but his voice kept penetrating her semi-conscious state, and she made the effort, and lived.
In 1906 an opportunity came to acquire a farm in Zululand, so they moved down to Natal and started to grow sugar-cane.
Conditions were rough and at first, whilst my father was building the house Mother had to stay in a boarding-house in Durban with the two little children.

Many were the tales of those early days at Iniwa. There were crocodiles in the river and many snakes on the farm; deadly black mambas and pythons so big that one killed and opened up was found to have sucked down the missing baby donkey.

There were countless stinging and biting insects, pests and diseases. The climate being sub-tropical was pleasant in winter but in summer the humid heat was intolerable.

Horses and mules were the only means of transport and oxen worked the land. There was, however, a railway line to Durban. The Zulus, a fine warrior race were lazy and happy-go-lucky, used to their women doing all the hard work whilst they smoked and watched their cattle grazing. It was difficult to get them to work. Why should they?

The nearest neighbours were several miles away, shops and a doctor further. It was a far cry from the gentle English countryside where they had both been raised. They worked hard, planted trees, made a garden, even a tennis court. The cane grew, was cut and went to the mill. In spite of all the hardships they were happy. Mother told me that they were the happiest days of her life.

Mother during the Boer War, when engaged to my father who was away in Africa, volunteered to work as a nurse, and she was put in the children's ward at Barts (St Bartholomew's) Hospital in London. Coming from the country, she was shocked by the poverty and sickness in the city slums, and much moved by the little children, many dying from tuberculosis. During this time she picked up some medical knowledge, little as it was; this came in useful during the early days on the farm. Every morning people came and waited patiently on the back veranda. Mothers came with babies, people with horrible veldt sores, malaria, snake bites, toes gnawed off by rats. She did what she could to help with the few medicines available. There was opposition and some resentment from the Witch doctors, whose traditional cures sometimes worked, more often not. Some of these medicine men were evil charlatans, working with sinister potions, spells and curses on the superstitions and fears of the simple people. Mother sometimes took a seriously ill person to the European doctor at Empangeni.

Years later on subsequent visits to the farm, people came from miles away bringing gifts - usually scraggy chickens, in gratitude; they did not forget. Another kind of gift became quite an embarrassment. A present of a small boy could hardly be refused without insulting the parents. There became quite a gang of these boys - usually aged about ten. The donors of these gifts were being most practical: The children wouldn't be far from the family kraal; they would remain in contact with their people while being well housed and fed, and at the same time receive an early training. It was an excellent arrangement. The girls were never presented, being worth a varying number of cattle for which they were traded when married.

It seemed that there was only trust and friendship in those days between the white farmers and the indigenous people. Certainly on our farm there was mutual respect and no fear.

Here, in this simple rustic house on the sugar farm Iniwa I made my first appearance on the second of June, 1913. Yes, a Gemini! I was something of an after-thought; nine and seven years separated me from my brother and sister.

I was not a good baby; I cried and protested all the time- poor Mother. The doctor had a crazy idea that I needed the colour red to calm me down, so my cradle was draped in red cloth and not surprisingly, I cried all the more.

Why the strange name? No one had ever heard of a girl called Unity. My mother said she just like the meaning of the word:"If everyone was united, there would be no more wars." I must admit I have never suffered from having a name that sounds like a Communist slogan; in fact I rather like having such an unusual name- although at times I called myself by other names.

My mother used to tell me how my father took me on his shoulders every evening to look at the oxen. "Surely you remember how you loved the cows," she would say. Sadly I remember nothing of those days. I was only two when we left.

They told me that one day a pure white heifer was born and presented to me by the herd boy. When in 1920 we returned to Zululand I owned half the herd.

I have always been lucky in the choice of procreating animals. I once had a hen called Speckley who laid two pure white eggs every day. And what about all those rabbits? And the cat that had a hundred and fifty kittens, perhaps that was not exactly lucky!

The happy life on the farm was not to last. The year after I was born the First World War broke out: My father, although over forty and under no obligation to join up, felt compelled to rejoin his regiment.

A manager was found for the farm and we sailed for England. It was my first of many such voyages between the two countries.

My father, Captain Edward Mason Grantham, was killed on the twenty seventh of February, 1915 on the western front in France, leaving his shattered widow and three small children.

Chapter 2

WEST KEAL HALL

West Keal Hall was a big, beautiful Georgian house. It was the ancestral home of the Granthams. Originally it had been a large estate, but most of it had been sold off and there remained, with the house, a forty acre park and some acres of gardens, orchards, outbuildings and stables.

My Grantham grandparents were both dead by the time we came to live at Keal, and so was the eldest son Valentine, who had died whilst serving in the Indian Army.

There were some strange characters on both sides of my family. There were crazy ones, religious ones, suicides, homosexuals, adventurers, frustrated old maids and not so closely related, a judge and an admiral.

The Granthams were an old Lincolnshire family, supposedly descended from the Vikings. They were typical landed gentry of that time, already a disappearing breed, with no idea how to survive in a changing world. Their interests were farming, horses, dogs, shooting, fox hunting and the army.

My mother's family the Sales were more cultured and studious, their education classic and artistic. The girls all played a musical instrument or sang. They were a Gloucestershire family, but at the time my parents met they were living at Halton Vicarage in Lincolnshire.

My Sale grandfather; I was told, was a dreadful 'hellfire' preaching clergyman. His wife was worn out with child bearing – nine children survived. They were all terrified of their father and hardly knew their mother, being always in the nursery or at boarding school, but they managed to have quite a lot of fun amongst themselves. Mother was one of the middle ones.

Of my uncles, Mother's brothers, two were in the church – one an Arch Deacon, the other a simple village priest, one a doctor, one a sheep farmer in Australia. Several were in the Territorial Army during the First World War.

The one I found the most interesting although I never knew him was the youngest, Uncle Charles. He was a rebel who couldn't get on with his father. He also went to Australia, where his farm was destroyed by a fire started by a spark from the railway. He escaped by standing in the river holding a group of horses, whilst he watched the flames destroy the house, tear through the dry, brown grass and burn up all the sheep. He sued the railway company, won his case and was paid a substantial compensation. With the money he went to America, became involved in some business project in San Francisco, where he disappeared. His brothers went to look for him in vain and came to the conclusion that he had been murdered. .

We were closest to the Croome family. My mother's sister, Aunt Grace was also a widow. Her husband had died of appendicitis whilst farming in an isolated part of Canada.

Mother's eldest sister, Aunt Edie, I remember as a nervous, fidgety old lady. For years she chose to live in small hotels with a paid companion. She eventually found the courage to gas herself at the age of eighty. The family were horrified but, I thought it was a brave way to end such a futile life. Aunt Mabel was also unmarried. She had a nice house and garden but she was a sad, lonely person. She had had a fine contralto vice. When I stayed with her she would constantly advice me not to be too fussy choosing a man, and to be sure to get married so as not to be alone in old age.

As a result of the war there was a whole generation of frustrated spinster ladies, with no hope of living a normal, fulfilled life. The strict Victorian upbringing and narrow upper middle class rules meant that any sexual activity outside marriage was unheard of. This situation was strongly brought home to me when visiting the battlefields in France and seeing the thousands of war graves, with their little white head-stones. For each one there was a sad woman waiting forever for her man to come home.

Keal stood on the first rise of the Lincolnshire Wolds, with a sweeping view looking down over the fens to Boston, where on a clear day we could see Boston Stump (the cathedral tower).

The two main reception rooms with their big, bay windows and the bedrooms above looked over this view. There were about a dozen rooms upstairs: bedrooms, nursery, schoolroom, maid's rooms, box room, two bathrooms and a W.C. with a great wooden throne for a seat!

One of my first memories is of finding myself on the sofa in the drawing room in the middle of the night. The entire household was gathered there, I was most mystified. Later, I was to learn that it had been an air-raid warning. The Zeppelins were coming over, heading across The Wash, having dropped their bombs. They were evidently guided on moonlit nights by our church on the hill, as they often passed over the house. Once, a bomb did fall in a nearby field.

Another occasion I remember was driving in the pony cart, waving flags. There were bonfires on the surrounding hills. It was Armistice Day, November the eleventh, 1918. The war was over.

My nurse Betty had come with us from South Africa. She was a tough little Scottish lady, staunch and good natured. She was nothing like the stereotype English dragon nanny. I could get away with anything!

We had three maids, cook, parlour maid and house-maid - there being no man in the house as we didn't need a butler. But, there was a gardener and a handyman. There were endless chores. The parlour maid was responsible for looking after the downstairs rooms. She waited at table, answered the door, cleaned and washed the silver and glasses in the pantry. The housemaid cleaned the upstairs rooms; she had to carry jugs of water up to the bedrooms and many other chores. There were fireplaces to be cleaned, fires to be laid, lamps to be cleaned and trimmed (as we had no electricity), washing and ironing; the irons were heated on the kitchen range.

Butter was made in the churn, which was kept in the dairy; there were also vats of preserved eggs to be used for cooking. A great many eggs and much milk was given away. Here also were shelves of bottled fruit and jam. The meat safe was also in the dairy. It was cool and dim and smelt of butter-milk.

The cook would be busy in the kitchen where there was a large central table, and the big coal-burning range. Twice a week there was the marvellous smell of newly baked bread. I was always given a little roll straight out of the oven. There was a larder, pantry, store rooms, cellar, back stairs and a passage with hooks for hanging game, which led to a yard where the washing was hung to dry. No one ever stopped me from going through the baize door which led to the kitchens - I spent a lot of time there. The maids were young and spoilt me; they taught me to do a lot of things. I was particularly proud when I learnt to skin a rabbit- funny thing, as I adored rabbits.

The kitchen garden was very large and every kind of vegetable and fruit grew there. In the middle was a great solid yew hedge, as big as a house, I have never seen anything like that hedge. It was my secret hiding place: I used to crawl into it when I wanted to disappear and would lie there listening to people calling me. The hedge acted as a wind-break and sheltered an area where tomatoes grew in frames.

There was the spring garden, small, sheltered and secret, with its romantic summer-house and mossy banks where white violets grew and small birds nested.

The orchard was full of fruit trees, mostly apples, old fashioned delicious dessert apples and big green ones for cooking. The lawns were bordered by herbaceous borders, and paths with pergolas arched over them, covered with rambling roses. There was a grass tennis court and croquet lawn, a see-saw and a swing. Also a monkey puzzle, a silver birch and many other trees and shrubs.

Rhododendrons grew beside a steam in the water-garden, and there at the top was a little gate which led into the big wood – fascinating, mysterious, forbidden territory. Sometimes the bang of guns came from that direction, but more dangerous perhaps were the fierce stinging nettles which grew among the snowdrops. This was the home of foxes, badgers, rabbits, squirrels, pheasants and many other animals and birds.

There were out-buildings and stabling for several horses, although only one pony lived there then. The little brown pony pulled a pony-cart, a tub-like affair called a governess cart, in which we went about. It could safely take a couple of adults and a few children but going up hill we would get out and push to help the pony. The only other method of transport was the bicycle and we all had these when old enough to ride them. But I insisted on riding the pony from the age of about four. Had my father been alive we would have kept some horses, a couple of hunters at least, but as no one in the family was interested in riding at that time, it was left to me, the little one, to inherit the Granthams love of horses.

I loved all the animals, of which there was always a collection. Blighty the dog,- a cross between a bulldog and a bullterrier, white with a brown patch over one eye- was my constant and much loved companion. I had tame rabbits, guinea-pigs, numerous cats and other animals. There was a large netted enclosure for chickens. They had nesting boxes and were allowed to sit on their eggs and hatch our baby chicks. They ran loose in the field during the day but had to go back in their enclosure at night because of the foxes. We kept two Jersey cows for milk and a pig. I was not encouraged to become friendly with the pig as he was killed and eaten in winter.

I remember clearly the drawing-room, cosy in the evening with a bright fire, the tall standard lamps giving a warm, mellow light, watercolours on the walls, and bowls of flowers and plants. Mother, perhaps, at the piano playing Chopin.

In the dining-room there was a big mahogany table which could be made longer by adding leaves. This was laid with a white damask table cloth. Here we had breakfast and lunch all together, supper was in the nursery.

There was a great gilt mirror in the hall, several chests and oriental carpets and the grandfather clock, which struck the hour and half hours. There was also a gong which was struck to summon us at mealtimes. On the hall table there was a collection of candles and lamps ready to be taken upstairs at bedtime.

Every morning my mother sat at her big desk working over accounts, business things and plans for the future. All the responsibility of running the household and bringing up three children was hers alone. She was sad; she missed her husband horribly and was never at any time interested in another man. I think she got satisfaction from bringing us children up in the family home; it was a challenge. She refused to take her war pension pittance, as it would have helped later when we needed money, but she didn't want to benefit in any way from her husband's death.

I think it was an ideal place for a child to grow up. I don't ever remember feeling lonely, and have only happy memories of my childhood. I was mostly alone as my brother and sister were away at school. Their holidays were fun, but I never missed other children; in fact when very young I was shy and rather anti-social.

The day started at 8.30 a.m. with family prayers. This was quite a short affair, but the entire household were expected to attend. Mother read the lesson for the day from the big bible and we recited the Lord's Prayer. On Sundays we walked up the lane to the fine old Norman church for the morning service. I was usually bored with church, except that I liked to sing the hymns loudly. It was fun when my brother Jim was home. He was very naughty! The dog also sometimes caused a diversion by following us to church, which delighted us as the parson was terrified of him. He had to be hidden in the pew and was encouraged by Jim to make an appearance during the sermon. Poor Blighty, he was the most amiable and good natured animal: looks can't always tell!

I hope the church at West Keal is still there, proudly on the hill and that the clock in the church tower, presented as a memorial to my father, still strikes the hours. And that the graves of my grandparents lie undisturbed looking over the fens.

Once a week someone would take the pony cart into Spilsby - the nearest town, to buy meat, fish, groceries, oranges and bananas. These were about the only things not home-produced. Sweets were purchased too, sometimes at the village shop. I was very interested in the sweets which were only given out after lunch. I'm afraid I used to steal them. I also stole baking-powder from the kitchen cupboard; I liked the way it fizzed on the tongue.

There was no telephone at home, or in the village. When the doctor was needed someone was sent to fetch him by bicycle, then he would come in his car. Our Dr. Mann lived at Revesby several miles away. His son Fred was Jim's best friend and Fred was to me like another brother.

Every year, the first sign of life in the garden was the appearance of clumps of yellow crocus, dear little golden flowers bravely breaking through the bleak frozen ground. Then came the snowdrops massed in the wood. Soon daffodils and narcissus would be out everywhere and the birds would mate and start to build their nests. A joyous chorus of bird-song would greet us in the morning. I was always fascinated by bird's nests, and had a fine collection of eggs. I had a special cabinet for them with drawers full of compartments each one labelled with its name. I was very careful not to upset the sitting bird. Not more than one egg was ever taken, and that most carefully; only the ones I needed for my collection. I never did have an owl's egg, as they only lay one, and I couldn't take that. Neither did I have a woodpecker's, though not for lack of trying: our hands were too big to get in the holes they make in the trees. When my Croome cousins came to stay, the littlest one, Marjory, was sent up ladders to try but she would get her hands pecked. Lois was rather clumsy and used to bite the eggs that we brought down trees in our mouths; she was always spitting out bits! When I had an egg for my collection I made a little hole at each end and blew out the contents.

There were always chores to do. I fed and brushed my rabbits and cleaned out their cages. I groomed the pony and fed the chickens, collected eggs, helped in the garden among many other things. Also of course, there were lessons. At first my mother taught me, I can't recall what I learnt; I suspect like most children I was always trying to escape.

A circus came to Spilsby. It was the first time I had seen an elephant and I was completely enthralled. Then and there started a life-time affection for these noble great beasts. From that day on elephants joined the horses in the toy cupboard; I never had much use for dolls.

It was of course before the time of Freudian theories, and I am sure no-one thought it odd. But to admit that eggs and elephants were my favourite things does sound a bit erotic! Let me say before you come to any lewd conclusion, that at my advanced age I might have lost interest in sex, but never my affection for elephants and eggs.

June, my month: the comforting lazy sound of pigeons cooing in the early morning. On my birthday I would be presented with a bouquet of my favourite flowers: Delphiniums, peonies, roses, lilac and laburnum. The pagodas were a mass of climbing roses. There was the sound of the mowing machine and the smell of new-mown grass. The fruit was ripening in the kitchen garden: Strawberries, raspberries, currants - red, white and black. Golden gooseberries on their prickly bushes- Blighty the dog, liked to suck them off the lower branches, leaving the skins hanging. The strawberries in their large beds had to be netted because of the birds who liked them too. I got up early and ran down there to try to unravel the ones that were caught up in the nets, before the gardener came and wrung their necks. This was not always easy; they were often horribly tangled up. Sometimes I had to resort to using the scissors, for which I was scolded having made holes in the nets.

In the meadow when the grass was high, I'd love to lie down in it and savour the scent of cowslips, meadowsweet, and clover, and observe the busy insect life going on all around me. Soon we would be helping with the hay-making, praying that it wouldn't rain. The grass was cut and spread out to dry. Then raked up, forked up onto a cart pulled by a big shire horse, and taken to the yard to be stacked for winter feeding

Summer was a happy time, Jim and Barbara came home for the holidays. The house was full of young people. Friends came to stay, there were tennis parties. I was spoilt and had a good time. I learnt early how to get round my brother and his friends. Both he and Fred Mann both teased me mercilessly and called me Prune. They used me as the go-between with their girl friends It was not so easy with my sister Barbara. Always during the summer some of my cousins came. There were two families with children in my age group. The Croomes: Jock, Lois and Marjory and the Sales: Peggy, Robert and Ann. Both their mothers were widows, so with my mother in the same state there were hardly ever any older men in the house; for years they were a strange breed to me. We cousins all got on well and had a great time. We got up to all sorts of naughty things, teasing the older boys and girls, sewing up pyjama legs, putting prickly things and frogs in the beds. My special close friendship with Lois lasted all our lives.

The pond was our great delight. It was down in the field in front of the house. It was quite a large pond; if it had been cleaned out it would have passed as a lake, as it was, a large part of it was completely blocked with reeds and water lilies. On the part where the water was clear we had a punt, a flat-bottomed boat in which we used to go over to the island, pushing it along with a pole, which was often stuck in the mud. There was a grove of big trees on the island, which was dry and secluded. Here we children had a house. I don't remember when it was built or by whom but it was quite a solid construction. What a great time we had there, especially when the cousins came to stay. On one occasion we invited our families to tea there. All was ready, but we had forgotten the milk. I took the milk jug, poled to the bank and looked around for a cow. There was one grazing near by. A most co-operative cow, she stood quite still whilst I milked her with one hand, holding the jug underneath with the other. The people duly arrived and were ferried across. Jock Croome had made a fire and was busy frying birds eggs (his idea); he broke them into the pan chucking out the bloody addled ones. There were leaves and sticks in the tea, but the guests were very polite and ate and drank it all.

Each year in September we took a house by the sea in Skegness, in the part facing the sand-dunes near the golf course. We went by train with Blighty the dog and the cats protesting in the cardboard hat boxes. I remember insisting that we take the cats, which would probably have been better left at home. I did not trust whoever was left to feed them, I worried that they would go after rabbits and be caught in traps, which sadly often happened. Usually Aunt Grace with her children or Aunt Con with hers would join us there. Needless to say we had a good time doing the things that children always do on beaches. The sea went miles out at low tide, leaving creeks in which we played and caught shrimps. These creeks filled up quickly as the tide turned and were quite dangerous. I can't remember when I learnt to swim but it must have been there, in the murky, cold water of the North Sea. There were also nasty currents. Once Jim, who was a strong swimmer but had just had his appendix removed, was swept right out to sea. We desperately watched him going further and further away. He had the sense not to fight against the current and was eventually brought back to the beach, about a mile up the coast.

Skegness already had a fun-fair, roundabouts, freak shows and a big dipper (we called it a figure of eight), in which we flew up and down in breathless excitement. There were various entertainments on the pier including a Pierrot show - people in white pyjamas with black pom-poms dancing about and singing. There were lots of shaggy little donkeys on the beach for children to ride, and a dance hall which the older kids frequented.

Back at home again when Jim and Barbara returned to school, the days closing in, fires lit, the leaves changing colour, we picked blackberries, crab-apples and mushrooms, the big horse mushrooms which sure enough come up in old horse droppings. The young cart-horses in the fields were frisky; their great fringed hooves thundering dangerously close as they chased Blighty, who stayed prudently at my side. They were only playing and would veer away at the last minute.

I went for walks with Betty, sometimes to the village shop to post letters. A bell tinkled when you opened the door and inside there was that unique smell of 'village shop' made up of the weird selection of goods on sale. Blighty always came too but he had to be put on the lead at the bottom of the lane. On the way to the shop we passed the blacksmith's. Sparks flew from the forge in the dim interior, and horses waited patiently outside to be shod.

The village had its idiot and its' bad girl! There was much talk about her in the kitchen. What a disgrace to her family it was, when they found out that she could do very nicely by doing what she liked doing best. She went off to London and was seen no more.

About this time I was fascinated by a dirty, bearded old tramp that lived with a dog in a broken-down cottage on the other side of the village. Poor Betty was persuaded to walk past there regularly. This old man paid no attention to me, even when I tried to make friends by giving him a cure for his dog's worms - which were embarrassingly obvious. He was the most disreputable specimen in every way. I can't think what the attraction was. When I ran away, which I did from time to time - when I was scolded, I always made for this cottage but luckily I was picked up before I got there.

The gypsies also fascinated me. They camped in a green lane not far from the house with their painted caravans, skinny horses, skinnier lurching dogs and beautiful brown children. Dressed in colourful clothes, with gold ear-rings and bangles, they came to the house selling clothes-pegs. The maids were full of stories about how they stole children. Betty could never be persuaded to go near them. So one day I ran off bravely on my own to visit them. I don't know if I was hoping to be stolen but the visit was not a success. I was sent on my way by a very grumpy lady, who made it quite clear that the prim little girl in the sun-bonnet was not welcome in the gypsy camp. I was ignominiously escorted home, very hurt.

Our relationship with the village was very feudal, very old fashioned. Today it would be considered most patronising. There was a responsibility towards the village people. If someone was in trouble, there would be visits; help and advice would be offered. Garden produce, milk, eggs and butter were freely given.

On wet days or when I was kept in with a cold, I was sometimes allowed to explore the box-room. Among the cobwebs and decades of dusty debris, there were leather trunks filled with treasures: Indian army officers' uniforms, complete with turbans and swords. Long silk dresses with bustles and tiny waists. And many petticoats, lace-up corsets, flowered waist-coats and top hats; the finery of a bygone age, just perfect for dressing up.

Long before Christmas the preparations started. Christmas puddings were made and left to ripen. We each had a stir at the cake and a wish. On Christmas Eve there was a big pile of holly and Mother, wearing thick gloves, made a long rope of holly which was draped across the hall with a big bunch of mistletoe hanging in the middle. There were other decorations in the living room but no tree, for the Christmas tree was considered a barbaric, heathen custom and was not yet popular in England. But I do remember there were big lit-up trees in some of the grand houses in the district where I went to parties. Father Christmas however was not excluded, and we left stockings hanging at the bottom of the bed. I was of course up at the crack of dawn to see what was in mine.

Early on Christmas morning the school children came, singing carols. It was my job to take round a basket and give each one a packet of sweets. I was very shy and didn't much like doing this. After breakfast the great moment arrived when we could open our presents. The best present ever, the only one I can remember, was the year of the white rabbits. I was led into a back room and there, in a cage, were the two most beautiful rabbits I had ever seen. White Angora rabbits with long silky hair and pink eyes. They were uncommon at that time and I had never seen one before. I called them Trusty and White Rose. And so I became a breeder of Angora rabbits and started my first business. They were most prolific and I made pocket money brushing them and selling their fur. They were very tame and I used to let them loose on the lawn where Blighty guarded them.

Sometimes over the Christmas holidays it snowed and this was very exciting. All wrapped up in boots, scarves and woollen hats, we battled with snowballs, and made a snow-man on the drive. We tobogganed down the grass slope in front of the house on tin trays and went skating on the pond when it froze.

At the top of the lane, where it turned right to go to the church, there was a house called the Rookery, where my Grantham aunts Sage and Elsie lived. The two aunts were very different. Elsie was an unconventional character. She was a farmer famous for her herd of prize-winning Lincoln Red cattle. She always wore some sort of brown overalls, farmer's boots and an old felt hat, under which there were a few wisps of grey hair. She was fat and shapeless and her unfettered breasts hung down to her waist. It was hard to believe that she was from an old county family until she spoke. She was, in fact, very snobbish, and disapproved of her sister Polly marrying an industrialist, even if he was rich. Aunt Sage was quite the opposite. She was a neat, rather conventional little person, always tidy, with pretty grey hair. Unfortunately, she was stone deaf. She had nothing to do with the farm, but kept order in the house, which was surprisingly tidy and full of antiques. The dairy was always overflowing with sour milk. This bothered Aunt Sage and she and Elsie were forever squabbling. I loved going to see them because they were so different. Aunt Elsie often took me to the farm with her. Every morning she walked there with her two dogs, a very spoilt bull terrier that slept on her bed and a woolly Old English sheep dog which was not allowed in the house. The farm was about half a mile away through woods where the trees almost met over the road making a leafy tunnel in summer. She showed me the animals. The main attraction was the bull, I always wanted to see him; he was a beautiful great creature with wild eyes and a ring in his nose. I was constantly warned not to approach him; I was actually rather scared of him but admired him tremendously. Because I liked these things I got on well with Aunt Elsie. There was no nonsense about her; she was quite unsentimental and down-to-earth. She talked to me, the child, and all the animals as equals. She would stand with her back to the fire holding her skirt up to warm her behind. It was difficult to communicate with Aunt Sage because of her deafness. There were many jokes about "Sage and Onions" as they were called behind their backs. They were good friends who helped me when I needed help and I think of them with affection even if they did get away with all the family antiques.

The relationship between these two sisters-in-laws and my mother was always strained. They resented her for marrying their favourite young brother (the older one had died in India), and they had hoped to have him at home running the farm, instead of which he went to South Africa and married mother. Then when we did come to live at Keal he was no longer with us. Later on they transferred their affection to my brother Jim and he too would disappear to South Africa. Jim wanted to go into the army but his foot was crushed in an accident when a loaded wagon went over it. This put an end to a future career in the army and pointed him towards Africa.

The farm in Zululand was being run by a manager. Over the years there were various ones, most if not all of them did Mother down, so there was not much benefit from the farm. Her family didn't understand why she kept the farm, but she insisted that one day it would be worth a lot and her children would be thankful she kept it. How right she proved to be.

In 1920 she decided to go to South Africa and see for herself what was going on. Her brother, my Uncle Bill who was sheep farming in Australia was coming on leave, with his wife and four sons. They were to live at Keal while we were away.

Chapter 3

THE SUGAR FARM

We sailed for the Cape and Durban- Barbara came too. Jim for some reason didn't come.

I don't remember much about that trip, I was only seven. I remember it was quite a small steam-ship and there was only one other child about my age on board. We met on deck and I asked her name, she answered Unity. I said "That's my name, what's yours?"
What a coincidence! Two little girls called Unity alone amongst the grown-ups on a voyage to the Cape. She was the first of the very few I have come across in my long life.

We docked at Durban and went up North coast to the farm by train; a distance of about a hundred miles. There is a long bridge over the River Tugela and on the other side is Zululand.

The farm was a new experience for me and very different. The house was the same small bungalow, with wide mosquito proof verandas and tin roof where I had been born. What impressed me most was the little hut down a path. It was my first experience of a "pop and drop" earth closet. I was frightened of going there because there was sometimes a snake in it.

There were lots of farm animals: oxen - many coloured with huge horns, horses, mules, and milk-cows, dogs, chickens and ducks. There were also cheerful smiling black people everywhere. There were masses of lovely fruit: pineapple, paw-paw, mango, bananas and great big juicy tangerines called naarchis. We also ate a lot of mealies (corn on the cob). The trees my father had planted had grown up well. In front of the house was a flamboyant bush which was covered with a mass of flame coloured flowers. It was beautiful, looking across the valley behind the house to the hills beyond. At the bottom of the valley ran the stream from which the farm took its name, The Iniwe. On the other side of the stream was Native reserve country, no cane was grown there, goats and cows grazed freely amongst the beehive Zulu kraals. Smoke rose from their cooking fires and there was singing and drumming at night.

I was always scratching, bitten to bits by fleas, mosquitoes and other insects. I had a monkey, a little brown bush monkey; it was very tame and friendly, I loved it dearly. I also had a baby crocodile. A friend from a neighbouring farm had found the eggs on the river bank (they were not unlike hens' eggs) When they hatched he gave me one. I called it Chaka after the great Zulu warrior chief.

I rode a big, grey horse, suitably quiet and reliable. It was not good country for horses, they became infected with the dreaded 'horse sickness'.

When we went to the nearest town, which was not much more than a village then, we travelled in a dog cart. The driver and one passenger sat high up above the horse, and behind there was a slippery little seat facing back the way we had come. I once fell off this seat and landed in the middle of the dusty road. There I sat and watched them trotting away in the distance, but at last they realized I was missing and came back. I was made a great fuss of and rather enjoyed the experience. The main street in Empangeni, in those days, looked like an American town in western movies but without the saloon bars; just ramshackle stores with verandas facing the dusty street. We went to see an Englishman who lived in a nice house on the outskirts. This was of great interest to me, as he had trained a team of zebras to pull a carriage - zebras are supposedly not trainable.

In the cool of the evening we walked or rode beyond the stream into the native reserve, or went for a picnic to an outcrop of rock called Mamba Rock. The people we met were always happy to greet us. We also rode down the cane-brakes with the sugar cane growing high on either side. When the cane was ready to be cut it was set on fire to burn away the leaves and the chaff, leaving the blackened cane standing. Then it was cut by hand with *pangas*, and piled high on trucks, which linked together, were pulled by oxen or mules, on narrow tram lines to the mill at Felixton. In the cutting season a strong, sickly sweet smell came from the mill and wafted across to us at Iniwa. After the cane was cut, clumps of scarlet lilies appeared immediately on the blackened ground.

We must have been at the farm about six months. I do not recall very much, but one exciting occasion is unforgettable. We were invited to a Zulu wedding at a big chief's kraal. We went in a wagon pulled by a full span of sixteen oxen. The boy, who drove them, had a long whip with which he could flick accurately any member of the team which was not pulling its weight, at the same time shouting its name. The manager of the farm was with us and several Africans. We had to ford the River Umfolozi, which bordered our property. There was a causeway where we crossed, so it was not deep there. The boys went into the water splashing and banging tins to frighten away any crocodiles that might be lurking near. Travelling over a rough track by ox-wagons is very slow, and it took us a long time to reach our destination. The wedding was in full swing when we arrived. We used the wagon as a grandstand to watch the most fantastic spectacle. They were dancing - hundreds of Zulu braves in full battle regalia., naked, except for their skins and beads, their feather head-dresses waving, their fringed leg decorations shaking over stamping feet. Line upon line they came dancing forward brandishing assegais and knobkerries. There were young girls among them; bare breasts bouncing, ululating, screaming encouragement. On and on they came stamping till the ground shook, chanting to the frantic beating of drums. We were alone amongst all this wild energy. There was a time when I thought my last moment had come. A line of warriors charged towards us assegais raised high over their right shoulders to stop dead as one, a foot in front of our faces. It was beautifully rehearsed. Big, black bowls were handed round and everybody drank in turn - a loving cup going the rounds. It contained something that looked like grey soup and smelled foul - it was home made beer. Mother hissed at me who was starting to complain "Pretend to drink". She was afraid of offending our hosts by not participating. There was the smell of roasting meat as whole oxen were cooking over open fires. Warriors were now coming forward in pairs and leaping at each-other, their weapons passing a few inches from each other's heads. The man with us said we had better leave. The party was getting rough and there would soon be accidents.

When it was time to leave the farm and return to England, I was told I could not take the monkey. There were restrictions; also it was sure to get ill and die in a cold climate. I was upset about this. Eventually a compromise was agreed upon. I could take the crocodile. He was then less than a foot long. He was kept in a tank which had to be tilted so that he could crawl out of the water and lie on dry land, which was also where he ate. He was hardly a suitable travelling companion. The only place on the ship hot enough for him was the engine-room. He was a great diversion for the sailors, who over-fed him and teased him. Never exactly friendly, he then became quite vicious, snapping and swishing about with his knife-edged tail. He travelled in a strong wooden box with air holes and a handle. On the boat train going from Southampton to London I was in a bad mood at leaving the boat and the friends I had made during the three week voyage. When an old lady asked me:

"What have you got in there little girl, is it a pussy cat?" I answered abruptly

"No it's a crocodile." It was left to Mother to explain that it was in fact a crocodile.

Uncle Bill and his family were still at Keal when we returned, with Aunt Daisy and four boys. Bill and Gurney were a few years older, Peter and I were the same age and Geoff was a baby. I had a great time with these boys and they let me join them in all kinds of escapades. Another thing that made their stay exciting was that Uncle Bill had a car. We were all delighted with this, and it gave mother the idea that we could have one too.

I missed them when they left; it seemed very quiet.

That winter there was trouble with the crocodile. He lived in a tin bath in the heated greenhouse, but when it got really cold it was not hot enough for him, and he would be lying still on his back, his white belly exposed, half frozen. We moved him into the kitchen and housed him on the plate rack over the massive coal-burning range. He liked this but nobody else did. There was a terrible stink in the kitchen as he would lie on his meat until it was rotten before he ate it. The cook said he would have to go or she would.

There was nothing for it. We gave him to the Regents Park Zoo in London. They had never had such a young crocodile and were very pleased with him, but he didn't last long, as the following winter was exceptionally cold and even the reptile house was not warm enough. We were informed that Chaka was dead. Poor little crocodile, he should have been gobbling things up in a river far away.

Chapter 4

THE GOVERNESSES

It was about this time that the first of the governesses came. We lived in the country and at that time there was no suitable school available; the choice being between a boarding-school or engaging a governess to give lessons at home. The first one was young and pleasant. She stayed a few terms and left to get married; nothing unusual about this one - but then the dramas started.

Miss C. was from London, she was well qualified, young, clever, sharp and neurotic. She taught well and was quite a success until she came back from the summer holidays, when she was in a nervous state constantly crying. She eventually confided in Mother that she was frightened. During the holidays she had become involved with her brother, who was a dangerous criminal. He was head of a gang that went round the country breaking in and robbing big houses. She could read in the personal column of the Times newspaper, messages sent in code, making arrangements for their next 'hit'. Some of these she translated to Mother who thought that the police should be informed, but at this suggestion she became quite hysterical. He knew where she was he would come and kill us all, he would think nothing of it. Doors were carefully locked at night but there was no visitation. I was kept in the dark about all this, but I was aware that something was going on; especially when Miss C. disappeared in the middle of term - she had been hidden away with some relations. What was it all about? Was it true, or just a story? But if so what did the girl gain by it? The mystery remained unsolved.

Next, came Miss J. She was a dead loss: A middle-aged religious spinster. She was a town lady, not used to the country. We had to walk on the roads because she was afraid of the cows in the fields. I didn't like her at all. The first time we went for a walk, I ran off and nipped home through the woods and hid to see what would happen. The poor thing, after wandering about calling and calling, had to return and report that she had lost me. She didn't know that no one would worry about that, and I was the one to get the scolding. She only lasted one term.

Miss N. was the most exciting and dramatic of all. She was a red-headed, blue-eyed lively girl from Wales. Her background was a terraced house in a drab coal mining town. She had won a scholarship to college where she had done brilliantly. She was bright, musical, clever and fun. She also had an over-active imagination. We all loved her and called her by her Christian name 'Margaret' from the start. She went everywhere with us, met all our friends and soon lost her Welsh accent. Best of all she liked to dance. The 'His Master's Voice' gramophone was a solid box with a large horn, and a handle to wind it up. We would put on record after record and dance, improvising to the music.

She had been with us for about a year, when she came to Mother very excited with a letter. It was from a titled gentleman saying that he was her father; she was his illegitimate daughter. He had just returned from abroad and was going to settle in England. He wanted to recognise and accept her on her twenty-first birthday, which was approaching. She would be the Honourable Margaret Carlisle. What a fairy tale, what excitement and drama. Next, Mother received a letter from the same Gent: Margaret had written so warmly about Mrs. Grantham, who was obviously a lady of good taste. Would she be kind enough to help his daughter prepare for her debut in society? Would she, as a favour, take her to London and help her choose some suitable clothes? All expenses would of course be paid. The letter was correct in every detail and posted somewhere in the south of England. The research had been well done: "Who's Who" informed us that there was such a gentleman. Mother was delighted to take Margaret on an excursion to London, staying overnight at a hotel and buying with her a whole wardrobe of expensive clothes, all being put down to Mother's account at various shops. Margaret spent a few triumphant weeks. The Grantham's little Welsh governess had turned out to be a titled lady. The local people, revoltingly snobbish, made a fuss of her and she was radiant.

Margaret told us that she had received a cheque from her father. She bought us all expensive presents. Mine I remember was a special tennis racket that I had been coveting. When the term ended she went off in floods of tears, to her castle in the clouds - in reality to the terraced house in the mining town. We wondered why she was so upset, she was going to come back for one more term; she loved us all so much she couldn't bear to leave us. She had overdone it a bit! The end was inevitable. I think it was Barbara, looking in her room for some missing object, quite unsuspecting who came across envelopes addressed in different hand-writing on the now familiar stationary. Then the shop people from Spilsby came with bills. None of the expensive presents she had given us had been paid for; Mother had to pay for everything. How could we have been so taken in? Looking back it seems incredibly stupid, maybe we deserved to be hurt. I have often wondered what became of Margaret. I wish that at some stage I had tried to get in touch with her. I would have liked her to know that I became a dancer, and that she was the first to encourage me.

We now had a car. It was a green-blue Austin touring model, with a canvas roof and side curtains, and it boasted a silver bulldog on the radiator-cap. The odd-job man (I think he had been a tank driver during the war) doubled as chauffeur. Mother and Barbara also drove. Jim had a motor bicycle with a side-car, in which he took out his girl friends. He was very good-looking and never lacked girl friends. Later, on her twenty-first birthday, Barbara had an Austin Seven, which was a little box on wheels and must have been the smallest car ever made.

My cousin Marjory Barrow was well known in the 'horse world'. She bought young horses, trained them as hunters and sold them to selected clients, among them the then Prince of Wales. The Barrows lived near Nottingham. Aunt Polly was my father's sister – married to a rich industrialist. We didn't see much of this family but Marjory was very close friends with Aunt Elsie and was often at the Rookery. She was a big, jolly, impressive woman, bossy and good company. She swore like a trooper, went to bed with her bullterrier and eventually got too fat to ride. Needless to say I liked her.

I had grown too big for the little brown pony and Marjory was commissioned to find me a good, bigger pony. She found it pulling a butcher's cart in Nottingham. She was a good-looking bay mare called Bess; she had only just been broken-in and had never been ridden. Marjory helped me to train her. We taught her all she needed to know to be a perfect children's pony. We entered in classes at horse shows round the county and won many prizes. Bess was always in the first three 'Best Pony Class', behaving with perfect manners till after her rosette had been pinned on. Then I would communicate to her and we would career round the ring putting on a rodeo show, and I would usually win the prize for the best rider. We also entered jumping classes and gymkhana events. There were no money prizes at these shows; we were usually presented with a small silver cup. One year we were entered for Olympia, the best horse show in England. It would have been a great experience but we were unable to go to London owing to an outbreak of 'foot and mouth' disease, and travelling with animals was forbidden.

I once rode one of Marjorie's horses in a lady's hunter class. I rode side-saddle, dressed in an old-fashioned habit and top hat. This was the only occasion I remember riding on a side-saddle. I did not like it. At that time many of the ladies riding with the hunt were on side-saddles. Some of them rode very well and it was certainly elegant, but the younger ones were starting to ride astride like men, and this no longer caused a scandal. The Southwold Hunt met on Saturdays in our district. If the meet was within riding distance I would attend. I rode there alone and joined friends; intrepid children on tough ponies at the meet. My friend, Margaret Maddison, was usually there with her father, Major Maddison, who kept an eye on us, otherwise we were free. Nobody fussed over us. We knew the rules and were careful not to get in the way, and if we did we were shouted at. There were other children in the charge of grooms and even some on leading-reins, which we thoroughly despised. Our ponies were marvellous.

I am sure they enjoyed it as much as we did. If the fences were too big for them to jump, we found a way round or pushed through a gap and somehow managed to keep up with the hunt. We had falls of course but we picked ourselves up and went on, we never seemed to get hurt. Sometimes there was a long ride home at the end of the day and it was often dark when I got back, and then I would have to rub down the pony and feed it.

The hunt was part of my first early life, to be left behind with all the rest when I left Keal. I never wanted to go back to it, but I do believe that those days spent hunting as a child, helped me to be tough, resourceful, independent and responsible. I suppose in some ways I was spoilt, but I did work hard at what I wanted and succeeded; this gave me the self-confidence which was so important when things were not so easy.

We were all at home at the end of the summer holidays, when one Sunday morning we found Mother unconscious on her bedroom floor. The doctor was baffled; it was not a heart attack or a stroke. She regained consciousness at last but she was quite 'out of her mind', shouting and talking rubbish. To see my quiet and always gentle mother behaving in this way was truly shocking. We were most upset and frightened. After a few miserable days during which she did not improve, she was taken away to a hospital in Lincoln. It was a mental hospital - she should never have been sent there. Her illness was of course called a nervous breakdown! Later she had a thrombosis in her leg; she herself came to the conclusion that she had suffered a clot of blood on the brain.

What could we do? We had no idea if she would ever get better. Barbara went back to school, Jim to college. Uncle John, Mother's good-looking youngest brother who was my Godfather, came to Keal from Australia with his wife Aunt Olive and two small children. Aunt Olive was horrid to me and I was literally turned out of my home. No one had ever been unkind to me before and for the first time I knew what it was to hate. I went to the Aunts, the ones that lived up the lane at the Rookery. I used to sneak down after dark to care for a cat I had hidden in the stable, (it had been caught in a trap and its foot had been cut off. but I never went near the house. It was the last straw when I saw Aunt Olive driving my beautiful prize-winning pony in a trap. My cousin Marjory Barrow came to the rescue (she and Olive were cousins but there was no love lost between them), she sorted it all out. I went to the village of Partney to stay with my friend Margaret Maddison and shared her governess. My pony was rescued and came with me on the understanding that I looked after it myself.

The Maddisons were kind to me. They had a lovely old house with many rooms, some not even furnished, but we spent most of our time in the kitchen (there was no living-in maid). Margaret was an only child but her cousin Betty stayed in term time, and we shared the governess Miss Callis, a rather prim middle-aged lady. We also had a French teacher, and piano and painting lessons.

Margaret and I were tom-boys; we galloped about the fields on our ponies, jumping fences and doing circus tricks. On Friday nights we cleaned the harness, polishing the bits and stirrups, in Major Madison's den, ready for the hunt on Saturday.

One day in spring I had a letter from my mother, a perfectly normal letter. She was convalescing with the Barrows at Norminton Hall near Nottingham. Soon after this, my cousin Val Barrow (Marjory's brother) came in his smart car and drove me there for the weekend. He was so kind and understanding. He sensed how shy I was and how worried as to how I would find my mother. He reassured me that I had nothing to worry about. I soon found out this was true, to my great relief my much-loved mother was just as always.

Chapter 5

A VERY DIFFERENT SCENE

Jim had gone to South Africa. Barbara had finished school. Mother decided we needed a change. We would go to the French Riviera for the winter. We had the car and we now had Miss Callis, safe, reliable Miss Callis - late of the Maddisons, who was prepared to undertake the adventure and give me lessons.

We crossed on the ferry from Dover to Calais and set off towards the south. A car full of females; it was quite an undertaking in 1925.

The first night in the strange French hotel, we were woken by blood-curdling screams from next door. We thought Miss Callis was being murdered and rushed to the rescue, but she was only having a nightmare.

We wound our way slowly through France enjoying the countryside. We drove through the Maritime Alps to Grenoble where we spent the last night. The next day we were climbing up and up the mountains till we reached the very top, where we got out of the car to have our picnic lunch. It was a bright morning and there before us, down below the Mediterranean Sea was shining and sparkling. I was enchanted with my fist sight of the sea I was to spend half my life beside. We arrived safely at the Beaurivage Hotel in San Raphael, a charming old fashioned hotel on the sea-front, with a palm court where a string orchestra played in the evenings.

We soon found a house to rent; it was called the 'Villa Rosa'. It was a two storey house with large windows and a terrace overlooking the sea.

I began a new and very exciting life. San Raphael was a small town with a fishing port and a graceful palm-lined promenade. It was not as yet a popular resort. Outstanding were the huge church and the casino. There was a small beach. One could also swim from the rocks in front of our house. The house agent supplied us with two maids. The cook insisted on doing the shopping and it was soon evident that she was stealing in no small way. Mother gave her the sack, and found herself in court accused of unjust dismissal. Imagine the scene: The poor, honest, hard-working French peasant being unjustly accused by the rich foreign woman. It seemed that we didn't stand a chance, but we had not counted on Ines, the other young maid. She got up and told the judge in detail what articles had been taken away each night in the cook's basket. It was a walk-over. Ines now insisted we did not need another cook; she would do everything. She lived in the house with us, she did the work alright but she was a bit crazy. She was in love with Mother. She once woke her up in the middle of the night crying "Oh Madam, thank God you are alive, I dreamt you were dead". We had to put up with Ines, we were deeply in her debt.

Mother could speak French, Barbara and I were working at it. I should really have been at school, but I learnt a lot of things that winter which I would never have learnt in a class room, not least was a reasonable fluency in French. Mother was relaxed and enjoyed herself. She liked doing the shopping. She had painting lessons and soon started painting some attractive water colours. I have two pictures that she painted there in front of me now - a poignant reminder of a happy time. She also enjoyed the Casino, where she played a modest game of roulette in the afternoons. I also loved the Casino. There was a *té dansant* with a cabaret show; girls danced on a glass floor with coloured lights under it. I was allowed to go into the Casino and watch this show with the others. Being only twelve I was not supposed to go into the gambling room, but in a dim light with a bit of make-up on I passed for more. I stood behind Mother watching her play. The chips were placed on the numbers; the Croupier called for no more play, the ball went clattering round and finally came to rest. I asked for some chips, I put one on red and it came up. I had won five francs and just discovered a life-long interest. Sometimes I went by myself, there were two men on the casino door at different times, one let me in the other did not. It was rather a small time casino.

Miss Callis too, was having the time of her life; a typical middle-aged spinster from a vicarage somewhere, always living in other peoples' houses, teaching other peoples' children, with a dismal future in front of her. Those six months were a revelation; she really enjoyed them. One day during the fiestas she was caught and kissed by a group of young boys. Shocked, I went to her assistance, kicking one boy on the behind and hitting another on the head with a tennis racket. I need not have worried; she enjoyed it. She confided to Mother that she had a list of boys who had kissed her: "Would it be alright to add these".

Barbara and I joined the tennis club. I had lessons from an excellent coach and my game improved a lot; I was of course playing with grown-ups.

One incident which deeply impressed me and may have had an influence of my later life-styles, happened one morning, when I was sent to fetch a girl with whom I was supposed to be playing in a tournament at the club. I went along a country path to a cottage where she stayed with her sister. When I knocked they opened the door and there they were with their boy friends, all in dressing gowns drinking coffee. They invited me to join them, they were friendly and not in the least embarrassed. I had never been in such a relaxed and informal situation and decided immediately that that was how I was going to live in the future.

I was also being a go-between. There was a Lady so and so staying at the hotel with her grand-daughter, a girl a year or two older than I. This girl was in love with a waiter from the hotel. Their meetings had to be very secret. I carried notes and messages between them, until the grandmother found out and horrified, whisked the girl away. I was at the railway station to pass, unobserved, the farewell letter. It was most romantic and exciting.

We went to Cannes and bought coloured raffia hats and table mats in the Croisette. We went to the ballet and the opera. We visited Roman ruins at Frejus. We went on excursions to the delightful ports of St. Tropez and Sante Maxime - they were simple picturesque villages then. We dressed up the car and joined in the 'Battle of Flowers'.

The sun shone, the rocks were red, the sea bright blue, the mimosa bursting into flower, oranges and lemons on the trees, the smell of pine trees after rain - All very heady, very intoxicating to an impressionable little girl from the country. I felt quite grown-up and worldly wise. I would have liked to stay there for ever but in front of me loomed the dreary prospect of boarding-school.

When the time came to leave and the car was all packed up, I ran back to the terrace to say farewell, and make a vow to return one day.

Chapter 6

A WASTE OF TIME

I am not going to say much about school. I always considered it a waste of time, not to mention money. I think I was sent to Battle Abbey because two of my friends from Lincolnshire were there. Mother also liked the sound of it because it was supposedly democratic and religiously unbiased; there were Catholics, Jews and a few foreign girls there, though most of us were standard Church of England.

It was certainly a most imposing place - An old abbey on an historical site with exciting ruins in the grounds. There was a Monk's Walk, very spooky and dark, under a tunnel of closely growing yews where ghosts were said to walk. Also reputed to be heard was the clashing of swords, for this was the site of the Battle of Hastings fought in 1066.

I was not unhappy at school. I was good at games - that was all it needed to be popular. I was a mousy, ordinary, quiet girl, but I was tennis champion and played hockey and lacrosse for the school. I couldn't be bullied, and I didn't care much what anybody thought. In class I did as well as anybody else, no better. I liked writing essays. My work always came back marked "Excellent work, spoilt by bad spelling and punctuation" with a mark of eight or nine out of ten. It is still the same; I have never learnt to spell.

The school was good for musical tuition. The head mistress's father was a conductor and her husband gave piano lessons, some girls complained that he pinched their bottoms. I had no talent for the piano and never had my bottom pinched. I did, however, sing in the choir. This was interesting because every year there was a music festival in Battle, and the school choirs were allowed to take part. I fancied one of the choir-boys, with whom I flirted.

During the summer term we spent a lot of time doing things outside in the beautiful grounds. In winter it was freezing. There was no heating in the dormitories and very little anywhere else. We had two baths a week; there was a list of bath times, which could be almost any hour. There were few bathrooms and no showers. We walked in crocodile two by two through the wet dreary country roads, lined by leafless trees or, slightly better, played games on soggy wet grass. What did I learn? - Nothing important really, just to be one more silly school girl among a lot of others.

I never finished my education, having to leave school before I took the final matric examination.

At home during the holidays I continued to ride and play tennis successfully. Playing at a tournament at Woodhall Spar, when I was fourteen, I met a young man who was to have a profound effect on me for the next two years. The older girls, Barbara and her friends were all talking about this good looking man who was playing in the tournament. Who was he? I was normally quite shy but could be audacious at times. I went up to him at a suitable moment and said,

"The girls are all talking about you; they want to know who you are".

That was the beginning of a strange relationship. He invited me for a drink and later when they were looking for me to go home, I was found in the bar drinking gin and tonic (for the first time) with the man they wanted so much to know. I told Barbara his name was Brian Garfit and he was coming to tea next week. He was new in the district, living in Boston working for an oil company and travelling round the country in his smart little sports car. He was pleased to be invited and introduced to our friends. He became a regular visitor and was often a house guest. He went to dances and parties with Barbara and her friends; I was too young to be included, but there was always something special between us. He was twelve years older than I, a sophisticated man with something of a reputation with women. I still have his photo - I took it to school to show off. Of course I fell desperately in love.

The following summer Brian got round my mother to let me go dancing with them at Skegness dance hall. He also partnered me in tennis tournaments. There was a shortage of young men around, and here was this child pinching one of the best. You can imagine I was not too popular.

In the autumn of that year I played tennis at the Junior Championships at Wimbledon. I got through several rounds and then won a battle lasting two and a half hours. There was no tie-break in those days- the final score was 10-12. The following day I had to play again. I couldn't move and ached all over and there was a bad pain on my right side. I was quickly beaten. Mother saw that there was something seriously wrong with me, put me in the car and drove straight home. I had rheumatic fever and my heart was seriously affected.

I had to spend six months in bed. At first I was not allowed to wind up the gramophone. I was moved into the best spare room, where a fire was lit when it got cold. Mother and friends sat round the bed and taught me to play bridge. I had a radio, books and records. It was not too bad. Best of all were Brian's visits. He came faithfully every week bringing presents: records, books, games - anything he thought would amuse me and help to pass the time. When he left, I lay listening to his car pop-popping away down to the fens, and I would start to dream and fantasize. Pure innocent romance, I knew nothing about sex. When I was better the next summer he asked me to be his partner in various tennis tournaments, and we continued our friendship 'till he went off to a job in Malay. I was sad at his departure. He should have been my first lover, but things were different in those days (what a scandal it would have caused). He was far too honourable to take advantage of my obvious infatuation, and never did anything more than hold my hand in the back of the car.

    I duly forgot him, and if I thought about him at all it was to think, what a nice man to be so kind to a silly little girl. Many years later when he was red-faced and round I met him again. He told me, to my astonishment, that he had seriously considered asking Mother if he could propose marriage to me. What stopped him was not my youth but to use his words: "You were so headstrong I thought I would never be able to manage you." So he must have loved me all the time.

Chapter 7

LAST DAYS AT KEAL

It was 1929 and the depression was on. My brother Jim was now married and running the farm in South Africa, there was a sugar slump, and no money was coming from there. Mother's investments were at rock bottom. Funds were badly needed. Something had to be done, for we could no longer afford to live at Keal.

That summer the ghost - we had a house ghost- was very active, walking about in the night and opening bedroom doors at dawn. Various people experienced this in different rooms but always at dawn; there was a knock on the door which opened but no one was there. My mother was psychic. When she was a girl a gypsy fortune teller on the sands at Skegness had once refused to take her money, making the sign of the cross she told her that she "had the gift". Encouraged by this experience she studied palmistry, told fortunes, had experiences with ghosts and sometimes had dreams that came true (once she won on an unknown horse she dreamt came in). We all believed in these weird things, I think I still do. Strange unexplainable things have happened in my life. I am certainly superstitious and believe in luck. But I have never, to my disappointment, had any dealings with our ghost, or any other. We did not know that we would not be coming back to the house, that no Grantham would live there again. Perhaps the ghost; who was certainly one of the family, knew this and was protesting.

Talking of strange happenings, I made the acquaintance of a witch about that time. I was playing tennis in the county junior team. An important match was coming up a few days ahead and I had a bad arm known as a 'tennis elbow' and could hardly hold a racket. Mother had heard of this witch curing people, so we went to see her. It was a long drive to the solitary cottage on a wind-swept moor. An old peasant lady came to the door; she looked disappointingly unlike a witch. We sat down and she took my right hand in her left and ran the fingers of her right hand up my arm quite firmly but not using force. I could feel the prickling sensation as the energy came from her to my arm; I was in no doubt that she had power. After about ten minutes she said,

"Rest it tomorrow and the next day you can play tennis".

And so I was cured.

I played again at Wimbledon that September. I stayed with friends who lived at Reading. They had a son my age called Jack who partnered me. We didn't have any success in the tournament but we had a good time. We imagined we were in love and became secretly engaged.

Some friends were coming from India and were prepared to rent our house. It was an opportunity not to be lost. We prepared to leave for South Africa. It was sad to have to find homes for the animals, and I was loath to leave my new boy-friend, but he was back at school and we didn't have many opportunities to meet.

I was excited at the idea of the trip but I would have been very sad had I known that we would never come home again to live at West Keal Hall.

Chapter 8

BACK IN AFRICA

At the farm things soon became strained. It was an impossible situation for everybody. Lack of money forced us to stay at Iniwa for the time being. It was the first time we had met Jim's wife Flora. Flora was one of three sisters, daughters of a neighbouring farmer. She was a very pretty girl who played the piano beautifully; she had given up the idea of becoming a concert pianist when she married. Their daughter Elizabeth was a little baby. For mother, Barbara, myself and a cousin, Betty Sale, to descend on this young family must have been horrible for them, but the farm was after all Mother's and she had every right to be there.

We were still living in the old house with the WC down the garden. Barbara and I shared a room and fought most of the time. She had always done everything with our brother Jim and was jealous of Flora. I was in the middle trying to make peace unsuccessfully.

I don't remember how many months we were there, but I did have quite a good time. The local boys, mostly sugar farmers, were interested in new girls. We went to dances, played tennis and golf – a lot of our time was spent at the golf club and we went for picnics to Richards Bay, our nearest beach. There were just a few cottages there and a rickety old hotel. We played about on the edge of the surf, not going far in, for fear of sharks. Behind the beach was a jungle of vegetation and trees full of monkeys.

I learnt to drive the car - we had bought an old Chrysler with a canvas roof at an auction in Durban. I made my own clothes as I couldn't afford to buy them.

I soon became bored with life. I couldn't understand the way the men all went into the bar at the club, where they lined up drinks and told dirty stories whilst the girls, not allowed in the bar, sat in the lounge talking about babies and servants. I remember shocking one girl by saying that I would divorce my husband if he behaved in such an uncivilised way. I wanted more than playing games and flirting with country boys. I wanted to earn my living. I wanted to study dancing. I was seventeen.

Durban was an attractive city with plenty of space, popular with tourists from inland places. There was a busy port, a long sandy beach flanked by hotels and apartment buildings, several attractive shopping streets and tree-lined avenues in the residential areas.

The Royal Hotel, in the centre of town, was the haunt of the Zululanders. It was a popular meeting place, and there on the wide veranda one was sure to run into friends. Another graceful old fashioned hotel was the Marine, which held popular dinner-dances in the Palm Court every Saturday night. It was all rather cosy and provincial if one was white and belonged to the privileged upper-crust.

There was already a thriving Indian community with several streets full of Indian shops, mosques and colourful covered market, smelling intriguingly of spices. The Indians being quick, bright and generally better educated, had most of the best jobs; they were almost exclusively waiters in the hotels and restaurants, whilst the Africans did cleaning and manual work. It was long before the word 'Apartheid' was invented but it was working just the same in most respects. A strict colour bar was taken for granted. House servants were generally well cared for and looked on as part of the family, sometimes remaining in the same family for generations. But for the most part Africans were exploited and ignored except as a source of cheap labour. How short sighted!

Durban in those days was a white city; there were not many Africans in the streets. I don't think they were yet aware of what a bad deal they were getting; they seemed cheerful and relaxed. Near the beach the much photographed rickshaw boys outdid each other in finery and fantastic head dresses. It was a safe town then.

The Berea where we lived was an attractive district on a hill overlooking the sea. It was close to a park and a tram ran past the door.

Neither Barbara nor I were trained or in any way equipped to earn a living. She soon went off to Nyasaland where she had friends and managed to get a job as a receptionist. I heard that there was an opening for a tennis coach at a girl's school- the Durban Lady's College. I got the job and went there every afternoon. The pay was very little but I was allowed to use the court on Saturday mornings and give private lessons, which helped. At last I was able to go to a studio and take ballet lessons.

As popular belief has it, it is much too late to start seriously training for ballet at eighteen – I disproved this by, within four years, dancing with one of the best companies in the world. I have to admit that I was never very strong on my points and owed it to a lot of luck, but mostly it was just hard work. I also took Spanish dancing with a girl who had been studying with the best teachers in Madrid and Seville. I enjoyed this much more than the ballet. I became friends with my teacher who was not much older than I and became intrigued with everything Spanish. Kay became a most successful business lady owning together with her brother the Oyster Box Hotel at Umhlanga Rocks. I owe Kay a lot for teaching me a dance with which I had a great success, and which helped me to survive the early days of my career.

Mother insisted, rightly, that I took a typing and shorthand course. At the technical college I made another long-life friend, Pat Lindholm - she was then, daughter of the Swedish Consul. Over the years we shared many experiences and adventures and at one time a house.

On the other side of the hill where we lived it was just country. There were a number of shacks and some racing stables there. One day when I was for some reason feeling depressed, I walked up and over the hill to the nearest stable to talk to the horses. I have always found it comforting to caress and fondle the velvet nose of a friendly horse. There was one horse there that I was particularly friendly with, he would nuzzle me and work his teeth gently up and down my arms pretending to bite, teasing. This day I saw a little man watching. He kept very quiet smiling to himself and then he said

"I would never have believed it. Come away and see what happens when I go up to him".

'Bust Up', for that was his name put his ears back and tried to grab the man who jumped back.

"He does that to everybody, no one except his stable boy dares go near him, but he has obviously taken a liking to you," he said. The man introduced himself, he was Major Bickley, the trainer. I told him about my experience with horses. He said that I could come down to the beach where they exercised the horses and ride if I liked. Did I like! I was thrilled. And so I became a jockey.

Most mornings at five thirty or six the horses were led down to the beach or the race course, by their black stable boys. I went with the trainer and some of the boys by car. Riding as a jockey was a completely new technique. At first I thought I would go straight over the horses head. One perches with very short stirrups on a tiny saddle, bottom in the air and all the weight on the legs; hands firmly holding the reins, crossed, each side of the neck, so that the horse pulls against his own muscle, and you take the strain with your shoulders, not your arms. You sit still until the moment comes to forge ahead and then you use your arms in rhythm with his stride, using all your body as well and encouraging him with the whip when the winning post it in sight. The horse gets the message and lengthens his stride; the great powerful body stretches out beneath you. It is exhilarating work.

The beach was well away from the bathing beaches. It was beautiful there in the early morning, the beach littered with horses, grooms, trainers and jockeys. We usually took several horses about a mile down, close to the sea, turned and galloped back at half pace. The horses took some controlling as we turned; they were trained to race, enjoyed it, and wanted to go at full speed.

Training horses can be a dangerous occupation. Young thoroughbreds sometimes resent being ridden - older ones may have hard mouths and a will of their own. I was in no way restricted. I rode all the horses in the stable. One morning I was told to take the last horse for a gallop. He didn't want to go by himself and went straight into the sea. I had not taken a whip and no one was looking. I kicked and shouted to no effect; we reversed steadily backwards into the waves. I wasn't noticed until he started to swim, then there were cries from the beach, at last I was rescued. I swore never to ride without a whip again.

The race course was much more dangerous than the beach. The ground was hard and in those days a road ran straight through the course. On race days the two sections where the track crossed the road were fenced off, but in the early mornings on the days that training took place, there were no barriers; the track, where it crossed the road, was simply sanded over. I was riding in a trial gallop against another horse one morning. We were beaten but when I tried to pull the horse up it bolted and went flying round the course again. I could do nothing with it; it was quite out of control. When we came to the road intersection it swerved off the course and careered onto the main road amongst all the traffic and crashed down on the concrete. I was pinned underneath the horse. Everything went dark and I couldn't breathe. I thought it was the end of me. But quickly people ran up and dragged the horse off me and I stood up not much the worse but soaked in blood, though not my blood. The horse had broken a blood vessel and had panicked at the smell of blood, which was blowing all over me from its nose, as we galloped. Poor Mother got a fright when I appeared at the door covered in blood. I had some skin missing here and there and I had a cut on my head (I never wore a hard hat), but I was soon back in the saddle.

My favourite ride was my old friend Bust Up. He was a champion over a mile but he was so temperamental he would only try when he felt like it. Time and time again a well-known jockey was engaged to ride him and he would do nothing, and then win when ridden by the stable apprentice. He went well for me but no women or blacks were allowed to ride in professional races. I could only take part at gymkhanas and amateur race meetings. Some of these were small country events but the ones held on the race course at Pietermaritzburg, were semi-professional, with bookies and tote betting. At first I only rode in the ladies race, but soon I became known and was offered rides in most of the races. I would just get up on a horse I had never seen before and ride it down to the start. It was quite tough going, the boys would try to push you over to get through on the rails, use their whips on the wrong horses in the wrong places and use all sorts of dirty tricks not to mention language. It was very exciting!

A handsome young man once offered me a ride on a pretty chestnut mare, he was carrying too much weight to ride it himself. What he did not tell me was that she had been barred from the professional race course for being quite mad and causing havoc at the start. Havoc was certainly caused that day with the animal, eventually rearing up and crashing over backwards with me. The young man was most contrite; he thought he had cured her. We became friends and I often rode the mare round the farm he was managing, when she was as good as gold.

I got paid nothing for riding the horses at work or in gymkhanas, but it turned out to be quite lucrative. You see, I was friends with and worked with jockeys, and when all is said and done, it is mostly up to the jockeys. They don't always know if they can win but they always know if they are not going to try to win.

There was a meeting every Saturday at one of the courses; I had a free pass to the member's enclosure at all of them. And there I went with the money I earned from the tennis coaching, and with tips supplied by the boys.

I think I must have been pretty cocky and full of myself in those days. The girls I knew were mostly all so lady-like and well behaved. I liked to shock. I consorted with racing touts and jockeys, I drank brandy and smoked a pipe, I played poker and went out with married men. It was all very innocent really. The married men never got very far, I was just having fun.

There was one young man belonging to a rich Catholic family who interested me, chiefly because he had such a bad reputation. The girls talked endlessly about how bad he was, and none of them would be seen with him. I met him one night on a drunken party. Prostitutes were being brought in and I had had enough. I asked him - his name was Bill - to take me home, he drove me apparently quite sober, apologised for the rough party and said he hoped to see me again. When next I ran into him he invited me out. He was good hearted; there was nothing bad about him except that he was quite mad and what's more quite mad about me. I was fond of him but he was so jealous and possessive that I daren't greet old friends or speak to anybody when I was with him, or he would get upset and start drinking. He had an ulcer and it was bad for him to drink, but he would go off on binges and would not be seen for days. His mother would phone me to see if I knew were he was. I went looking for him, on one occasion to a brothel near the docks, where I had once been with him - drinking after hours. I remembered the place because there was a monkey in the garden.

"No, Madam had not seen him." He landed up that time in hospital having crashed his car. He kept a loaded revolver in the car and one night he took it out and pointed it at me. I thought he was going to shoot me and I didn't even know why. I had given up all my friends, and had even told him that if he gave up drinking and straightened himself out, I might marry him, which was what he wanted. Sometimes he was a sweet and loving person and I did my best, but he would still have fits when he would drink and then spit blood. I was becoming a wreck, the situation was impossible. I felt I had to get away, but I hadn't any money.

Bickley the trainer started to get funny about my riding, making lame excuses and putting me off going to the gallops. I was hurt, I had been riding for him a long time and he had always shown every confidence. It didn't occur to me that it was Bill behind it. Later after Bill died Bickley told me that he insisted that I stopped riding, he was so afraid that I would get hurt.

One unforgettable Saturday I was in the flat when Mother came in from shopping. She was surprised I had not gone to the races. I told her that I only had thirty shillings and there was no point in going with that. She said,

"Oh come on, I will make it up to three pounds."

So I went off to Grayville racecourse. By the time the second tote double came up I had one pound left. I took two 10/- tickets. The first horse won and I had it doubled with two outsiders. Together these two horses fought out the finish in front of the rest of the field. The grey, a rank outsider called Claudia won. It was about the most exciting moment of my life. I collected a cheque for five hundred pounds from the tote. It doesn't seem much today, but in 1933 it meant freedom.

They both came to see me off at the boat; the two people who loved me the most, Mother and Bill. I felt awful. I never saw Bill again, he died six months later.

My luck continued on the voyage. I played bridge every day and made enough money to pay my bar bill, tips and all expenses on the trip.

Travelling on the big liners in those days was great fun. People were not yet generally flying, so everybody went that way. The boats usually made a stop at Madeira or one of the Canary Islands. On one trip we visited St. Helena and saw the house where Napoleon dragged out his last lonely years. When the ship stopped at these places, people came on board and set up shop on deck, selling all sorts of exotic things. Spanish shawls, wicker work, baskets, painted fans, carpets, leather work and beautiful hand-embroidered table cloths and bed-spreads. On that trip I remember buying a white ostrich feather boa!

There was dancing every night, deck games, plenty of good food and drink, and flirting on the top deck in the moonlight - Durban to Southampton; three weeks of fun and games. I think it cost thirty pounds.

Chapter 9

DANCE & WORK

No more fun and games now, just work, work and work. It was winter in London, cold foggy and dark by four in the afternoon. I bought a little bunch of bright anemones in the street to cheer up my small room in Moscow Road off Queensway in Bayswater.

I had enrolled at Margaret Crask's Ballet School in West Street off Cambridge Circus. I went by bus in the morning and attended classes all day: ballet in the morning and afternoon, character dancing, limbering, and more ballet - everything that was available. I did not enjoy it, but I wanted to get it over quickly, get with a company and go off and see the world. I got no encouragement from Miss Crask In fact she made it clear that she thought I was no bloody good, which I would not dispute. But I was working at it, working as hard as my body could take. The method taught at the studio was the 'Cechetti', very strictly technical, dry and uninspiring. There were exams that qualified dancers to teach, this did not interest me. I later found out that the Russians found this ridiculous. There was much more freedom of movement with the Russian teachers I worked with. I never enjoyed ballet class. I only enjoyed dancing, never endless exercises at the *barre* or in front of a mirror. I would have been better suited to modern dancing but there wasn't much choice in those days; it was kicking, tap dancing or ballet.

I usually went with some of the other students to lunch at a Chinese restaurant in Wardour Street, where we had a good meal for 1/6d (18p). Soho was a district with a Continental flavour with many foreign shops, restaurants and clubs. It was conveniently placed for many theatres. Theatrical agents and film companies also had their offices there. It was colourful and pleasant (before it was taken over by the porn industry). West Street was on the edge of Soho; when I stayed late in town I envied people I saw getting in and out of smart cars and taxis in evening dress, on their way to theatres and restaurants. I knew no one and wished I was back in Durban; what was I doing here? In my lonely room I would boil an egg on a tiny spirit stove for super.

Of course this situation did not last for very long. I made friends, went to cinemas and theatres - queuing for seats in the gallery, and often spent weekends in the country, with the Croomes particularly. I spent that first Christmas with them at Greenhouse Lodge near Painswick. Dear Aunt Grace, Lois and Marjory, they were always so welcoming and kind.

I was still living in my humble room when it was suggested that I join up with two sisters, vaguely related to the Croomes, who were coming to London to study flower arrangement with Constance Spry. I liked this idea and started to look around for accommodation. I had met an old gentleman who was going abroad and wanted to let his flat in South Kensington. I saw at once that it was much too grand and expensive for us and thought no more about it, till a few days later when I had a call from the man's solicitor, who said that before leaving he had given instructions that if the flat had failed to be let, we could have it for what we could pay. This seemed like good news. I got in touch with the others and we made an offer which was agreed on with the solicitor. I moved in the next day. It was Heaven! Comfortable, spacious, beautifully furnished and a maid came in every morning to clean. Things were looking up.

I was there alone for about a week, till the day before the girls were to arrive. I came back from the studio that evening, to find a furious couple there with a pile of luggage. The woman said that she was the niece of the old man, who had offered them the apartment whilst he was away, and that he knew perfectly well that they were coming. What was I doing there? I was to get out at once. They were quite the nastiest people I'd ever had any dealings with. I tried to explain, but they wouldn't listen. They obviously thought I was up to something with the solicitor, who of course could not be contacted. They kept insinuating that I was lying. I got madder and madder and refused to go that night - where could I go? The man weakened a bit, I think he believed me, but the woman was a bitch.

I was faced with finding a place for the three of us to live, in one morning. I sent a telegram telling the girls that I would meet their train, and went in search.

I was lucky I found a place that I thought would do, in a house near Gloucester Road tube station. It had one nice big bed-sitting room with two beds and a pokey little attic with a high-up window for me. Actually it wasn't bad and quite cheap. The big room was always full of discarded flowers from Constance Spry, which we arranged in chamber pots.

Coming back on the train, after having spent a weekend at the Croomes, I saw a peacock in a field. I felt a cold shiver of premonition. I am superstitious about peacocks. Sure enough there were two letters waiting at the digs: One from Mother telling me of Bill's death and one from him, written whilst waiting for the operation on his ulcer. It was a goodbye letter: very, very sad.

I was working as hard as ever. Forcing my legs to turn out, stretching them up to my ears and down into splits. Strong legs from riding - controversial this - dancers are not supposed to ride horses, it is said to bend their legs in the wrong direction. Rubbish! This was my favourite topic later when talking to the press.

The Col. De Basil Ballet Company was at the Covent Garden Opera House. We students went to many performances. Starting in the gallery, we knew how to get down to the circle in the first interval. From there we observed if there were any unoccupied seats in the stalls, usually ending up there for the last ballet. If there was an attempt to stop us we pretended we were from the company and couldn't speak English. It was an exciting company, most exotic and Russian. The English Sadler's Wells was making a brave effort but lacked the spark and energy of the Russians. (There was no Royal Ballet yet.)I remember particularly two of Léonide Massine's Ballets; Symphonie Fantastique and Les Presages, with the three beautiful and very young ballerinas Tamara Toumanova, Irina Baranova and Tatiana Riabouchinska. I was later to work with Massine.

The studio was closed for August. I bought an ancient Ford two-seater for 5 pounds and drove round the country visiting friends and relations. Then I went back to London and sold it for 8 pounds. I have to admit it broke down a few times.

I was beginning to get worried. There was not much left in the bank. I had to get a job. There was just about enough money to get back to South Africa but that would be a terrible admission of defeat, especially as I was beginning to feel like a dancer.

I sometimes used to rent a room in the same block as the ballet studio, to practise Spanish dancing. I was not taking lessons and did not want to get out of practise; I obviously couldn't do anything so noisy in my digs. I had my castanets in my handbag that afternoon. I ran into some friends in Charing Cross Road. They were going to an audition for the Léon Woizikovsky Ballet. They asked me if I was going too. I had not considered trying to get into this company; frankly, I did not think I was good enough. I knew he only wanted a few extra dancers for the London season, but he was doing a Spanish ballet. I didn't have any practise clothes with me; however, I went along with the girls to see what happened at an audition.

It was a big rehearsal room. There was a piano and a table with several people sitting behind it, facing the room. The others went off to change, I sat down and waited. I watched girl after girl and a few boys give their music to the pianist and do their 'bit'. They were nervous, not very impressive. I was thankful that I was not competing. When they had all finished Léon Woizikovsky came to me and said,

"And you. Are you not going to dance?"

I explained that I had come unprepared, but then I said on impulse,

"Is it true you want Spanish dancers? I can do Spanish dancing".

He gestured to me to get up. So I took my castanets out and danced my Spanish dance in my street clothes and high heels, with no accompaniment. When I finished he grinned at me and asked:

"You also dance on zee point?"

I assured him that I did. I was in. I couldn't believe my luck, it had been pure chance. Delighted as I was, I was also terrified, what would happen at rehearsals when he found out that I was not very strong on zee point?

Léon Woizikovsky had been one of Diaghilev's dancers. Now, after a time with de Basil he had started his own company. Paris-based, mostly with Russian dancers, this was his first London season.

Léon wasn't young, tall or handsome, but he was vital, full of taut energy and charm.

The rehearsals started. I was nervous, very green with no experience amongst seasoned dancers who knew exactly what they were doing. What should have made me happy but which in fact made it worse, was that Léon had taken a fancy to me and placed me in front in a prominent position, where I had no one to follow. I would have been happier in the back row watching the others.

We rehearsed the ballets, Les Sylphides, Petrouchka, Prince Igor and the Spanish ballet L'amour Sorcier to the Falla music. This ballet was produced and danced by Woizikovsky himself with great success.

We opened at the Coliseum in late September with Les Sylphides.

Sitting in front of the brightly-lit dressing room mirror, I put on the heavy make-up that ballet demands. First, light coloured 'Leichner' greasepaint, powdered over, then dark blue eye shadow, lashes built up with black to twice their length, black lines above and below the eye slanting slightly upwards on each side, a blob of white at the outer corner and one of scarlet on the inner, of each eye. Eyebrows were blocked out at the sides where they curved down, and filled in straight with a black pencil. Lips were bright red lightly outlined in black and hair pulled back in a bun with a wreath of small white flowers, pinned in place. Arms and neck were powdered over light for a white ballet. Next were the pink silk tights and small white pants. Then the pink satin ballet shoes; these I had darned before they were worn to make a more substantial platform and to make them last as long as possible. Like all the other dancers, I hated hard new shoes. I tied the ribbons and tucked in the ends. Lastly, I took down the calf-length tutu for which I had been fitted, put it on and stood whilst the dresser fastened it. The call-boy knocked on the door and called "Beginners on stage". Up we went to the stage and took our positions. The overture finished - the overture to the Bartered Bride always reminds me of that moment - pristine white, we poised on points, waiting frozen with fright. There was a creak as the curtain rose on a silent house.

It seemed that the world changed, I was vulnerable, exposed. I could feel the lights hot on me. Out front a huge cavity of darkness with white blobs of faces in the front row. Behind and above, in the vast darkness the massed public, every single person looking at us. The orchestra starts playing the Chopin Nocturne. We move smoothly forward on our points. Concentration takes over from nerves. We are sylphs, dancing in a moonlight fairy-tale world.

When Fokine created the Polovtsian Dances from the Opera Prince Igor for Diaghilev, he wanted to make a ballet for the girls and boys of the Corps de Ballet. I danced in this ballet with three different companies; with Maestro Fokine himself and once with the Monte Carlo Opera. But the first time was there at the Coliseum with Léon Woizikovsky dancing the Tartar Warrior. What an exciting experience! I think only Russians can do this ballet properly, it has to be danced with complete abandon.

The company was made up of exotic young dancers from different countries. Many languages were spoken though the common language was French. It was a success, the public liked it, and the critics were good. I enjoyed being in this environment but my contract was only for the season, and to my great disappointment it was not extended.

I went to see Léon, he was kind but he told me to go back to school and come and see him in a year's time; when he hoped to return to London. I cried all the way home in the tube.

Two years later I did see Woizikovsky again, when I had the pleasure of telling him I was now with the Ballet Russe de Monte Carlo.

Chapter 10

PARIS

Disappointed as I was at least I now had some invaluable experience, which I was soon to make good use of. I heard that the Ballet Russe de Paris was looking for dancers. They had been on tour in England and were returning to Paris for a season at the Opéra Comique. I gave an audition and told them I had recently danced in several of the ballets that they were doing, and they accepted me.

We left for France immediately on the ferry. Arriving at Calais I joined the others lining up to go through the immigration desk. When asked my purpose in coming to France I proudly said that I was with the ballet, where upon the man asked to see my work permit. Of course I had no work permit. I rushed to our manager Eskoldoff in a panic, imagining myself being sent straight back, when I was right on the threshold of an exciting new life. Eskoldoff said,

"Stupid girl, go back and tell him you make mistake, you just student, you not work with us." I went back trembling to the man,

"Pardon Monsieur, je n'ai pas compris." He let me through without another word.

The Ballet Russe de Paris could have been a good company if it had been properly financed. Money or rather the lack of it was always the trouble. The two Russians who ran it were always scratching around for funds. But it was a splendid training ground. Many good dancers were there for a time, only to move on to better and surer opportunities. There were people of all ages and nationalities - Russians, Poles, Finns, Danes, Yugoslavs, French and English. The ballet master Tadek Slavinsky was a Pole.

We rehearsed at the Opéra Comique: a huge old theatre with stacked galleries. The rehearsal room was on top of the building, up hundreds of steps. The first time I went to the WC it was dark and there was no light and I fell straight in the hole - for that's what it was, a hole with a place each side for the feet. I became quite used to these stinky holes, which are still to be found in some countries.

The work was not hard. Two of the ballets I already knew, Les Sylphides and Prince Igor. Then there was an easy Straus ballet called Souvenirs de Vienne, a ballet to Ravel's Bolero and a lively romp called Suite Caucasienne. There was not much point work which suited me. Our dressing rooms were so high up that we couldn't hear the orchestra. We were always dashing up and down stairs, frightened of being 'off cue'. When looking up from the stage, there were so many galleries it seemed as if there were people sitting on the ceiling.

We all lived in Montmartre, which was almost like living in a village. We were within walking distance of most places we wanted to go to. The hotel - just a rooming house - was in the Rue de Clichy. It was one of those typical places to be found in all French towns; terrible blazing wall- paper, stuffy old-fashioned plush upholstered chairs and curtains, a comfortable three-quarter bed, a gilt mirror and in a corner, a basin and bidet. The latter was usually unattached - a moveable one: There was a receptacle to fill it with and you squatted over this rickety arrangement to wash the lower regions. If you were foolish enough to sit on it, it would overflow on the carpet or collapse altogether. It was easier to do the feet one by one in the basin. There was never a bath or a shower in any of these hotels. The WC was a smelly little cupboard on each landing. The beauty of it was it was always warm. Unlike the freezing English house there was always the 'chauffage'- a lovely hot radiator to keep the room warm, and invaluable for drying stockings and underclothes. In the hall of such houses there was usually a fat old lady concierge with a fat old dog. Gentlemen callers were never discouraged, especially if they gave a small tip. It was stuffy, comfortable and somewhat decadent. The tooth glasses were accustomed to being filled with champagne, and the beds were well bounced on.

I started taking classes with the famous Madame Preobrajenska at her studio in the Salle Waker on the corner of Place Cliché. This building was something like a club. There were a number of ballet and music studios there and strains of music were distinctly heard everywhere. There was also a café which was a meeting place for people connected with the arts: Painters, musicians and dancers, singers and impresarios looking for talent, all gathered there. Interesting and famous people were to be seen drinking coffee, although at the time I didn't know who was who. Once when I turned down an offer to be painted, Eskoldoff said in his usual way,

"Stupid girl, you might have been famous."

I forget who the Russian painter was.

Dancers came from all over the world to study with Madame Preobrajenska. The studio was not very big and was always crowded, especially when one of the big ballet companies was in town. One had to stand sideways at the *barre* to do the grand battement. Madame would not allow the window to be opened, so it was unbearably hot and there was a heavy aroma of sweat and cheap perfume. The piano was on a dais and Mme stood in front facing the class - the once great ballerina from St. Petersburg; very tiny, very old, banging on the floor with her stick in time to the music, and every now and again poking a foot outwards or taking a swipe at a leg. She was a great character, her whole life was ballet and she went on teaching till she was a great age. She was a kind hearted woman. I know that when some of the Russians were out of work she took them free, and always gave all of us credit to pay when we could. I was proud to be one of her pupils and always returned there, until I discovered Victor Gzovsky.

I loved Paris. Nowadays just the smell of coffee and black cigarettes brings it back. The delicious croissants and brioches, the Camembert and petit Suisse, the yards of fresh crisp bread, the good food and wine in small inexpensive bistros, and the people who were always kind to 'les artistes'.

There were certain things unique to France, and there were many new sensations to be experienced in Paris. To hell with the plumbing; one could keep quite clean without a bath. As for showers, I don't think they had been invented yet in Europe; I certainly didn't come across one till much later. We rubbed down with eau-de-cologne, in dressing-rooms after class. We were really quite clean and non-smelly. The boys were not always so hygienic; indeed some of them were very gamey - these we tried not to get partnered with. They looked so handsome and glamorous with their beautiful athletic bodies and painted faces, but not quite as good at close quarters. I think it was the constant sweaty physical contact that put me off. We were altogether too familiar with the bulging padded tights to be interested in what was inside them. They were good friends and hilarious, often outrageous companions. Most of them were bi-sexual, some went where the money was, all were good company, but not for my bed. I hate to admit it, but opera singers were my weakness.

After the season at the Opéra Comique, we went on tour to some provincial towns in central France. I got along fine with the other members of the company, I don't remember any discords. I made friends with a young English girl who danced under the name of Manya Zarina, and her mother Boula, who helped with the wardrobe. Manya was very beautiful and sexy and needed an eye kept on her. There were several mothers travelling with young dancers, who were either themselves dancing in the corps de ballet or working in the wardrobe. The latter was hard work, always packing and unpacking the skips and ironing, cleaning and mending all the costumes and hanging them in the correct place, ready to be put on in a hurry.

Both of the two Russian business men had a not-very-young mistress in the corps. Mme Krassovska - who was with Eskoldoff, our manager, was the mother of a most promising young dancer, Natalia Leslie, who was to become a big star in America dancing in her mother's name (Natalie Krassovska). I think these couples lived together for comfort and economy more than for passion. They were like long-married couples. There was great consternation when, in Germany, they were not allowed to share rooms in the hotel, not having the same name on their passports. We were much amused about this.

Our ballet master Tadek, also had a girl friend in the corps the ballet, an English girl; Nadine. She had a hard time as he was sometimes nasty to her, shouting at her when he was drunk. We got shouted at quite a lot too, for he was bad tempered and a heavy drinker. In the past he had been a good character dancer and was still dancing, but he was lazy and getting a bit old. I think he was disgusted by being in such a second rate company and took it out on us all. I respected Tadek, cynical and lazy as he was, he was a very experienced artist. He could also be amusing. He had the physique and face of a middle-aged jockey. He would sit up all night talking and drinking, and sometimes he told wonderful stories about witches, ghosts and werewolves. Once after he had been telling us a story in our digs, I was teasing one of the girls for going out with a man named Wolf, when there was a terrible wailing noise close at hand. We all went straight under the table - We didn't know that there was a big dog shut up in the room next door. Tadek's tales were very effective!

The tour over, we returned to Paris. There were no engagements in the offing, but we rehearsed a ballet for the film 'Mayerling', which was in preparation with Charles Boyer as the star. The shooting was postponed, and we were never paid. When the scene was eventually shot we were away somewhere. So we were in Paris with no work and no pay.

Every evening we met at a café opposite the stage door of the Opéra Comique, where we were handed out ten francs each, just enough to keep us from starving. In the café the waiter would rush to remove the bowls of lump sugar before we demolished them all - we were so hungry. Temporarily solvent we searched for the cheapest place to dine. There was one restaurant on the Boulevard des Italians, where we got a four course meal with wine, for four francs fifty.

Thanks to our Russian friends we got to know a different Paris 'by-night'. We wandered all night visiting little bistros and clubs run by other émigré Russians. There was a big café where a balalaika band played. When we walked in, they always broke off what they were playing, and greeted us with the music from Prince Igor; they would also invite us to a drink. Another place was a small dark night-club in Montparnasse called 'Djiguite', where there was a cabaret of Cossack dancers and knife throwers. The young Russian who owned it was a friend of mine.

The place we frequented most was a small Russian restaurant not far from the hotel, where we went for a good cheap meal and vodka thrown in. This all-night bistro was more like a club than a restaurant. Artists working in cabarets in the district came in for a meal after their performances.

Russian taxi drivers and paper sellers dropped in at all hours of the night. Most of these people had fled from Russia during the revolution and landed in Paris, where they worked at whatever employment they could find. It was quite usual for an ex-general to be driving a taxi, or a count to be a commissionaire at the night-club. They talked endlessly and laughed a lot when they were not in the depth of despair. Their biggest problem, apart from money, was 'papers'. Many of them had no proper passports or documentation, which caused them to be in a constant state of worry. A different type of immigrant was also arriving in Paris - many Jewish people were coming in illegally and quietly from Germany.

Most of the dancers that I knew at that time in Paris eventually made it to America where they formed a colony in New York.

We often bought a yard of bread, some cheese, pâté and a bottle of wine and ate in our rooms. One night we were picnicking like this in Manya's room when she read out a letter from her friend Paula, who was in Spain with my ex-company, the Woizikorsky ballet. Spain, where I longed to be and where I should have been - and here I was half starving in Paris. I felt discouraged and depressed.

It was at this point that a man came looking for me. I made no secret of the fact that I disliked this man, but he insisted. I listened to what he proposed: A couple of dancers from our out-of-work company were going to do a trial act at a smart nightclub. He wanted me to go along as an added attraction, to meet the owner of the club and see what I could do to persuade him to engage them. He was plainly pimping, but I thought; 'what the hell', I might at least get a decent meal out of it. So I put on an evening gown. Going in the Metro I felt somewhat out-of-place dressed like this and thought he might have rung for a taxi, but no. I was escorted, a lamb to the slaughter, in the Metro!

I was quite intrigued with the night-club owner. He was tall, elegant, rather handsome and most sophisticated, from Warsaw or Budapest. He was immaculately dressed in a dinner jacket, he wore gold jewellery and his black coat had an Astrakhan collar - a monocle would have suited him. He looked a bit like Count Dracula on a good day.

We sat at a table in the front of a gallery overlooking the very glitzy club. An excellent dinner was served with champagne, followed by vodka. I struggled to make conversation in my Russian-accented French. I was not exactly relaxed but he seemed happy enough puffing his cigar. When the dancers came onto the floor and danced a ballet *pas de deux* he hardly looked at them, he was looking at me, clearly pleased with his little present. I did my best for my friends, but he was not interested, he just said that their act was not suitable for the place, which I had to admit was true. I was getting worried as to how I was going to extricate myself from this situation. I was tempted by the good life, and thought I would like to string it out for a few days, if I could do so without getting any further involved, but how? It was late when we left there. I told him that I had an early call for rehearsal, hoping he didn't know we were not working. He took me home and we made a date for the following night. It was good whilst it lasted. He took me to dinner at Maxim's. We lounged in arm-chairs in the front row of the Folies Bergères. The next night we ended up at the Russian night-club Scheherazade. We had dinner and plenty of champagne, and now we sat in this exotic oriental setting with a bottle of vodka on the table, and we drank it all. Who could drink vodka like wine? Not me. This night he did succeed in getting me to his apartment, but when I got there I just lay on the bed and passed out. Poor man, he must have been fed up with me. The next thing I knew, it was midday and I was in his bed with a terrible headache. He was a creature of the night; I had never seen him in the daylight before. He looked grey-faced and old in his brocade dressing-gown. He had given up on me by this time, so I never did become Count Dracula's bimbo.

Once recovered from the hang-over I felt quite cheered by my adventure! It had broken the monotony, but it was a long time before I could face vodka again.

One evening, when I arrived at the usual café, Eskoldoff handed us four English girls tickets for the Dieppe-Newhaven ferry, for the following night - We could spend Christmas at home. I had no home in England but I knew Aunt Grace Croome would be pleased to have me. I sent her a telegram and – as was the custom - left a suitcase at the hotel, as a guarantee that I would pay what I owed them on my return. On the ferry, we naturally left our things in the third class compartment and went through to the first class, undetected as usual!

Chapter Eleven

AMSTERDAM

Early in January I received a letter enclosing a ticket for the return overnight ferry to Paris. I didn't really want to go just then, as I had a date to go to a dance with a young man I fancied. He was due to return shortly to India and I wanted to see him again. I never did. My first priority was to return to Paris and go back to work. Every one of us returned to that second-rate company without a second thought.

It appeared there was an engagement in Amsterdam.

After an uncomfortable night on the train from Paris to Amsterdam we arrived early in the morning. Leaving our luggage at the station, we started to look for somewhere to stay. I was with Manya and her mother Boula, we were tired and it was freezing cold. The addresses we went to were all occupied or too expensive; we were paid in French francs, which didn't change well into Dutch guilders. We were sitting at a café having espresso coffee and discussing what to do next, when a young man sitting next to us overheard our conversation - He spoke to us in English:

"Pardon me, but I understand you are looking for somewhere to stay. I think I can help you." He told us a friend of his - an actress - was away on tour and that we could have her apartment, which was in the same house where he lived. I didn't much trust the man, but it did seem a reasonable suggestion and we were desperate.

The house was one of those tall ones overlooking a canal. There was a garage on the ground floor; our apartment was over that and the man and his girl-friend were over us. At first sight it looked quite attractive. It was one large studio room with a pretty view over the canal. It would have been nice in the summer but this was mid-winter. We agreed to take it; there was no time for discussion as we had to rush to the theatre.

We were not performing in a proper theatre but in a large modern cinema. In between the showing of the film we danced one ballet - Bolero. We danced this over and over again, starting at mid-day and going on till midnight - five times I think it was. Nothing could be more repetitive than Ravel's Bolero, and to have to do it every two hours or so was desperately boring. There was hardly time to do anything between shows, we just dashed out for a meal or paid a hurried visit to a museum or art gallery. Most of the time, we spent without taking our make-up off in the cinema café; it was at least warm there and snowing outside. In our apartment it was freezing. All we had for heating was an oil stove; one of those old fashioned round ones. There was always a kettle on it, for making tea in the morning and heating water to wash with, as there was no hot water in the bathroom. There was just a cupboard for a kitchen with no stove. There were a few rugs on the floor and these we put on our beds at night. There was also an unpleasant smell of stale petrol from the garage underneath. The only advantage was that it was near the theatre.

Our young man upstairs was at first most attentive, very willing to show us round the town and meet us after we had finished work. We saw no reason not to pay him the rent in advance when he asked. He took us to some weird places where there were some very freaky people. One night-bar I remember was painted with pornographic murals. His oriental girlfriend was never present on these outings, and we usually ended by paying for him. Things changed when Manya refused to respond to his persistent passes. One night he grabbed her on the dark stairs going up from the garage and there was quite a scene.

We would sometimes buy things in a delicatessen, to have for our supper when we got home. Imagine our feelings when one night the cupboard was bare? It was late and we were cold and hungry. We marched upstairs and asked for an explanation.

"Oh yes" he said. "You see, we are Communists, we share everything. What is yours is ours and what is ours is yours. You can come up here and take what you like."

We tried that, but of course there was never anything there. So we could never buy anything in advance for our supper. There was no lock on our door and weird people used to walk in, when we were in bed in the morning, and wander around as if it was the most natural thing to do. They usually wanted payment for something that had nothing to do with us; all this, naturally in Dutch. Our relations with upstairs became rather strained but we couldn't leave because we had paid the rent.

The last night we were there, we had a meal before coming home. It was late and we had to do our packing; ready for an early start the next day. We found the house in total darkness and nothing happened when we turned on the lights. They had deliberately gone away and left us in a black-out. We guessed there must be a meter somewhere and after fumbling about, with only a box of matches to light us, we eventually found it in the garage. It needed a coin to be inserted and then the lights came on.

I felt sure that the girl, whose flat we were using, would certainly never see any of our money. All her belongings were there and I am sure she probably never intended to let the place. We left her a note but I don't expect she ever got it.

After Amsterdam we went back to doing proper ballet programmes, performing in various towns in Holland. What I most remember is the cold.

There were never any baths available where we stayed, so on occasions we went to a public bath-house. I didn't like this idea but after the others had been and assured me it was all right, I risked going. It was actually quite clean; a big, hot bath-tub with a great white towel provided.

We were in The Hague when we heard that King George V had died. Boula said we should go to the British Embassy to sign the book. She said this was something one did at a time like this, to show sympathy and patriotism. On arrival we were ushered straight into a reception - a sort of wake party. All the British residents in The Hague were there, dressed elegantly in deep black. We were in our usual clothes, quite unsuitably dressed; muffled up in coloured scarves, woollen hats and old fur coats. The Ambassador came forward to shake hands - all polite and correct - and didn't turn a hair. Poor Boula explained that we had just come to sign the book. Outside again in the snow, we fell about laughing. I thought it was a pity we hadn't grabbed a few canapés before retiring.

Chapter 12

HITLER'S FIRST MOVE

We were in Bonn when I woke up one night to the noise of marching in the street. I got out of bed and went to the window. There in front of me was the German army, marching through the narrow dimly lit street. Line after line they came, hour after hour, foot soldiers and horses pulling gun-carriages. They were silent except for the noise of their marching feet. The houses were dark and quiet on either side of the street. Were the people asleep? Or were they watching as I was from behind closed shutters? What was happening? I knew that the Rhineland was a de-militarised zone since the end of the 14-18 war. Why were they marching secretly through in the middle of the night?

There were two English girls and two Yugoslavs staying in the house. The Yugoslavs were cousins, a boy and a girl, their rooms did not face the street and they had heard nothing. There was great consternation in the morning and now everybody was talking. Hitler had occupied the Rhineland during the night. It was a complete surprise. Was there going to be war? What should we do? The Yugoslavs, who spoke German, were afraid - they were Jewish; they were all for going straight back to Paris. We went to our respective consuls for advice. They told us that there was no immediate danger; we should stay where we were and keep quiet.

We gave a performance as usual but it was poorly attended. It was quiet but there was tension in the air. The Germans were not yet celebrating, no one was sure yet what might happen.

That night the Yugoslavs suggested we hold a séance. They were worried about the future. We were all in a highly emotional state, as we sat round a table with our hands touching, and the lights out. I did not expect anything to happen, but almost immediately the English girl, Olive, began to moan and cry "They are all dead, they are all dying"- She was seeing death and destruction on every side, it was very frightening. We didn't know what to do to bring her out of the trance; we knew it could be dangerous to give her a shock. We put a light on and massaged her hands lightly. After some minutes she sighed deeply and opened her eyes. She was exhausted, but remembered nothing of what had passed. We all felt depressed and subdued.

Our next stop was Cologne, where the mood was of wild jubilation. The streets were full of celebrating Germans. A great event was about to take place: Hitler was about to make a triumphant entry.

We were advised not to be out in the streets. I was in digs with several friends. We went to a hotel, where some of the others were staying and from where, on a balcony on the second floor, we had a fine view of the main street, which was decorated with flags and banners bearing the Nazi swastika. The street was packed with people, all waving small paper flags; red with the black swastika emblem - We had some of these too. The road was cleared by the police, who then lined it joining arms one facing in and one out, down the whole length of the street. We had a long time to wait. Down on the side-walk below us, two men were trying to attract our attention. They were jumping about and miming that they had seen our show and recognised us. They were funny and we were bored and tired of waiting, so we joined in the fun. With gestures, they made a date with Manya and me to meet them that evening opposite the hotel, at seven o'clock.

Now the great moment was here. The motorcade was approaching. The crowd was shouting –"Heil Hitler" and raising their right arms in the Nazi salute. Adolph Hitler was standing in the first car, with his arm raised. Three other men were seated with him in the open car. Behind came about a dozen more cars driving two abreast. I quickly aimed my camera and took a photo. How easy it would have been - a gun instead of a camera from that spot. How many lives would have been spared? How much misery and suffering would have been saved. And there we were waving paper swastikas.

There was no point in giving a performance that night, everyone was in the streets. There were loudspeakers blaring from every corner with the ranting, shouting, hysterical voice of the Führer drowning every other sound.

Manya was nervous of keeping our date. I suggested we sit in a café across the street from where we could see them arrive; if we didn't like the look of them we didn't have to join them. On the stroke of seven a huge, long, low, white car drove slowly up and stopped at the curb. We were duly impressed and went out to them. And so it happened that we took part in the celebrations and festivities, in honour of the occupation of the Rhineland by Hitler. What a terrible thing to admit! One of the men was in uniform, good-looking and spoke English; the other was nondescript and did not. We went from beer-hall to beer-hall. Both men were singing, drinking, toasting and getting more and more drunk. We had had enough, we wanted to go home. We had lost the little one but the big fellow had other ideas. Once in the car he headed out into the country. Luckily we were two to one; he couldn't cope with two furious females and turned the car round. We were very foolish and could have landed in a nasty situation, but although not an enjoyable evening, it was an interesting experience.

Chapter 13

KISSING THE BLARNEY STONE

When we got back to Paris there were some changes in the company. The ballet master Slavinsky left. His place was taken by an American woman called Margaret Severn. I think she bought a share in the company - probably saved it going broke. She also got Eskoldoff and a good deal of say in the company. She did some clever numbers with masks, which she made herself, but was too tall and angular and not suited to some of the roles she danced.

We did a tour of the British provincial cities. We also went to Ireland.

I was now doing my Spanish dance in the Divertissement Programme and having quite a success. It was the first time I had been to Ireland. It was so different and I liked it. We started off at Cork in the south. I don't think they had ever seen a ballet there before. They laughed when the male dancer came on in Les Sylphides, but the theatre fairly exploded with applause after my Spanish dance. There is an affinity and some shared blood between the Southern Irish and the Spanish. This they demonstrated by not letting me off the stage. I came back to bow again and again until Margaret Severn hissed "Do it again". So I danced all over again. I could see she was furious, her mask-dance always went down well but she never had to repeat it.

The theatre in Cork was strange and old-fashioned. There was a small bar back-stage where people from the audience came in for a drink during the interval. It was very cosy, the people so friendly and keen to buy us a drink. It was a new experience to get to know some of our audience.

One day we were taken on a picnic in a side-cart and pony, to kiss the Blarney Stone. You hang upside-down and make a wish. We were the only people there.

Wherever we went I stole the show, though never quite as dramatically as at Cork. It was really quite out of proportion to my talent. I had good write-ups in the papers and began to feel like a star.

We were in Dublin at the Gate Theatre for two weeks. The first week business was bad, on the Friday we were not paid our salaries.

I was renting a room from the family of one of the stage-hands at the Gate. They were friendly, warm people, very Irish. The bath was in the kitchen; it did double service with a board over it as a table. One had to make arrangements in advance, so that there would be nothing spoiling in the oven whilst you were in the tub. When I told them we had not been paid, they were most indignant. The man, who of course had seen me dance, had an interesting idea. He told me there was a cinema, where on Sundays they ran a variety show between pictures. He suggested I could work there for two performances the coming Sunday, and make up the loss of salary. He told me who to see, and sure enough I was engaged. I rehearsed with the orchestra, a much better and bigger one than we had at our theatre, the conductor was good too. I only had the music for one number, for the second I asked him to play a *paso doble* to which I improvised with castanets. I had taken my costume and orchestration from the theatre without telling anyone.

Most of the dancers from the company were in the audience to see the Bing Crosby film that was showing. What a surprise when, after a big build-up from the orchestra, who should come on but an all too familiar figure doing the same old dance. I could see some of them sitting there. I did enjoy it.

The next day Margaret Severn sent for me, she said,

"Do you realise you signed a contract which says you are not to appear anywhere else?"

"Yes," I answered. "But my contract also says that I get paid five pounds a week and last week I got nothing."

I went on to ask for a small raise; after all I was using my own costume and music and contributing to the success of the company. She did not agree, so I decided to leave. The company had lost a lot of its sparkle anyway and I had a much more ambitious plan.

It was at this time when I returned from Ireland that I had the unpleasant job of clearing everything out of our house at Keal. The local county council were taking it over. I, being the only one of the family in England at the time, had to deal with it. Aunt Mabel came to help me - she was marvellous; I could never have managed without her. I stayed with my old friends the Maddisons at Partney and bicycled over to Keal every day. Aunt Mabel stayed at a hotel in Spilsby and came by taxi. We filled packing case after packing case with things, and it all went together with the furniture to store. It was a heart-breaking job. Riding back the last evening in the dusk, I cried bitterly to think I had lost my beautiful home. I could imagine how Mother must be feeling and was determined to see her as soon as possible.

The house was turned into an old people's home, and during the war it was used as a billet for soldiers. It was actually sold after the war at a compulsory price fixed by the LCC. We were virtually forced to sell it at the meagre price of seven thousand pounds. I wrote to the Times newspaper protesting which resulted in them giving one thousand more. It was a ridiculous price, but under a Socialist Government there was nothing we could do about it. My mother gave me the extra thousand pounds. It was the first capital I ever had.

Chapter 14

THE BALLET RUSSE DE MONTE CARLO

The Monte Carlo Ballet was the most prestigious ballet company in Europe at the time. M. René Blum, brother of the French Socialist Prime Minister, Léon Blum, had started this company in Monte Carlo that spring, with the great Russian Choreographer Michel Fokine. Fokine had created some of the most beautiful ballets for Diaghilev, working with Nijinsky, Pavlova, Karsavina and all the other great dancers of that time, in cooperation with the best composers, artists and musicians. They had taken Paris by storm when they had first appeared there in 1919 at the Theatre Châtelet. Diaghilev had died in 1929 and the dancers were all dispersed. Fokine had been for many years in America in comparative obscurity. Now, he had returned to Europe, persuaded by René Blum to come to Monte Carlo and re-make the ballets he had created for Diaghilev, as well as produce some new ones. They had opened in Monte Carlo, then Paris and London with great success.

Every dancer wanted to be in this company. People had come from all over Europe and America to try for a place. I felt it was presumptuous of me to think I had a chance of joining them, but I was determined to try, because in September the company was going to South Africa for the Centenary Exhibition in Johannesburg. Unfortunately, I had not been able to see a performance as their London season had been in June when I was in Ireland.

I was now living in digs in Ladbroke Square, Bayswater. It was a homely place run by a big-hearted Irish lady. My friend Jane Newman from Lincolnshire was also there and various other young people who had jobs in town. We used the kitchen and generally behaved as if we owned the place. Our land-lady cooked a big lunch for those who were at home on Sundays. It was the nearest thing to a home I had had since leaving South Africa.

In August London was hot and empty. The Monte Carlo ballet people were on holiday, most of them in Paris. I made inquiries. René Blum's secretary was still in London arranging the South African tour, staying at the Tavistock Hotel in Covent Garden. I went there. The hall porter told me that he was rarely in and that the only time of being sure to get him was at breakfast. In the dining-room I asked what time M. Raymond came in for breakfast. Eight thirty or nine, I was told.

It was a bright sunny morning as I made my way through Covent Garden market. I was wearing a yellow dress. The fruit and vegetable porters whistled and made cat-calls:

"'Allo Canary", one shouted, "Sing us a song, love."

My heart was beating fast, as I walked into the hotel and through the foyer to the dining-room. I hadn't met George Raymond and didn't even know what he looked like, so I asked a waiter which was his table. He was already sitting there alone, reading a newspaper. I introduced myself. He did not get up but indicated a chair. He was tall, slim, dark, youngish and French. I sat down and started to talk. First I told him that I was South African and wanted very much to go on this tour. I explained what experience I had and produced press cuttings. I insisted that my family was well known there, that I was bound to get good press coverage, especially in Natal. He listened, looked at the press cuttings and didn't say much. He was very nonchalant, very laid back. I got the impression that he was not in the least interested in me. When I had finished he said,

"There is no room in the company, we don't need any dancers." I said desperately,

"Perhaps someone will fall out."

"That is not likely" he replied. But he took my address and phone number.

I was disheartened; it had been such an ordeal. I am not by nature a pushy person and had forced myself to take such desperate action - all, it seemed, in vain. I felt empty and let down. I couldn't face the cheeky porters and walked back to the tube station another way.

Eskoldoff called me. Didn't I want to change my mind and rejoin the Ballet Russe de Paris? They were going to Germany to dance at a Gala performance in Munich. Why didn't I want to go? What was I to do? If I refused this offer I could find myself without a job. I had to decide quickly but couldn't give up the idea of going to South Africa. It was two years since I had seen my mother, and this was such a perfect opportunity to return triumphant with such an important company. I turned down Eskoldoff's offer to be called once again,

"Stupid girl."

One day I ran into a friend called Olive. I remember this occasion because she gave me some much needed encouragement. When I told her what I was trying to do, she said,

"Of course you can do it. Just go for it and I am sure you will make it. Go and see that man again, don't let him forget."

And so, next morning I was there again. This time I had to wait for him. He did not seem surprised or angry to see me. It was a quick interview. He just said that nothing had changed; there was still no place in the company. But, he did add,

"I haven't forgotten, I have your address."

It was about two weeks later when the phone rang for me.

"George Raymond here, do you still want to go to South Africa with the Monte Carlo Ballet? *Bien*, come now to Odaninos Hotel in Regent Street and sign your contract with Monsieur Blum."

M. Réne Blum was a tall, distinguished-looking, middle-aged man with iron grey hair and moustache, charming and polite. He asked me a few questions about my past dancing experience and I signed a six months contract, it was written in French and I hardly looked at it. It took about five minutes and once again I had fluked my way into one of, if not the best companies in the world, without giving an audition.

I have to explain here that my luck was largely explained by the fact that I looked like a dancer. I was not especially good looking or beautiful. I just looked like everyone's idea of what a classical ballet dancer should look like. Unfair though it is, it doesn't matter how well you dance - if you are not the right type you don't stand a chance. Things may have changed since then but it used to be like this in my time.

I could hardly believe my luck. I bought a bottle of whisky on the way home and celebrated with my friends in the house where I lived. I had three days in which to get ready.

We sailed from Southampton on the Union Castle Mail Boat, the Edinburgh Castle. I knew a few of the dancers from the previous Company. Manya was there without her mother.

At first I was put in a cabin with an English dancer called Barbara Barrie, who was not very friendly and didn't seem to think much of sharing a cabin with me. She had been the girlfriend of George Raymond (of the breakfasts) but had been ditched for another beautiful blonde - whom he eventually married. Understandably, she was not in the best of moods and soon got herself moved to another cabin. Manya took her place. There was no indication that Barbara would become one of my long lasting friends.

The first few days on board were cold and rough. I felt a bit lost among so many strangers who all knew each other. There were about seventy of us. The prima ballerina was Vera Nemtchinova, partnered by her husband Oboukhoff. They were older than the other dancers, aloof and kept to themselves; they had seen it all before. Amongst the girl soloists was a beautiful American dancer, a new find, called Nana Gollner; a pupil of Balanchine and Maria Ruanova. There was also Nina Tarskanova, a lively and attractive Argentinian with amazing elevation and the very young Nathalia Leslie. Some of the principal men were André Eglevsky and Michel Panaieff - both beautiful - and character dancers Nicholas Beriosoff and Simon Sapero. There were sixteen girls in the corps de ballet including five English girls and one South African from Cape Town. Among the male dancers were two English boys, Stanley Judson and Jack Spurgion, who were both good fun. There were two conductors, a pianist, stage manager, and wardrobe and business staff. René Blum was there with his secretary and business manager. The ballet master, who gave us classes, was a M. Gué. The most powerful person was the Régisseur; one Yazvinsky, known as Ivanivanivitch, who took rehearsals in the absence of Fokine - who would not join us till the following spring in Monte Carlo.

When the weather improved, we did a ballet class before breakfast on the top deck, the ship's rail substituting for a *barre*. The sun came out and so did all the young people. It was very lively. There was dancing every night, deck games and forbidden parties in Officer's cabins. We called at Madeira and had a riotous time on shore, sampling Madeira wine and hurtling down the famous flower-linen toboggan ride.

I was getting worried about all the new ballets I would have to learn. I was the only new dancer and would have to learn quickly. All the attention would be on me. Was I up to it? I asked some of the girls to show me some of the dances but they wouldn't help. They were on holiday and couldn't be bothered.

"Wait till we get there", they said.

There was to be a ship's concert, and we were asked if any of us had numbers we would like to dance. It was the very last thing I wanted to do but Leonard Pierce, one of the conductors who knew me, talked seriously to me. I could see that what he said was true. All the rehearsals would have to be held for me alone and I would have to learn at least six ballets in a short time. As I was not a very strong dancer and as Yazvinsky was a most impatient man, it was going to be difficult for me. I realised this only too well. Leonard suggested that I did my Spanish dance at the concert to show what I could do, and give a good first impression. He said he would play the piano for me. I was appalled at the idea but it made sense. I agreed to do it.

On the night I dressed in the cabin and, sticking my castanets down the front of my dress to warm them up, I ran up to the smoking-room, and drank a whisky quickly. I had never felt so nervous. The bar was deserted, all the passengers, including the whole ballet company, were down in the saloon waiting for the entertainment. God help me, what had I let myself in for?

The ship was rolling, the floor was slippery. I felt I had never danced so badly. It was agony, I felt sure that everybody was laughing at me. There was some applause but it didn't seem much. I slunk back to the cabin to change back into evening dress. I wanted to hide or jump overboard, but I knew I had to go out and face up to it. The first person I saw coming towards me along the corridor was Monsieur Blum. I felt like bolting in the other direction and then I saw he was smiling. He put his arm round me and said

"*Très bien, ma petite, très bien.*" My friend Leonard had given me good advice. From that day I was always included in the divertissement programme. There were other people with Spanish dances but they never got a chance to show them, Monsieur Blum liked my dance.

We had come to South Africa for the Centenary Empire Exhibition in Johannesburg. My mother had given up the apartment in Durban and was now living in Johannesburg, to be near my sister Barbara who had a job in a girl's school. She had a room in a very pleasant guest-house with a big garden, where she arranged for me to stay with her. This meant that she had to drive me into town to the theatre for rehearsals, or I drove myself in her car. This I found rather embarrassing and tried to park the car round a corner out of sight, but someone saw me and soon they were all gossiping. I was sure that they would not understand that everybody in South Africa had cars and that I had been driving since I was sixteen. The two worlds were touching and I didn't like it.

The rehearsals were just as bad as I had anticipated. All the others knew their parts and were bored with going over the same things just for me. I struggled on with Yazvinsky constantly shouting at me; sometimes I went quite blank with nerves. Somehow I survived the first night, but my self confidence was at very low ebb. One day when I was feeling particularly depressed, an experienced character dancer called Simon Sapero, whom I had never spoken to and who was not in the least interested in girls, came up to me during the evening performance. We had been doing Swan Lake during the matinee and he said he had been in front watching. He said,

"It is you I watch." He said it again smiling,

"It is you I watch, you understand?"

I did understand, it was a great compliment. I began to feel better at once. I mentioned this, as before with Olive, because I never forget the people who helped me when I needed encouraging. It is so important to encourage and help young people.

Again the Spanish dance came to the rescue. I got applause, flowers and press cuttings. The other South African girl, Yvonne and I had a lot of publicity. It pleased me that Kathleen O'Connor who had taught me the famous dance in the first place was in town, working with her band-leader husband.

There was no longer a relaxed holiday atmosphere about the company, now we were working hard. Strict discipline had taken over. Yazvinsky saw to that. He had it in for me for a long time and once even tried to get me sacked, until one day, as I came off to heavy applause, he flung his arms round me and said,

"*Quelle artiste.*"

We were friends at last.

We stayed six weeks in Johannesburg.

Next we went to Durban, where I stayed with our old friends the Caneys, in their house overlooking the bay. We were only there for a week and it rained all the time. Jim and Flora came down from the farm but there was no time to go up to Zululand. Many old friends came to the theatre to see me and sent good-luck telegrams and flowers, some of which came with no sender's name attached - That was interesting; which of the old flames had sent them? It was all too quick. In no time we were off by train to the Cape.

In Cape Town I stayed in a private house near the Mount Nelson Hotel, where I shared my room with a rabbit. The land-lady said she hoped I didn't mind the rabbit. It ran loose all over the house, but it was usually under my bed or on it, sharing its fleas with me. It was a most friendly rabbit.

Being near the end of our tour, we were not taking too seriously the clause in our contracts about not getting sunburnt. Up till then we had covered ourselves when lying in the sun. This did not apply to the boys, who to our envy, all had beautiful tans. Now we had fewer rehearsals and more free time. I had a friend with a car and we went on some excursions along that beautiful coast, and then inland to see the Old Dutch houses and the vineyards. Surely the Cape is one of the most beautiful places in the world.

We sailed back to England, once more on the Edinburgh Castle, so we knew all the ship's company who made us very welcome. We had a marvellous Christmas on board.

Chapter 15

MONTE CARLO

I was so happy to see the Mediterranean again; to wake up and look at the shining blue sea as the train ran along the coast on its way to Monte Carlo. It was like coming home again.

Several of us got rooms in a pension up the hill from the casino, in the not-so-fashionable part of town, but still quite close to the centre.

As I walked down that first evening the gardens in front of the casino were brilliant with cinerarias; masses of cerise, blue, pink and purple. The fantastic building shone with golden radiance in the amber flood lights. The fiacres stood one behind the other opposite the entrance, the horses shining chestnut, grey and brown. Palm trees waved gently in the breeze. Bright lights shone from the Café de Paris, the Sporting Club and the Hôtel de Paris opposite. It was an enchanted world as fantastic as a fairy story, bursting with riches and romance. And I was to be there for four months.

One of the first things I did was visit the casino. Ever since Diaghilev's days when some dancers had gambled away all their salaries, the members of the company had been banned from the gambling rooms. I reckoned that if I went quickly, before I was known, I might manage to get a pass, and so it turned out. I showed my passport and was given a card which gave entry for a month, after that it was simply renewed. I went in and out as I pleased, no one ever stopped me. If I had started to play seriously it would doubtless have been a different story. When I saw Monsieur Blum there he greeted me politely. As it was I mostly just watched, fascinated, as people won or more probably lost, what to me was a fortune.

I had time to go to the casino because at first we were only rehearsing the minor ballets for the opera season, which preceded the ballet season. This was not very taxing work, but we rarely got to rehearse on stage with the opera people. The result was sometimes hilarious; one never knew what was going to happen on the night. The director of the operas did not take us dancers seriously.

I used to enjoy watching from the wings. I fancied one Italian tenor from the Paris Opera, but he was strictly guarded by his wife, who was well aware of his roving eye. He told me he sang my favourite aria from Tosca just for me. This encouraged me no end but no further progress was made.

We practised and rehearsed every day in the big studio under the casino. To get there one walked along the sun-drenched terrace overlooking the sea, and through a wrought-iron gate which led to the musty dimness of the underground studio. This huge rehearsal room with its *barres* and mirrors was the work-shop of the ballet, the birth-place of many masterpieces. It was with a feeling of awe that I entered there for the first time and stood before the great mirror, where so many famous dancers had stood before me.

We were expectantly waiting for the arrival of Fokine. We were sitting on the floor, resting after class one morning, when the great man walked in. We all leapt to our feet immediately. He was held in such respect, that the company always stood up and stopped talking when he entered. He greeted us in Russian. Fokine was then approaching sixty; he was quite bald, with bushy eyebrows and piercing eyes. He was as always accompanied by his wife Vera Fokina; they had been a famous dancing couple in their youth in Russia. She was a rather large, overpowering lady, very protective of her husband.

The rehearsals started in earnest now. We went over the entire repertoire and started a new ballet, 'Les Elfes', to Mendelssohn's A Midsummer Night's Dream music and violin concerto. This was an abstract ballet; it had been performed in America but never in Europe. The elves were based on Shakespeare's fairies in 'A Midsummer Night's Dream'.

There was never any doubt that one was working for a master. Fokine was a perfectionist; every movement had to be perfectly executed. He spoke little, showing more often by movement than words what he wanted from his dancers, moving gracefully and lightly to the music, never counting. He was patient and took endless trouble to get every detail as he wished, unless he was upset; then, he would become red in the face and angry, whilst the unfortunate victim stood quaking in front of him. Thank God I never had to suffer this. If I did something wrong he would quietly show me again, a little smile on his face as if to say,

"You're a bit of a fool", but I felt he quite liked me.

I once saw an unfortunate girl dance a version of the waltz from 'Les Sylphides' at an audition. He was so livid I was afraid he would have a heart attack

"What is that?" he shouted, "Is that supposed to be my waltz?"

Fokine had reformed the ballet by using expressive mime instead of the old fashioned conventional gestures. He was the first to use pure dance in abstract form. To him, dance and music were inseparable components in ballet; he had an extraordinary sensitivity to music, and he had no use for the type of modern dance which uses noises for accompaniment. He had also improved the corps de ballet, by picking out individuals and couples to dance small parts; it was not just a question of dancing always in line - you were studied and put in the right place. He is still considered to be the most important choreographer of the century and many of his ballets still live. I was very privileged to work with him.

The season opened with all the glitter and glamour of days gone by. Every seat had been sold before the first performance. There were no cheap seats in the house, all were the same price. Squinting through the special peep-hole in the curtain, I could see the sleek, well-groomed audience; the glint of diamond tiaras catching my eye. The opera house with its rich Baroque opulence was actually part of the casino. There was no gallery or circle, just three boxes, the centre one was the royal box where the Prince of Monaco sat with his guests. On the right of the theatre from where I was looking, were three great gilded mirrors which reflected the stage and opposite, on the other side, were three long curtained windows, which I knew looked over the terrace, where ruined gamblers were said to go and shoot themselves.

I was delighted when Monsieur Blum asked me if I would like to dance at a 'Soiree de Gala de la Légion D'honneur' which the Prince was hosting in the casino ballroom. Several other members of the company were taking part in this most exclusive cabaret performance and it was a great honour to be invited. I felt good after my dance, standing there bowing, holding a bouquet of roses in front of such an illustrious gathering. When I saw Monsieur Blum the next day he told me,

"You danced last night for five kings." He sighed,

"I doubt if you will ever do that again."

I wished I had been given a signed programme instead of the roses. Who were the five kings? I have forgotten but I think several of them were already dethroned.

Our lodgings were quite comfortable and we were well fed. The only problem was that the rooms on the top floor were let to prostitutes. We had to be careful to lock our doors or we had unwelcome visitors. Everybody knew us in the town; wherever we went to shop we were recognised and given a large discount. The bars and cafés were pleased to have the young people from the ballet as customers; it was an attraction, which meant we could afford to patronise all the best places. Especially delicious, were the cakes at Madame Pasque's famous patisserie, which we passed on our way to work. Opposite the tea shop was an equally prestigious perfumery, where we were encouraged to spray ourselves with the most expensive French scents.

There was no time for social life now; we were working nearly all the time. We started with class at nine, followed by rehearsals for the rest of the morning and afternoon, and sometimes at night if there was no performance. We were rehearsing two big ballets: 'Les Elfs' and 'Les Elements'- the latter to a Bach fugue representing air, water, earth and fire. This ballet was to have its world premier in London in June. Several smaller ballets were also being prepared; I had a small solo part in one of these.

We did have some spare time when only the soloists were needed, this I usually spent in the casino which never failed to fascinate me. The players also interested me; they came from all over the world to play at this most famous of all casinos. Some looked what they were; Greek shipping millionaires, Arab Sheiks or rich industrialists. Men with fine aristocratic faces and hands, greasy fat men with diamond rings, elderly ladies heavy with jewellery and some people who looked as if they shouldn't be there at all - all of them deadly serious and intent. "Rien ne vas plus" called the croupier. There was a deadly hush as everyone concentrated on the little white ball, bouncing and skipping merrily round the wheel, tottering on the edge of one number and finally coming to rest on another. The croupier called out the winning number and raked in the losing chips. One more game was over. The croupiers were professionals, the play perfectly controlled. There was no getting away with grabbing other peoples winnings; certain old ladies with claw-like hands would try this, to be told politely:

"No Madame, ce n'est pas a vous, c'est à Monsieur."

I saw a sad thing once. A young man came and sat down at the table. He put a chip on red, black came up and he doubled his money on the red. Black won twenty-two times in succession and each time he doubled his stake. In just a few minutes all his money was gone. He went white, got up and left. Then everyone started to back red. Poor fellow, I felt so sorry for him, I could see he was hopelessly inexperienced to play such a fatal system.

The season in Monte Carlo lasted through April, and then we went to Paris for our season at the Theatre des Champs Elysées. Here I had a little attic room overlooking a leafy avenue near the theatre. The acacias were in bloom and the scent drifted in the window. Paris in May is light hearted and gay. We were walking along the Champs Elysées eating cherries, I had one dangling by the stalk from my mouth, when a hand came from behind and stole it. To my surprise it was Fokine – even he was feeling in a boyish mood.

At the theatre there was a continual flow of costumiers, painters, writers, musicians, photographers, patrons and admirers. Jean Cocteau and his friend Bébé Bérand were often there. Mistinguette came to rehearsal and sat in a box looking like an aged and wrinkled monkey. Many other famous people came. The theatre was packed every night.

At the end of May we opened at the Coliseum Theatre in London.

What I remember best about that season was the World Premier of the ballet 'Les Eléments'. It had already been postponed once because the costumes were not ready. On this night it was again delayed from second to last ballet on the programme. Up till the last minutes the costumes were coming, one by one in taxis. This ballet, representing the natural elements, had been well rehearsed in Monte Carlo but we had never seen, let alone had a chance, to practise in our costumes. I was one of the earth characters. Our dresses were enormous crinolines, most of which were in quiet brownish colours but mine was a bright conspicuous purple. The dresses had off shoulder bodices held up only by elastic shoulder straps, which seemed inadequate, but we had no time to do anything about it - we had to go straight on. When the curtain rose, us earth girls were lying stationary on stage with our dresses over our heads, looking like mounds of earth. I soon felt pins sticking into me in various places, I had not realised that all the beautiful, applied flowers on my skirt were only pinned on. I had to endure! Slowly we had to rise up, as flowers growing out of the ground, and moving down to the footlights go on one knee and bend right back facing the audience. The King and Queen were in the box just above me to the left. As I bent back, I felt the elastic pulling, giving and the bodice slipping down. I was sure I was exposing my left breast to the royal box. To look down to check would make it worse. I continued to hold the pose, looking over the right shoulder, praying for the best. As it turned out I was not quite exposed, just on the brink, but one of the others was not so lucky.

Things got even more hilarious when our boys (partners) came on. They wore sort of round pantaloons which had not been strapped properly between the legs, they swung backwards and forwards as they moved, like crazy lampshades. We burst out laughing.

Chapter 16

THE TOUR AND AFTER

After the London season we toured until January of the following year; first in England and Scotland and later on the Continent. We usually stayed a week, two in the bigger cities like Manchester, Birmingham or Glasgow. It was a major operation moving a company of that size, with all the scenery, props and skips full of costumes plus wardrobe staff and dancers. Two conductors and a first violinist came with us, and we used the Symphony orchestras in each town. There were usually six evening performances and two matinees a week. We travelled on Sundays, when the train services were slow and infrequent, but at least in Britain we did not work on Sunday. On the Continent we worked seven nights a week, and travelled after the show on Sunday night; often travelling all night, in third class compartments, reserved for us. When this happened we had a method; the luggage was put in the middle of the carriage and six people would sleep stretched out with their legs on the suitcases. Two others went up on the slatted wooden luggage racks to sleep - the latter was where I preferred to be.

We travelled, danced, rehearsed, washed tights, darned ballet shoes, gossiped, drank a bit, ate, slept and went to movies when not working in the afternoons. We stayed in a variety of digs and hotels, some good, some bad. There was nothing glamorous about it.

It was winter and we were back in Amsterdam again. It was freezing cold and people were skating on the Amstel Canal. This time our rooms were beautifully warm and our Dutch housewife fed us well and fussed over us - so different from my last visit, two years before. We were performing at the Carré Theatre. I had a friend in Amsterdam, a young man I had met on the Edinburgh Castle coming back from South Africa. He invited me and Nina Tarakanova out to dinner several times after the show. He had a friend with him and the four of us went to all the best night spots during our stay there.

That Christmas we were in Switzerland. It was the coldest Christmas I can remember. My nose felt as if it was freezing on my face. Some of us tried to go to church on Christmas Day but by the time we found the church, the congregation was leaving. So instead we went to the nearest café and had delicious hot chocolate with lots of whipped cream on top. We had a party in our digs that night, our friends all brought bottles and we got a bit drunk and had hangovers the next day.

Funny things happened in Zurich. We were always being warned to be careful of the white slave dealers, who were active in certain countries at the time, but one didn't expect it somehow, in smug respectable Switzerland. A strange man walked into Manya's room early one morning when she was in bed. He offered her some fantastic sum to model some fur coats. She was naturally interested but became suspicious when the man called again ostensibly to measure her for the coats, and let slip that she would never want to go back to the ballet again as she would make a fortune in South America. She sent him packing. I had a phone call from a stranger along much the same lines.

We all got a shock in that cold city, when we were called to a meeting and were told by Mr. Blum, that we were to have a month's unpaid holiday before going on to Monte Carlo. There were to be changes too. Mr. Blum had sold a share in the company to the American Theatre Manager, Hurok. We were to have Massine as Ballet Master instead of Fokine. This was unsettling news. Some of the English girls made a protest about not being paid, I did not join them; I knew from previous experience it would be hopeless and only cause trouble. Most people went back to their homes for that month. I joined some friends from England who were at the winter sports not far from Zurich. I was taking a chance, I could easily have broken a leg and spoilt my career but I went all the same. It was great fun and I learnt to ski well enough to enjoy it.

I thought it would be best to go straight to Monte Carlo for the last two weeks and ask for an advance on my salary, having spent what little money I had. However, this was not necessary. I arrived at Monte Carlo and found some of the others there already, busily rehearsing for the Opera ballets, so I went straight to work.

When the rest of the company arrived, we found that some of our old stars had left and others had taken their place. Massine brought a group of American girls; they were referred to as students. It did not take us long to find out, that they were paying instead of being paid for the privilege of being in the Monte Carlo Ballet. They were pupils of Balanchine and had amazingly strong technique. The one to become the most famous of these was Rosella Hightower. Two very well known dancers, Alexandra Danilova and Igor Youskevitch came in the place of Nana Gollner and Andre Eglevsky and also the English dancers Alicia Markova and Freddy Franklin. Massine's present wife and various ex-wives and girl friends were also there. We were quaking, wondering who was going to be sacked to make room for all these newcomers.

I had seen Massine dance and admired his work as a choreographer; I thought it would be interesting to work with him. He was a small, lightweight man of about forty with great dark eyes that looked straight through one. I found him attractive in a way, but there was a strange sort of vacancy about him. He was not a compelling personality like Fokine; no one jumped to their feet when he came into the room and he had to shout for us to be quiet. I started rehearsing with him the first act of the ballet he was doing to Beethoven's Seventh Symphony - it was an interesting ballet about the creation of the world. He counted out loud to the music all the time as he showed the steps. I was enjoying it, when suddenly I was no longer called to rehearsals. Not only me, all the English girls were taken out of the rehearsals for the new ballets. The Americans and 'friends' were put in our place. It was painfully clear who were the ones to be dropped.

The next two months was an unhappy time, full of rumours and intrigue. We continued to dance and rehearse the old repertoire under the instruction of Yazvinsky, but none of us were in the new Massine Ballets. We got together and amongst ourselves decided that we would stick together and not go and talk individually to Massine. In consequence we knew nothing definite. All sorts of rumours were going round. The Russians love intrigue. They were all trying to find out what was going on for us. Daily, we heard different stories about which girls were being kept on and which were not.

Danilova and Youskevitch, the new stars, were friendly with us and interceded with Massine on our behalf. Alicia Markova, the English ballerina (Alice Marks), stuck up and unfriendly, ignored us completely. In this company there had never been any distinction socially between the stars and the rest of us. Now, there was a bad feeling in the company, a constant undercurrent of worry and intrigue. Monsieur Blum looked sad; it seemed he had very little say in the company any more. Massine, representing Hurok and American money had all the power.

My mother, who was back in Europe, came over to Monte Carlo and we took an apartment over a flower shop. It was nice to be looked after again and I was particularly happy to see how she was enjoying it. She went to the market in the morning, did the cooking, and enjoyed a little flutter at the casino. She was interested, sympathetic and never shocked by my friends.

As it became more and more obvious that our days in the company were numbered, we became rebellious and naughty, doing things we would never have dreamt of doing normally.

And so it came to the last night. We danced 'Les Elfes' for the last time. It was an emotional occasion, and several elves were in tears as we moved to the haunting music of the violin concerto. The last ballet on the programme was Coppelia. As we danced the lively Mazurka, at the end, I felt that one of my shoes was loose. I just let it go and a red shoe sailed right out into the audience. It was a dreadful thing to do but it seemed a fitting farewell gesture.

Massine sent for us after the performance. The first thing he asked was whose shoe it had been, I confessed and was duly told off. Then he went on to say how sorry he was to lose us, that it was nothing to do with our work and that in fact he liked some of us better than some of the ones he was keeping. He explained that he had to have the Americans because they had nowhere else to go. We, on the contrary, had ballets in England which we could join. We didn't say a word. We had also heard that the English backing had fallen through, which may have been a deciding point - money was always at the back of everything. And so the seven of us were officially told what we already knew; that our contracts were not to be renewed.

Before I left Monte Carlo I asked Massine to sign a photo for me.

"Are you going to stick pins in it?" he asked.

Chapter 17

LONDON AND MILAN

Mother and I took a little mews flat near Ladbroke Square. It was over a garage and smelt slightly of petrol but it had a nice, leafy outlook down the mews. It was fine in the summer but mother, who always felt the cold, wanted to find a central heated flat before the winter. The one we decided on was in a block in Porchester Road near Queensway, Bayswater. It had a fair-sized living room, two bedrooms - one big the other small - a dark kitchen that looked into a well, a hall with a cupboard and a bathroom with no window. It had central heating, boiling water, parquet floors and numerous built-in cupboards. It was modern and convenient and quite characterless. It was unfurnished so we got some of our furniture from Keal out of store and enjoyed fixing it up. We had a home of sorts again.

All that summer I was working up new numbers, and having costumes made. I didn't want to go back to the ballet, I wanted to work alone as a solo dancer. I also went to an agent and got a little film work here and there, either dancing or as a special extra. These jobs paid well but I could not rely on them.

The Indian dancer Ram Gopal was at the Adelphi Theatre. He was a beautiful dancer and most gorgeous creature. Indian dancing was a new experience for me and I was fascinated by it. I persuaded Ram to give me lessons. For these I went to his apartment, somewhere in Hampstead. He would appear bleary eyed in his pyjamas, straight from bed but still gorgeous. We drank tea attended by several little girls from his company, whilst he made fun of his latest admirer and showed his latest expensive gift. After that he would give me a lesson. It was delightfully informal. I was allowed also into the theatre to watch from the wings. When he went on tour, Ram suggested I joined his company, I would have liked to, but I was aware what I would look like, amongst those delicate little Indian girls with their fine bones. Ram Gopal was deadly serious about his dancing which was absolutely authentic. Indian dancing is a very big subject, every gesture has a meaning. I worked hard at it for the short time it was available to me but I could only touch the surface. I knew just enough to make a pretty dance.

I also learnt some South American dances at this time, and had a red and white frilly dress made with a Carmen Miranda hat - a white satin turban with a big bunch of red feathers on top.

It was around this time that Mother became friendly with the mother of a friend of mine. They were a well-to-do family with whom I had stayed when I was a student. This lady was involved in spiritualism. She was a widow and claimed to be in direct touch with her late husband, who talked to her and gave her advice on how to bring up the children and manage her life. My mother was very interested in this and we went to several séances. The most impressive was when it was arranged for me to see a well-known medium. She immediately got in touch with Bill my South African boyfriend, who had died three years before. Through her he sent a message to say that he had got my dog with him. There followed a perfect description of Blighty, the bulldog with his patch over one eye, he even said: "But doesn't he dribble?" Then he went on to say. "I go to the races here but the right horse always wins." It was uncanny, but somehow so superficial that it was hard to take seriously. I subsequently came to the conclusion that the medium must have been reading my sub-conscious.

One séance we went to was quite exciting. We sat in a circle holding hands, soft music played and the lights were put out. Various objects were lying on the floor in the middle of the circle between us: several trumpets and a mouth-organ, which were outlined in phosphorescent paint. These things rose up and sailed about the room, the mouth-organ played a tune. The trumpets hovered around people giving messages, sometimes in strange languages. It was eerie. I was disappointed that there were no messages for us. The people each side of the medium, holding his hands, had been told to keep hold of him until they were forced to let go, when this happened, he would be completely levitated. We could not see this but could sense his legs going slowly past, and then he bumped downwards into the middle of the circle. This phenomenon had been examined and authorised as genuine by the body who investigates these séances. I found it difficult to believe but on the other hand it would have been difficult to rig: If there had been a powerful magnet in the ceiling, it would have been detected at once.

After Christmas an invitation came from Monsieur Blum to go to Monte Carlo for the opera ballet. The ballet company was in America still and would not be back in time to do the opera season, so a separate company was being formed. In the middle of the English winter Monte Carlo was very tempting. I accepted.

We found an attractive villa overlooking the sea, which we shared with several other people, Mother kept house for us.

It was quite a good little company. The ballet mistress was Tania Chamié. An old fashioned lady in a long skirt gave us class. Amongst other things we did quite an interesting ballet to the Grieg piano concerto.

I did not like the idea of being in Monte Carlo when the ballet company came back from America, so after the opera season was over I went to Paris.

After years of boring ballet class I now found a teacher whose classes I enjoyed. Victor Gzovsky had been teaching in Berlin and had fled to Paris to escape the Nazis. His studio was in the same building as Madame Preobtajenska's. I think I was a little in love with him. His classes were different, full of expression and beautiful movement. I am sure that if he had not suffered from a drink problem he would have been one of the great teachers. As it was he went back to Berlin after the war, where I believe he died in penury. Victor spoke Russian and German, I English and French, but we managed to understand each other. I used to meet him with a group of friends at a pavement café in Pigalle, where we sat talking and smoking Gauloises cigarettes well into the night, as the saucers piled up in front of us - each drink came with a saucer which was retained for counting at the end of the evening.

It was 1939 and there was a lot of anxiety about the future. There were a number of people, like Victor, who had fled Germany. Some had no permission to stay in France: people would quietly disappear from the café tables, then a few minutes later, the police would come round checking papers - the absentees had been tipped off; they would hide in a back room and soon reappear when the coast was clear. No one ever remarked about these happenings.

Bed bugs were evident in the hotel; a common occurrence in the old buildings in summer. I was plagued by these little beasts, but as I didn't want to leave the hotel I tried to get rid of them. I soaked bits of cotton wool in methylated spirit, pushed them into the cracks in the skirting-board behind the bed and set fire to them. The Hotel de Palm was in danger of burning down, but it worked - no more bugs. In my room I had a tiny spirit stove for making tea and a small travelling iron. We were not supposed to iron in the hotel, if several of us did at the same time - usually on Sunday evening - all the lights in the hotel fused. We would hurriedly get rid of the evidence, hiding the iron under the bed before Madame came looking for the culprit.

I badly needed a job. Without a work permit I could do nothing on my own, so I joined a dancing act. We did some jazzy music-hall numbers, including a tango, a can-can and one ballet number.

We performed at a Paris Music Hall, shaking frilly dresses to the Offenbach can-can music, whilst old men in front rows peered up our skirts. It was a far cry from the Russian ballet.

That August we also went to Milan. The show - which was at a large variety theatre - came on late, so we had all day free. Most of the time we spent at a large swimming pool called the Lido. My only bathing costume was a two-piece, the forerunner of the bikini. I showed a discreet bare middle quite acceptable in France but apparently not in Italy. I was for ever being hounded round by the attendants. To pacify them I tied a scarf round my middle, which of course I removed when I went in to swim. I was surprised that they were so prudish in Italy. One of the acts in the show consisted of a couple dressed just in leaves who did a sexy Tarzan *pàs de deux*. The girl was annoyed when she was told to wear a bra and she crossly sewed something in the dressing-room. On the last night she tore it off and threw it away in the middle of the act.

Among our fellow artists were a bear and a dog. The poor bear was obviously very unhappy; he lived all the time in a cage behind the stage. We were told not to touch him, but I used to go and talk to him, although he didn't understand English and didn't like people. Who could blame him? The couple who worked with him said he was unhappy because he was used to working in a circus with other bears. The little dog was also in the act; he was terrified of the bear and trembled all over whenever he had to go near him. At the end of their act the bear rode round and round the stage on a scooter. At this point he expressed his feelings by peeing, so there were trails and whirls of bear-pee all over the stage. Immediately after this we posed in a group for the ballet number. We would put ourselves down wherever there was a dry patch, usually nowhere near centre stage. It was also very slippery. We made a fuss and eventually there was a delay while sawdust was put down and swept up. One night the bear was in a bad mood and clawed the arm of the girl who was working with him. She was very brave and kept her arm, pouring with blood, well behind her back, as she led the animal forward to take the curtain call. The moment the curtain was down her partner started bashing the bear, boxing it in the face. It was horrible. The girl tried to defend the bear. She had to have stitches in her arm.

The Russian woman who employed us looked like a fat witch. She always wore black clothes with a flowing cape. I did not like her or her little pet marmoset, which bit me whenever I tried to make friends with it. This little creature ran about the dressing-room doing its business wherever it pleased. Its owner thought it was very clever when it did it in someone's powder-box, but we did not.

I was enjoying Italy. I had scampi and strawberries every day for lunch. It didn't concern me what Mussolini was up to in North Africa, nor did I think about how close we were getting to war; I wanted to stay on in Italy. I was just a silly girl wandering in the hot streets of Milan, eating ice-cream and slices of cold watermelon accompanied by a handsome, flashy Italian. I had picked him up at the Lido. He was a Neapolitan, always most courteous and correct when he took me out to eat spaghetti, so I paid no attention when I was warned to have nothing to do with him. I was told that he had recently come out of prison for killing a man in Naples. This made him all the more interesting! I asked him if it was true, he said he had to knife the man in self-defence. I didn't know then that he was a drug addict. I told him I wanted to stay in Italy and he said he knew someone - a theatre manager, who might have a job for me. On the last night he insisted on taking a room at the hotel where I was staying with another girl. In his room he produced some white powder which we sniffed together. Apart from making me feel rather light headed it didn't have much effect. Then we lay on the bed and he showed me all the puncture marks on his arms from injections. This was by way of explaining why he was impotent.

The next morning he introduced me to the man who might give me work. The man resembled a fat toad.

"Sure I could work for him," he said, and threw a bunch of keys on the table. I suddenly realized what I was getting myself into. I was thankful to be on the Paris train that night with the others.

Chapter 18

WAR

I went back to London. Luckily I took all my costumes and things with me, for within two weeks we were at war.

I was in the apartment with mother on that fateful third of September, when Neville Chamberlain announced on the radio that we were at war. Immediately, the air raid sirens blared a warning. It was the first of many times we were to hear them.

I had an opportunity to join the Col. De Basil Company again, which was just about to leave for America, but the last thing I wanted was to leave England at this critical time. Instead I joined the London Auxiliary Ambulance Service, together with my friend Jane Newman. We were stationed at Putney Bridge, an awkward place to get to from where I lived. The ambulances were converted furniture vans, a varied collection of heavy, clumsy vehicles. One had to do something called a 'double declutch' to get them in and out of gear. There were lectures and a first aid course, and before petrol became scarce we had to do some practice exercises, the most spectacular of which, was driving down Oxford Street in a huge van wearing a gas mask. The mask soon fogged up and it was difficult and dangerous driving. People looked at us in horror – had there been a gas bomb?

Everybody was issued with a gas mask, which we had to carry with us all the time in a cardboard box. I was worried about Victor Gzovsky in Paris, in case (not being French) he did not have a gas mask. I wrote to him in Russian, with much reference to the dictionary - what on earth was gas mask in Russian. I told him I could send him mine, and then pretend I had lost it and get another. He never answered the letter, but when I saw him after the war, he told me that he had received it and shown it round the Russian colony where it had caused much amusement. It was my one and only attempt to write a letter in Russian.

One night there was a gas alert. All the residents of Peters Court were herded by the wardens into the air-raid shelter under the building, where we were crowded for what seemed hours. Mustard gas was supposed to smell like rotting vegetables. It turned out that there was some not very fresh produce at a greengrocer's down the street, which had been sniffed by an overzealous air raid warden. The experience convinced us that it was better to take a chance and stay in our flat, rather than go down to the basement when the siren went.

The black-out was strictly in force. We made curtains of black material and stuck sticky tape criss-cross on the windows to stop glass splintering. Food and clothes were rationed and we were issued coupons.

At the station we waited about, bored. We only functioned during air raids and so far there had been none.

It was Barbara Barrie this time, who suggested I join her in the revival of the Oriental Musical 'Chu Chin Chow', of First World War fame. We girls had not yet been officially called up so there was no difficulty about my leaving the Ambulance Station. I had been trained and would go back when I was needed.

'Chu Chin Chow' was a big production - A spectacular show with some good singers and actors, a chorus and about a dozen dancers. We had a numbers of dances for which we wore attractive oriental costumes. I was given a small Japanese solo which I arranged myself.

Although we opened in London, it is the tour that I remember best. I was in love with a bass baritone: Don was a big handsome fellow with a fine 'dark brown' voice. He was quite a bit older than I and an experienced lover. We shared digs and a double bed wherever we stayed. One night in Manchester, I woke up burning hot, to put on the light and find myself covered in a bright red rash. My lover was out of that room in two seconds flat. All the time I was in bed with German measles, he only put his head round the door a couple of times. I should have been warned that he was a very cautious man. It was watching his behaviour during the air raid later that finally put me off him; I could not admire a man who was cowering on all fours under the piano. He was also rather good at letting other people pay for drinks in pubs. At the time of the German measles, however, I was only nervous in case it might be the end of the affair. I need not have worried; as soon as I was over the quarantine period we continued as before.

France was falling. The German army, two million strong, had taken the Netherlands and Belgium and simply gone round the Maginot Line. The war was coming nearer and there was talk of a German invasion. We were on the train returning to London when we read about Dunkirk, where the Allied forces had been cut off by the advancing German army and all the little boats had gone across the channel so bravely, to pick up our soldiers on the beaches. It was the time of the Battle of Britain. The German bombers were attacking our air fields and our boys in their fighters – not nearly enough of them – were fighting back.

Chu Chin-Chow was at the Palace Theatre in Cambridge Circus, a stone's throw from my old dancing studio in West Street. It was a hot summer and sometimes we used to go up a ladder onto the roof to get some air.

One Saturday in September, we were lazing about in the dressing-room between the matinee and the evening performance, when suddenly there was a wail of the air raid siren from close by. It came as a shock after months of no action in London. We dressed quickly and went out to see what was happening. We could hear planes and guns in the distance, and then fire engines came dashing two abreast down Shaftsbury Avenue, sirens blaring. Something awful was happening somewhere. After a bit the all-clear sounded and it was decided that we give the evening performance (there had been a lot of advance booking), but we were told on no account, to go on the roof. Soon the warning sounded again. I was determined to see what was going on. In the middle of the show I just had time – dressed in harem pants and floating veils – to scramble up the ladder on to the roof. What I saw was awe-inspiring. It seemed as if the whole of the East End and dock area was on fire. Great flames reared up into the sky, some green and blue, where a chemical factory had been hit. The sky was alight with a red glow. High up above the inferno, planes were circling, the red light catching their wings as they wheeled. I could hear the 'woof' of bombs exploding and the clatter of ack-ack guns in the distance, but it was the visual affect that was so shattering and quite beautiful. It left me in no doubt what the future held for us in London. Over a thousand bombers and their attendant fighters took part in the raid that day, thousands of high explosives and incendiary bombs were dropped.

After the show we gathered in the theatre bar, where we waited not knowing what to do. We were told that we could stay there if we liked but that the underground trains were running. I walked down Shaftsbury Avenue to Piccadilly Circus. It was quiet and dark, with very few people about in the street. I went home on the underground to Queensway. As the train went through the stations, I saw for the first time, what was soon to be a familiar sight; people taking refuge, lying in rows on the platforms. Our theatre closed, as did all the others in London sooner or later, with the exception of the Windmill Variety Theatre which stayed open all through the Blitz.

I rejoined the ambulance service. This time I was stationed a short walk from home, in Moscow Road, off Queensway. Things were better organised now. We had proper ambulances, with four stretchers in each. At least two of us went with each vehicle, a driver and an assistant, whose job it was to go in the back with the casualties. I nearly always drove, which I preferred. At first we were about equal in numbers, but as the younger men got called up for the forces, we girls were left with just a few elderly taxi drivers. We were a mixed bunch at the ambulance station. Young girls from good families, older ladies who wanted to do their bit, out of work taxi drivers too old to be called up and a few young men, who for some reason were not eligible for the forces. I made friends with an interesting Hungarian woman, Terry Miller. She was married to an Englishman, very much in the news at that time; he was an oil man and had been abducted somewhere in Eastern Europe. I don't remember why he had sent her to England at the beginning of the war. She was in a strange country with no friends, and people were unkind to her because they thought she was German. I befriended her. She had a small flat near ours and we were friends for many years.

At first we were on duty alternate weeks, on day and night duty, changing at seven, morning and evening. Later it got dark early and there were raids nearly every night, shifts were then changed to twenty four hours on duty and twenty four off. This adjustment was made so that we didn't run the risk of going on duty during a raid. It was so dark during the black out on moonless nights, that I once walked into a lamp post. Luckily my tin hat clanged against it first.

At the station, the shift leader sat in an office with a telephone. There was a list pinned on a board. The two ambulances at the top of the list were on emergency duty, ready to go out first. After two hours, regardless as to whether they had been called out or not, they went to the bottom of the list. This way, on quiet nights, we could get some rest in a room with stretcher beds. Once the air raid siren went we were on duty for all ambulance work.

The ambulances were lined up in the garage with the office situated at the end. Just outside the office there were some tables and chairs where we waited for our instructions. This was a tense moment; you had to know the best and quickest way to get to where you were called, before running to your ambulance and driving out into a world illuminated by a red glow, with search lights criss-crossing in the sky, and noisy with bombs exploding, ack-ack guns firing, and bombers growling overhead. On dark nights it was probably quieter, but then it was difficult to see with the head lights blacked out, except for a tiny slit; the road often blocked by craters or rubble from bombed houses. We had of course studied the district minutely, and knew the quickest way to get to the hospitals but there was always a liability of hazards. It was essential to keep one's head. Once arrived on the scene, there was inevitably a wait, whilst casualties were brought out of the bombed houses and attended to. If there was fire, the fire engines would be there. The heavy rescue team went in first, with equipment for moving heavy objects and digging people out. The light rescue teams, assisted people to evacuate buildings when a time bomb was suspected. The first aid people tended the injured; they were a team usually working under a doctor.

Whilst all this was going on we waited by our ambulances, witnessing what was frequently a chilling, macabre scene. People covered in dust loomed out of bombed buildings in the red glow, the smell of burning pervading everything, and the dead left to lie, their feet sticking out pathetically from the blankets thrown over them. Distraught people would be looking for relatives. This for me was the worst time, I felt quite calm and dead cold. Once the stretchers were shoved in the back, we were off as fast as possible to the nearest hospital and back again for the next load. When once called out we stayed on the job until no longer needed. We were trained for emergency first aid, but I personally was never called to practise it. The girl, who went inside the ambulance with the casualties, had to try to keep them quiet - if they were conscious. They were always in shock and often hysterical, usually more worried about what had happened to their loved ones than their own condition. They would keep on asking questions to which we had no answer.

One of the first times I was called out, there was a nasty muddle. Four stretchers were put in my ambulance. I didn't examine what was on them and drove straight to St. Mary's hospital. Two of the stretchers were taken out and the other two shoved back in.

"We don't take stiffs" the attendant said.

"Well, what am I to do with them?" I asked.

He told me to take them to the hospital mortuary; this was not in the hospital but down a dark back-street. The other girl was in front with me but neither of us could see a thing and there was no one to ask. When we did eventually find the building it was locked, there was not a soul there. So back we went to the hospital again for another wait whilst someone was found to unlock it. Then we had to go back and help with the stretchers. It was not a nice experience and I took more care in the future what I carried. We were not supposed to take the dead but it was not up to us to decide who was dead! Later things were better organised. When we got back to the station after we had been on a job, the inside of the ambulance had to be cleaned. This was the assistant's job but if it was very dirty with blood and vomit I would help.

All that winter of 40-41 there were raids most nights; they were always worse on moonlit nights. What a relief it was when there was a thick fog; one could then catch up on some sleep. All Londoners suffered from lack of sleep; night after night we were disturbed. Ours was a bad area, we were constantly attacked because we were near Paddington Station and the stations were prime targets.

Many people went down into the tube stations every night with their bedding, and fortified by sandwiches and thermos flasks took up their regular parking places. It was all rather pally; I believe some of them quiet enjoyed it, the children certainly did. At least they felt safe down there.

They became so used to the racket of the trains coming and going and then rattling to a stop as the automatic doors hissed open and shut, that they slept through it all, in the stale, fetid air. I used to see them on their way home, as I went to work in the early morning; bedraggled and dirty, parents clutching their family's pillows and blankets and dragging sleepy children behind them. Sometimes we had to go down there to pick up people who had been taken ill. On one occasion a baby was about to be born, and we had the greatest difficulty in finding a man to start the automatic lifts to get the woman to the surface.

There was a notable change taking place amongst the population of London. People who normally never spoke to their neighbours were now friendly with everybody. There was a great exodus. Most of the children were evacuated and sent to the country to stay with willing families, often with bizarre results. City girls joined up as land girls and went to work on farms, with equally bizarre results. No one stayed in the city unless they had to. Amongst those of us who were left there was a feeling of comradeship; we were all in it together. The true Cockney was at his best, brave and tenacious, his marvellous sense of humour never deserting him. I am glad I was in London during the Blitz; I learnt to respect my British nationals. I think about it sometimes when people today seem so utterly awful.

Food was scarce and bad. We had our rations and no-one starved but it was very dull. I will never forget those horrible powdered eggs; there was no way of disguising them. Mother did her best to make edible meals out of our meagre rations and became quite inventive. She made marmalade out of the skins of our one orange per person a week, adding a little of the precious sugar ration. If there was anything 'off ration' at the butchers there would soon be a queue. A lump of dark red meat that looked like steak turned out to be whale meat. We tried it once but never again. Rabbit was not rationed, but on the rare occasions when it appeared, it was cut up in small pieces - very suspect, was it rabbit or cat, or rat? I met an old friend who was in the Ministry of Food. He asked me if I would like some meat. A brown paper parcel duly arrived by post dripping with blood - A delicious steak.

Barrage balloons appeared floating over the city, great cumbersome things, their function was to stop the planes coming in low and machine-gunning the streets. There was a tragedy when one of these got loose and floated down in a crowded area on a foggy day. It was mistaken for a land-mine; these came down slowly on parachutes.
People panicked, they dashed to the nearest tube station and stampeded down the stairs, to pile up at the bottom. Many of them were crushed to death. After that the entrances to the stations were sandbagged to prevent a headlong rush.

The dock district in the East End had taken a continual blasting. Drivers had been killed and ambulances destroyed. Some of us from other stations were lent for periods of twenty-four hours to the worst hit areas. I was interested to know what it was like down there and volunteered to go. I spent twenty-four hours in the Isle of Dogs. So near the heart of London, but we could have been in another world. There was intense damage to wharfs and warehouses and piles of rubble everywhere. The people at the station were friendly enough but we west Londoners felt outsiders - people from another club. Also, we had not been through what they had. There was no raid that day and somebody said:

"They are not going to come tonight; it's a bit misty. Why don't you go over and ave a quick'un at the pub, love?"

The pub stood in the middle of the rubble, miraculously untouched. The bar was full of Dockers and their ladies; some of the older ladies were wearing men's caps and smoking pipes. They were all talking in broad Cockney and knocking back their bitter, or was it gin? Where did they go to, all those lovely people?

One bad night, when there was a lot of activity and noise and the ambulances were coming in and out fast, I had just come in and was in the office reporting when the phone rang. I heard: "Peters Court, Porchester Road - Two cars right away." I froze. Ambulances were being sent to my block of flats, to my home where my mother was alone. I knew it was strictly against the rules to use the phone. I had to go. I told the shift leader that I would be no good until I knew what had happened. I was at the bottom of the list now to be called out and she didn't try to stop me. I went out into the noisy night and started running. There were planes overhead and suddenly two bombs screeched down and exploded one after the other, the second one very near. I threw myself down in the gutter waiting for the third, it came screaming over me and exploded even nearer, and then I was up again running. As I got to Whiteley's departments store, the plate glass windows came crashing down from the first floor into the street. I crossed to the other side and there I was stopped by an air raid warden, who wanted to know what I was doing out in the street. I told him why I was there and to my great relief he told me that no bomb had fallen on Peters Court. The pub on the corner, The Royal Oak, had been hit and people had been injured in the street. An emergency first-aid post had been set up in the foyer of Peters Court and the injured were being taken there. The rescue teams were arriving at Whiteley's as I returned to the Station.

My mother was marvellous through all this, she always responded to a challenge. She would not hear of going to the country to stay with one of her sisters. She was always calm and resourceful and if she was ever afraid she did not show it. I had a horror of being bombed in the bath and the building being blown away and my being stuck up somewhere, still sitting naked in the tub. In our interior bathroom, if you had the taps on you couldn't hear anything. I enjoyed soaking in the bath after twenty four hours on duty. I remember Mother knocking on the door and saying; "I think you had better get out dear that last one was rather near."

I was still seeing my boy-friend Don, the singer, whenever I could. He was not working. He lived in a flat near the Kings Road, his mother lived there too but she had her own quarters. I never stayed the night there as I didn't like leaving my mother alone any more than I had to, but I went there in the day time when I was off duty. We listened to a lot of opera records.

One day Don phoned me to say their windows had been blown out, and could he and his mother come and stay with us? My mother agreed of course, but I could see that she was not very pleased. She did not approve of Don, she thought with reason that he should be doing some war work. So when they came she made him sleep on a mattress on the hall floor. She was not having him share my little divan in the sitting-room, (his mother had my bedroom). Mother was no fool; he was somewhat put out by this treatment and the next day they went back to their boarded-up windows. Don soon went off touring with another show. I felt frustrated and jealous, imagining him living in the same digs, and sleeping in the same beds with my replacement. I sometimes went to see his mother but she never had any interesting news of him.

My sister Barbara had come back from South Africa. She had joined the A.T.S. and was stationed somewhere in England, but she had left that because of bad health and came back to London. She later joined the light rescue service. So we were both working in the Auxiliary forces. In South Africa my brother Jim was a gunnery instructor. He would rather have gone to the North African front, where many South Africans were soon to be taken prisoner at Tobruk. My cousins Lois and Marjory Croome were both working at the War Office, while Aunt Grace had some little East End refugee children staying at her house. There was constant sad news of friends and relatives being killed, among them my teenage boy-friend Jack and my cousin Dick Sale, who were both killed flying.

The night the Luftwaffe finally got Paddington station was the night they got us. It was a noisy night. Four of us were playing bridge, waiting to be called out. I was facing a big plate-glass window which was camouflaged with thick paint. Without warning the whole thing was coming at me. Apparently I yelled:"Down", (I did not remember doing this) and we threw ourselves on the floor. Then, came the roar of the explosion. The noise of falling masonry and smashing glass was all around us, as we lay cowering on the floor. It died away into an awesome silence and a great cloud of dust swept through the broken window and walls, enveloping us as we lay choking and coughing. The lights had gone; we crawled blindly about in the dark, calling out to one another. When eventually we stood up, we found that miraculously none of the four of us had been injured. The roof of the garage had collapsed, smashing some of the ambulances, but the roof above the office and rooms where we were had not fallen and nobody had been hurt. A block of flats next to the garage had received a direct hit from a heavy land-mine and had come down like a pack of cards. We were so close to the explosion, that the blast, going up and out and smashing everything within a wide radius, had missed us. It was just one of those flukes, a lucky one for us. It was a busy night. Next to our garages there was another garage where cars were stored and this was on fire. We had to get the ambulances out before the fire spread. Some could not be driven and had to be pushed out into the street. It was fortunate that there was a second entrance as the main one was completely blocked. There was no light of course and the phone was not working. People came running asking for ambulances. We worked all night with the few that were serviceable. Rescue workers were trying to find people in what had been the flats. Bodies were carried out and laid in a row. There seemed to be no survivors. In the morning, when our relief shift came on duty, they found a ruin and some filthy worn out ambulance workers. But we were glad to be alive.

We went to new quarters but it was never as bad again.

The raids became fewer after that, until they stopped altogether: The Luftwaffe was otherwise engaged, busy over Russia. Once again we had nothing to do but hang around and again I was bored.

Chapter 19

BACK ON THE BOARDS AGAIN

One day I ran into Eskoldoff (from the Ballet Russe de Paris). I had not seen him for several years. He told me he was producing a Russian opera and Ballet called 'Sorotchintsi Fair' with music by Mussorgsky. He said he had solid backing and he felt this was just the right moment: Russia was fighting on our side, everything was pre-Russian and this show was to be typically Russian. He asked if I wanted to join the ballet. I liked the idea very much and told him I would do so with pleasure, if he could get me permission from the Ambulance Service.

In due course I was given leave for three months. It was fun to be dancing again. I was out of practice but as there was no classical ballet involved it didn't matter much. The choreographer, Madame DeVillier was an eccentric old Russian lesbian, but definitely talented. It was typical of her that at the first rehearsal, when we were all trying to make a good impression, she made us girls do men's steps (doblers) with bent knees over and over again. With the result, that the next day, our legs were so stiff we could hardly move - Of course we never used those steps, the sadistic old bitch had done it deliberately.

We rehearsed a weird ballet with witches and demons to the 'Night on the Bare Mountain' music, and a lively Russian Gopak. The Principal dancer was Diana Gould, later to be known as Lady Menuhin; she had one solo in that ballet and I was her understudy. Among the singers were two Polish officers who came to rehearsal in uniform. The tenor, Edward Boleslawski, had a sweet and beautiful voice - Yes, I was already slightly smitten.

We opened in October at the Savoy Theatre to rapturous audiences and critics. The show was a huge success. It was original, colourful, beautifully staged and dressed with excellent singers (Russian, Polish and Welsh), and with an exciting and original ballet and full chorus. The Savoy was the ideal theatre and it should have run there for months but owing to some muddle, the theatre had only been booked for three weeks. So off we went once more on tour.

On this tour, I became friendly with a Russian soprano, Kyra Vayne, who had a remarkable voice. At that time, she was at the beginning of a career in which she did brilliantly. My old friend Gene Eskoldoff, spotting a winner, moved in as her manager and into her life as something more. Kyra and I would remain friends for the rest of our lives.

We were in Blackpool when I saw a bill, advertising a musical production at another theatre in the same town. There on the bill was the name of my ex-boyfriend, Don. I had not seen him for some months but had thought so much about him, and now he was here in the same town. I became very excited and nervous, thinking I was sure to run into him, when he would surely be with another woman. My name was also on our bill, so I reckoned he knew I was here too. The last time I had been in Blackpool we had been living together. After the mid-week matinee, he came to the stage door and asked for me. He was standing backstage when I came down. I took one look at him and thought 'What on earth did I see in him? How could I have been so silly?' The romance was over. He wanted me back, he even asked me to marry him. But, for me it was finished - dead from that moment in Blackpool. From then on I concentrated on the Polish tenor.

We had some fun on that tour. Plenty of affairs and back-stage intrigues were going on. The singers fought over their parts. One of the men soloists was caught red-handed stealing from the dressing rooms. I flirted with the Polish tenor who sadly did not come up to the promise of his voice. There were poker games in bedrooms with the old DeVillier - A wicked old woman but what a character!

Sorotchintsi Fair returned to London, not to the Savoy but to another theatre in the Strand - the Adelphi, I think - where regrettably it was not the same success as before.

My three months leave had finished by now, but I never gave it another thought, until one day a policeman came to the theatre, with a summons for me to appear at Bow Street police court, on a charge of being absent without leave. I was shocked! There were two of us in the same situation. The director of the company was most concerned. He should have asked for an extension on our leave but we had all forgotten about it. He engaged a most prestigious lawyer to defend us. The famous court room was filled with supporters both from the theatre and the Ambulance Service. I was hoping to be called to the stand: I planned to say that we were the only two girls in the company who had done any war work and were prepared to go back when needed - The head of my Ambulance Station was there to back me up. But I didn't get a chance to say anything. Proceedings took up just a few minutes. The Judge told us to be good girls and return to our stations or else we would have a prison sentence and still have to go back afterwards. So that was the end of Scorotchintsi Fair and the prospects of any other theatre job.

I had no intention of lazing about the Ambulance Station again. I would have to look for some alternative war work.

E.N.S.A., the organization for entertaining the Troops, was in Drury Lane. I went and saw someone there and arranged to be transferred to them, to work as a solo dancer in the variety section. Using my stage name 'Unita Granta' (generally called Nita) I was in various groups and departments during my time with E.N.S.A. I did work in Britain, but most of the time I was abroad. I experienced many exciting adventures and travelled to many weird places.

The first show I joined was a variety concert group. Artists doing their own individual acts, comedians, singers and so on, usually with a piano accompaniment. In this type of show I did two or three showy, popular numbers: A Spanish dance with castanets, a South American rumba or samba with maracas, a Russian dance and an Indian number - all things I could dance on a small stage. There was no hunting for digs; accommodation, meals and transport were all provided. The group usually stayed together in a house, sometimes in the country. There were very few expenses and the money wasn't bad. We were even issued with a uniform; khaki battle dress, shirts, coat and cap. We didn't always have to wear it but it saved a lot of bother.

With the first variety group I went to Northern Ireland. It was very cold and not very eventful. Most of the time there were troubles with the group. At one time we were staying in a place where by crossing an inlet in a small boat, we could get into the Republic of Southern Ireland. As they were neutral in the war, one could buy many things not obtainable in England. Someone suggested that we hire a boat to take us over to do some shopping. It was only a small village on the other side, the shops there were full of merchandise and the shopkeepers were obviously used to these excursions. We all spent a great morning choosing and buying. I bought chiefly material, of which there was a good choice. Then we were shepherded to a pub were we drank plenty of Irish whisky. We were advised that we had better hide our purchases because of possible customs inspection. So we went into the toilets where I draped the material round and round my body, underneath my coat. We came out looking a good deal fatter than before. By this time we were all a bit tipsy and hilarious. We waddled heavily laden down to our waiting boat. At that moment someone came running with the news that we must return to the pub, as we were about to be searched by the customs official. So we all went back and unwrapped ourselves. We were told that we could leave everything there at the pub and that it would be delivered to our hotel after dark. We did not expect to see our stuff again. But we were wrong. It all arrived safely with no extra charge. I think this is a very Irish story.

The next E.N.S.A. job I had was with a 'Gaucho Band'. This one was fun. It was a small band; one girl singer, five men and me. Three of the men were Cockney Italians. The leader, Johnny, was a funny looking little guy with gold teeth who sang popular Italian and South American songs.

Then there was Pepe, who could not read music but could play anything by ear on his accordion. There was no problem with my music, I just danced and he followed. They were all small-time professional musicians, very friendly and easy to work with and pleased to have me with them. Being Italian, they had not been called up to the forces.

We were scheduled to go to small camps in isolated parts of Scotland. Fortunately, we stopped on the way up north to do a few shows. The first performance was hardly as planned. There had been warnings about the pianist; he had been invalided out of the army, suffering, it was said, from shell shock. Johnny (our leader), in his easy going good natured way said not to worry, that he would be alright with us and so it seemed, at rehearsals. He was quite a good pianist and appeared to fit in perfectly. But, in the middle of the first performance, during one of Johnny's songs, he got up from the piano - which was on the stage - and wandered down to the foot lights where he stood making rude 'up yours' gestures to the audience, who loved it, thinking it was part of the act. Nobody knew what to do. Johnny tried to lead him back to the piano with no success. The soldiers in front laughed and applauded. Pepe eventually saved the situation with his accordion. Of course the poor pianist had to go; he just hadn't known what he was doing. A replacement was sent before we reached the wilds of Scotland.

We visited some lovely places in the West Highlands. During a spell of good spring weather, we roamed the country buying eggs from farms. How we enjoyed all those fresh eggs! There was good country food available everywhere and our motherly Scottish land-ladies made oatcakes and scones. In one place, there was a loch where one had to pick one's way amongst the sea birds nests, which were thick on the banks and among the reeds. It was like a holiday to us Londoners. In one place we were surprised to see American Indians, cutting down trees.

Sometimes the stages were so small that it was impossible to dance on them. On such cases they got me singing. Me, who couldn't sing a note. I did a number called 'And when you buy a rose from Margarita'. I held a basket of flowers and sang a verse, and then they all came in with: "From Margarita." I also sang some Carmen Miranda numbers like 'I, I, I, I, like you very much' and 'When I love I love' dressed in my red and white frilly dress with the hat, using the mike and putting on what I thought was a South American accent - Pretty corny, but it went down well with the soldiers.

It seemed a long way from the war and bomb-stricken cities but soldiers were training in these remote places, preparing to be sent overseas.

Chapter 20

WEST AFRICA

I heard that there were shows being sent to Africa. I went to the overseas section of E.N.S.A. (Entertainments National Services Association) and applied to join a group that was going to West Africa. It sounded interesting. I did not know at the time that I would be away for a year or I might have had second thoughts.

We rehearsed at Drury Lane and the opening song and dance number featuring the name of our show; 'Stepping Out'. We were fitted for some rather pretty long dresses for this, which we donned again for the closing number. There were nine of us: Once again the manager was a middle-aged comedian, Billy, who with his wife Alva did comedy numbers and sketches. Pat Kelly, was a pretty Irish blonde soprano. Sheila, who was a real beauty, did a bit of everything. Dorothy did point numbers and was good at leading sing-songs. May, was a little blonde cockney who played the squeeze box. Bob was the pianist and Stan played the violin. Some of these people acted in the sketches as well. It was quite a good little company. As it was, we endured each other's company, through every imaginable hazard for twelve months - real good troupers all.

We had a medical examination and various inoculations; anti-typhoid fever, typhus, cholera, yellow fever, smallpox etc. Some of these made us feel quite ill. As there was no vaccination against malaria, we were well supplied with quinine and given many warnings about wearing protective clothing, always long sleeves and boots after dark. We were issued with suitable shirts, pants, boots and sun-helmets, real Gunga Din pith helmets. These amused us greatly, we wore them at first but most of them soon got thrown away as being an unnecessary nuisance.

When the day came for us to leave, we had to assemble at Drury Lane Theatre after dark - our luggage had already been fetched during the day. We did not know from where we were leaving. I went home by bus. It was a very dark night and I felt profoundly sad and depressed. Looking down, I saw with a shock that the middle stone was missing from my topaz ring. I always wore it and thought this was surely a bad omen for the start of such a dangerous trip to darkest Africa.

We boarded a ship that night in London Dock. It was altogether cold and depressing. We six girls were in a cabin which had been meant for two, before the ship had been converted as a troop carrier. Once in bed, one couldn't sit up without banging one's head on the roof or the bunk above. There was a wash basin which pulled down and did double duty as dressing-table, with a mirror over it, and one hook each for hanging our clothes. The rest of our things stayed in our cases under the bottom bunks. It was extremely close quarters; we had to get up and go to bed in relays, two at a time.

When we got up the next morning we saw that we had been joined by other ships. We were sailing into the North Sea accompanied by Merchant ships of all sizes, and two destroyers were patrolling the convoy; going very slowly - at the pace of the slowest boat. There was a boat drill; we were instructed where we had to go if there was an alarm. We lined up on deck near our life boat. Now we knew the name of our ship, it had been erased from the ship's side, but it was painted on the lifeboats. We were on a Union Castle liner which had been converted as a troop carrier. She was a big ship, packed with soldiers. The soldiers slept in hammocks in the hold and during the day most of them sat on deck being sick. The officers, a few civilians and people like us had the cabins. It was obvious that there were far too many people onboard to fit in the lifeboats, in the event of an emergency. There was no hope of getting a chair to sit on either. We were lucky to find something to lean against while sitting on the floor of the saloon or on deck. Meals were served in three different shifts in the dining saloon. We sat on benches at long trestle tables, and were served with the worst food it had ever been my misfortune to eat. And we had to eat it, as there was no possibility of getting anything anywhere else, there being nothing to buy anywhere. The bread was speckled with weevils baked into it. The thin watery soup had maggots floating in it. The meat was as tough as old boots, the boiled potatoes mouldy and the eggs, needless to say, were of the cheapest powdered variety. There were no green vegetables or salad. Breakfast consisted of black pudding (blood sausages), the offensive eggs and weak tea. The only thing I found tolerable was on occasion a plate of rather greasy plain rice. I used to do a swap with Sheila, her rice for a slab of soggy pudding cut off a block. We were hungry so we ate everything, picking the weevils out of the bread and the maggots out of the soup. We were told to sleep in our clothes, which we did not do, but organised ourselves with essential garments nearby, ready to grab in an emergency. The first boat drill warning in the middle of the night caught us out. There were other warnings, but they were only practice alarms and we were usually tipped off in advance by members of the crew.

After dark there was a strict black-out and we were not allowed on deck. We crowded into the saloon to sit on the floor and chat or play cards. The bar was closed. There were very few women on board. I made friends with a group of young Naval Officers. The ship's officers were the only ones who had any drinks. They held late night parties in their cabins, which were strictly out of bounds to us. Little May got into trouble for attending one. May was already beginning to get over excited with so much male attention. She started to do strange things in her sleep. One night she woke us up by putting on the cabin light, getting out of bed, donning her pith helmet standing in front of the mirror and announcing; "I want to thank everybody, even the mosquitoes for the lovely time I am having." Then she went back to bed and in the morning she couldn't remember anything about it.

After several days we sailed into the Straits of Gibraltar. We anchored outside the port and soon little bum-boats appeared from the shore and surrounded the ship. They were selling booze and cigarettes. Hanging out of the portholes we negotiated for bottles of wine. Ten shillings and one pound notes were tied to the end of a rope and lowered, and on return came a bottle. It was a bit of a lottery, we didn't know what we were going to get but no one complained - all bottles were gratefully received. We hid the bottles and planned a party. Some of us sneaked up to the top deck that night and sampled our purchases sitting in a sheltered spot in the moonlight.

A lot of people including the naval officers left the ship at Gibraltar. The convoy went on into the Mediterranean. We continued on our own, going full steam ahead into the Atlantic. It was more comfortable now, not so crowded or cold. With luck it was even possible to get a chair in the saloon at night. We were also cheered that the bar was open now for a short while. By queuing for half an hour one could get a drink. With this lengthy process there was no fear of having too many but it made for a brighter evening.

We stopped outside the port of Dakar and saw the sad sight of French battle ships lying on their sides, where they had been scuttled in the harbour at the time France fell.

As we approached Freetown, the ship's engine died and we were immediately aware of the heavy overbearing heat, and a weird ripe, mouldy smell which came wafting from the shore. The coast was lined with beaches, miles of white sand, backed by thick tropical vegetation and palm trees. Once again little boats came out; selling great bunches of green bananas. I wondered why they were green: somebody enlightened me that in the humid sub-tropical climate they ripened so quickly there was not time for them to turn yellow. This, I found also applied to oranges and tangerines, also green and surprisingly ripe.

We were taken ashore in tenders. As we approached the quay, we saw that it was crowded with men dressed in shorts and bush-shirts, all staring at us. Our arrival was an event; they had come to see what was being unloaded in the way of girls. We soon found out that there were very few white women in Freetown; just a few nurses at the Military Hospital and a few remaining civilians - most of them had gone back to Europe. But there were thousands of men! Freetown was a sprawling, dirty, native town, shared at that time with the military.

We were housed in a transit camp outside the town. It was just like a stable; a line of rooms with stable doors looking onto a narrow veranda, beyond which was the bush. Each room had two windows - back and front - with mosquito netting covering them, but no glass. The camp-bed swathed in mosquito netting was in the middle of the room. The rest of the furniture was minimal. It seemed clean and spacious after the cramped conditions on the boat. With the stable went a two-storey house which served as our mess; a large room furnished with tables, comfortable chairs, a wireless, books and a bar. The mess was presided over by a bald-headed sergeant whom we called Pop, the rest of the staff were African. The food was simple but a treat after what we had been eating, with plenty of fresh eggs and fruit. We were pleased with our new home and set about unpacking everything. At last we could take off our uniforms and put on cotton frocks. We were warned not to leave any thing within reach of the windows - we soon learned why.

We were each allotted a small African boy to be our personal servant. Minie was a little teenager, very black, very nervous and immensely keen to please. These little boys had been told to do our washing; unfortunately this was not properly explained. The first time I went out, I found on my return everything hanging out to dry, on the veranda in front of my room. All the clothes I had left hanging to get the creases out, were dripping, including my favourite shocking-pink chiffon evening dress; it hung limply there, shrunk up to half it's length. No amount of ironing was ever to get it back into shape. I couldn't scold the poor little boy, he was new to the job and no one explained that it was only the dirty things that had to be washed. He used to bring me a cup of tea in the morning - early morning tea is a ritual in most parts of Africa. The cup came sliding about on a large plate. One morning he brought me a present of two limes. I was so appreciative of this gift, that from then on I was supplied with avalanches of limes. I even sent a parcel of them to England where they would have been greatly prized, but they took weeks to get there and eventually arrived dried up and brown.

Pop the Sergeant had a little monkey. It was very tame and entertaining but like most of the tame monkeys I was to meet, it was alcoholic. It had been spoilt and encouraged to drink. It was mad for any alcohol it could get hold of and went round draining the dregs in all the glasses. Consequently, it was quite tight most evenings and amused the company - it also had a daily hangover, poor little thing.

There were so many troops in and around Freetown that we were working most nights during the six weeks we were there. The boys were being trained here in this damp tropical heat for service in Burma. Our transport was an ambulance with blacked-out windows and we sat in it facing each other, so on the way from camp to camp we could see nothing of where we were going. The theatres - usually Nissan huts - were always crowded and unbearably hot. Each time I danced I came off soaked; I would tear off my costume and sit sweating in a towel. Then there was the Mess, where one had to make an effort to be amiable. Transport during the day was a constant problem. We either went to the beach in the ambulance or hitched a lift into town. The town was dusty, dirty and smelly but colourful. Open drains ran on each side of the unpaved streets. Children were everywhere begging, little hands held out, grinning.

"You dash me something Missis, dash me." There was a marvellous variety of bright cotton fabrics, beads and African carvings in the shops.

The only hotel had a wide veranda overlooking the street. It looked attractive, but we soon learned that to go there at any time of day, was almost a certainty to be accosted by drunken sailors. The only other place to go was the Officers Club, the Lion and Palm. This was a lively social centre, a large house with bay windows in a typical African street. The ladies cloakroom boasted several chemical loos scattered around the room. It was the Lion and Palm where we were frequently invited for lunch or dinner. In the mess after every show, we would be surrounded by men trying to make dates; men of all ages and ranks from the General down. Never had girls had so much attention paid to them, it was enough to turn any female's head. I found it embarrassing; altogether too much.

On the beach, soldiers walked up and down in swimming trunks showing off a variety of animals: monkeys, of all shapes and sizes, mongooses, squirrels, parrots and all sorts of weird creatures. They would come up to us and ask if they could take our photo with their animal. I could imagine it; a snap of 'happy time on the beach with girls and monkey'. Poor boys, many of them covered with prickly-heat, bored stiff after months of heat and lack of female company. No wonder they were dying to talk to a strange girl on a sparkling beach. And it was a lovely beach, with white sand, banana trees and coconut palms in the background.

I realised early on that the best plan would be to choose a man and settle for him, if only to keep the others off. There was to be a dance at the Country Club on the first Saturday night and we happened to be free. I was invited by several men but each time I said I was booked, until a few days before the dance when I chose my man. We were in a mess quite close to our camp, we had been talking for a while when he asked:

"I suppose you are going to the dance on Saturday?"

When I answered "Yes", he said:

"Who are you going with?"

"You", I answered. His name was Dick. He was lively, amusing, self assured, good looking, tall, and fair - not the dark type I usually fell for. He was a Captain and twenty eight years old. I made a good choice. I have happy memories of those six weeks in Freetown. We saw each other whenever we were both free and he could manage to scrounge a car. There were picnics on the beach, lunches and dinners at the Lion and Palm and late night swims. He was an excellent companion. He made no secret of the fact that he was married and I was in no doubt that he had enjoyed other light-hearted affairs; he was obviously irresistible to women. He was naughty and getting all he could out of life. It was not from him, but from one of his friends that I learned that he was from a rich and well-known family.

One night, when we had a date, came a message that he was in bed with a bad leg. It was a free night and the others were all out; I was alone in the mess. I decided to go and visit him. His camp was about half a mile along a narrow dusty road with thick tropical bush on either side. I hoped to get a lift but no car came by, so I walked. There was a moon so it wasn't too dark but it was still a bit scary. I knew there were some bad types about, as we were constantly being robbed by thieves who crept through the bush and with long poles fished things out through our windows; I had experienced this when I awakened one night to find one at it. Mosquitoes buzzed around me and there were strange jungle sounds from the bush. A few natives passed quietly by. I was relieved when I arrived at the camp, then I had to explain to the sentry on guard what I was doing there. Somewhat intrigued, he told me where to find Dick's tent. And there was Dick, lying in a hammock reading. He was laid low with a thrombosis in his leg. His fellow officers were all out too and he was very happy to see me. There was absolutely no diversion about that bare tent. I saw another side to Dick that night, it was the first time I had seen him in a serious mood. He was obviously worried, thinking about his family and fretting about the future. I did my best to cheer him up. I was glad that I had made the effort to go and see him, but perhaps on hindsight it was not such a good idea. Were we getting too close? For both of us knew the affair must not become serious. When I left, he sent his boy to escort me. The young native walked respectfully two yards behind me till we reached the sentry on our gate.

We did not always have to wear uniform, but we nonetheless came under army command. This was made clear to me when I was invited to lunch by the General. I told his staff officer that I didn't want to go and have a *tête à tête* lunch with the General; in fact I said I would not go.

"You must," the man replied, "you are in the army, it is a command."

The lunch part was all right, but when we sat on a sofa on his terrace having coffee, he started to encroach. I kept pushing him away and telling him not to be naughty. It was all very camp. The silly old thing was really quite easy to control and I managed to extricate myself without making an enemy, which was to come in useful later.

There were problems with May. She had a list of appointments. Starting in the morning, she made dates all day long, turning up just before we left for work, over-excited and exhausted. There was a sort of childish innocence about May; in spite of being a dyed blonde and not so young any more, she was not a tarty type. I was sure she wasn't having sex with all these fellows - where would they go to do it anyway; they were all living in camps and few had any transport. But there she was, making a great war-effort, rationing herself out all day long in that hot dirty town. We teased her and laughed amongst ourselves about her goings but Billy (our manager) was worried. May's room was next to mine in the stable line and we shared a communicating door. One night there was a tropical storm with flashes of lightning, deafening claps of thunder and torrential rain; the lights as usual had failed. Suddenly the door flew open and there looking like a zombie, was May, dressed in her nightie, with wild eyes and hair flying.

"They're coming" she cried. "They're coming" and before I could disentangle myself from the mosquito net and get out of bed, she had opened the outside door and rushed into the night in the pouring rain, straight into the bush. I dashed after her and when I caught up with her slapped her hard across the face. Then I took her by the arm and led her back to the house, by which time we were both soaked to the skin. The next day she remembered nothing about it. Billy was afraid she was heading for a breakdown and said he was going to send her back. Freetown was only our first stop and he felt he couldn't take the responsibility of taking her on the long tour we had ahead. I liked May and pleaded with Billy to wait a bit and give her a chance to settle down.

We were about to be temporarily split up. Some people were to go to Gambia but for some reason we couldn't all go. There was an Entertainments officer who decided these things. Billy asked me if I wanted to go but I was an obvious choice to stay behind, as I worked alone and did not take up much time on the programme: If only five people were to go, there had to be acts that could fill up the bill. In the end it was decided that the three men with Pat and Alva would go. So Sheila, Dorothy, May and I were left to stay in Freetown. We would join the others at our next stop in the Gold Coast - at least that's what we thought. The day before the others were to leave we were suddenly told that we would be departing too, that we were to go south and wait for the others at Takaradi. This didn't suit us at all; we felt at home in Freetown where we had friends and didn't want to leave. We saw this as the work of the Entertainments

Officer (whom we didn't like); he would be coming with us to show us off; four attractive girls, we had learnt, was quite an asset.

That night, which was to be our last, there was a party. Sheila, Pat and I had been invited. Dick was there but he sat with his leg up and wasn't dancing. I stayed with him in the garden and refused all invitations to dance - it was a sad occasion. When I saw the General was present, I had an idea. I found Sheila and we had a serious conversation. I smiled at the General as he waltzed by and he soon came over and asked me to dance. This time I did not refuse. I told him, as we danced, about us being sent away for no apparent reason, when we didn't want to go. I told him we were sure it was a plot made by the wicked Entertainments Officer to get us for himself. Then I said:

"You are the Boss aren't you? You could stop it if you wanted to".
He looked thoughtful. I handed him over to Sheila - she was an extremely attractive girl. When we got home about two in the morning there was an urgent message for us: we would not be leaving that morning. The old boy had done his stuff! Disgraceful manipulation by the General, but it had worked and I didn't think Sheila would have much trouble coping with him if he asked her to lunch.

So now there were only four of us in the stables. Sheila and I talked seriously to May. We told her that she was in danger of being sent home. This horrified her; it was the last thing she wanted. She pulled herself together, cut down her engagements and booze and from then on caused no trouble; in fact she was an asset to the company, always helpful and funny.

The four of us were on the beach one day when we were approached by a man who introduced himself as a Naval Officer. He was in command of a boat that was lying offshore. There was no harbour at Freetown and there were always a number of ships anchored out there. This officer begged us to do a show on board his ship; a converted merchant boat which was holed below the waterline and full of water. He told us that in order to repair her she would have to go to Gibraltar or Cape Town; a lengthy operation that would need tugs and would make her a sitting target for submarines. Due to this she was floating indefinitely off Freetown, with a full compliment of desperately bored sailors. We explained that there were just the four of us and that we didn't even have a pianist. He said that they could supply a pianist. The much-abused Entertainments Officer had left, and Billy wasn't there so it was up to us to make the decision. We wanted to help this nice man but we warned him that it wouldn't be much of a show.

On the day, we were taken over to the ship in the afternoon, to practise with the pianist. They had fixed up a proper little theatre with footlights. After the rehearsal we had a splendid dinner with the officers. I dreaded to think what we could produce in the way of entertainment but I need not have worried. It was a great success, mainly thanks to Dorothy, who improvised and told jokes and got everybody singing. We all did our best and they were a lovely audience. At the end, the four of us stood on the stage singing, 'Land of Hope and Glory', with the boys. It was quite moving.

From Freetown we flew to Takorade on the Gold Coast (now Ghana) in an army Dakota. We were again billeted in a military transit camp.

In Accra (the capital) the hotel was in the middle of the town. We slept in an annexe; a house with no running water. The loos were buckets, emptied insufficiently once a day. We went to the hotel for meals and to shower.

At any time of day or night there were these old Somerset Maugham-like characters, sitting in crumpled white suits with a glass in front of them, on the hotel veranda. Seeing them there late at night and again at breakfast time, made one wonder if they had got up early or been there all night.

I met a man at the hotel who had some horses preparing for a race meeting. I went riding every early morning with him on the track, which I enjoyed.

There was a lovely beach at Accra with white sand and palm trees, which we made full use of. It was as usual, extremely hot.

On Christmas Eve there was a ball at the Accra Club. We gave a cabaret on a tennis court; imagine doing a Spanish dance on a tennis court! There was however, an excellent buffet.

We went on an interesting trip up country. The town of Kumasi was particularly full of interest. We visited a Paramount Chief who put on a show of talking drums: The chief and a drummer sat on the veranda with us and a man was sent to the bottom of a field in front of us. The drummer, using his drum, would instruct the man - One of us for instance would say; "Tell him to climb a tree", or "fall down", or "run in a circle" and the man at the bottom of the field obeyed the drum's orders. This was the time-honoured way of spreading news from coast to coast.

We went by road to Lagos - a drive along the coast through thick vegetation with glimpses of golden sand and rolling waves. There was once a thriving slave trade in this part of the coast; one felt it was seeped in superstition and dark secrets. Wherever we stopped, little children with pot-bellies held out their grubby little hands

"Dash me; you dash me one time Missis."

'One time' was added to every sentence throughout West Africa. At one camp where we stayed, I was woken by a timid boy pulling at my pillow and the words:

"I made water one time Missis"- The bath was ready.

Everyone said how much we would like Lagos. I was disappointed, perhaps because we lived in a comfortable civilized house with a garden, some way from the centre of town, and so missed a lot of local colour. It was a more sophisticated city with better shops and hotels but I recall nothing of particular interest. It was a different story when we went up country, spending days on the train, getting off for a night here and there to give performances, staying overnight at a military hospital.

Chapter 21

ENUGU

We got off the train at last, one morning, to stay for a time at Enugu in the province of Biafra. I sensed that early morning that something important was about to happen; I had a quite unreasonable feeling of expectancy. It was the usual dusty African town, the European quarter tidy with bungalows and nice gardens. I stayed in one of these private houses.

In the evening we were picked up and taken to a Servicemen's Club to play bingo. When I saw the man who was driving the car, I knew why I had experienced those strange feelings. I had fallen in love, hopelessly at first sight. Why, amongst all those men I was meeting every day, did this particular one have such a profound affect on me? What powerful chemistry was at work? It seemed to be mutual. We sat together in a hall full of men - we could have been alone. We kept embarrassingly winning the bingo; if we had needed an omen, there it was. He asked me if there was anything special I would like to do whilst I was here in Enugu. I said I would like to ride, if possible, as we had been on the train for days with no exercise.

The next afternoon he got hold of two horses and we went riding, and after to his little bungalow. We did not make love then. We talked till it got dark. I felt that I had known him all my life, that I could tell him anything. I had never felt like that about any man before. He was a doctor, a Major in the Medical Corps. Before the war he had been at Scotland Yard, working on murder trials as he was a pathologist – a specialist in blood, presumably very clever. He was a little older than I, tall, good looking and dark, with a moustache and dark brown eyes. But it was not just his looks that attracted me – there were plenty of handsome men about.

We only had a few days but we made the most of them. I tried not to think about the parting but had I known him better, I would have guessed that he had no intention of parting then. There was nothing slow, dull or stupid about Jack.

At the last show we gave at Enugu, Sheila's teeth were chattering so hard she couldn't sing. After the show Jack took her off to the lab and insisted I went too. He showed me under the microscope the malaria parasites squirming about in a drop of Sheila's blood. The he took a sample of my blood and said,

"There you are, you have them too." I protested that I didn't feel ill, but he said that the malaria would surely manifest itself within a few days.

He told us we had both better go to hospital here in Enugu and be cured. I believed him then but later, knowing him better, I am sure he made it up.

So Sheila and I went into the military hospital for a few days. We were put into a double room and were pumped full of quinine, whilst the rest of the party went off up north in the train.

There were some funny incidents at the hospital. They were not used to having women patients; we were mostly looked after by African male orderlies, who were rather nervous and shy of us. I remember waking from a nap one afternoon and hearing a boy say,

"Matron say she want a stool, one time" and Sheila answering grumpily,

"Well go and tell Matron that there aren't any stools here, we have only got chairs." I explained that I thought she was referring to another sort of stool.

"What the poor fellow is trying to say is that Matron wants a sample of shit."

First thing in the morning when we were still asleep, one of the orderlies came in and sprayed noisily around and under the beds for mosquitoes, Sheila would shout,

"Shut up and go away."

There would be silence for a second and then the spraying would resume at half pace.

We were something of a curiosity in the hospital; everyone who passed our window on the way to the bathroom peeped in. Lizards scuttled about in the thatched roof. We played bridge with the two men in the next room and every evening we had visitors. One day the Army Chaplain came to see us, he told us some fascinating stories about the local people. He liked to go exploring in the wilds and he told us how he had come across a pagan village deep in the bush, which had never been visited by a white man. He had made friends with the chief, distributed a few presents and was always welcome there. The village, he told us, was seeped in witchcraft. We were fascinated, so he offered to take us there if we liked.

When we came out of hospital we had to wait a few days for the train which would take us to join the others, so we had a chance to go with the Chaplain to visit this village. We drove some miles and then left the car and walked down a narrow jungle path. As we neared the village we passed some little pyramids of hard dry clay, they were about two foot high. Half a coconut shell was imbedded on the top of each of these pyramids and the sides were stained with dried blood. Each one was separately protected by a small thatched roof. These were house ju-jus or family sacrificial altars. We were soon surrounded by children who ran to tell their chief we were there. He came out of his house wearing a blanket tied on one shoulder and an old felt hat. No one else wore anything except for little bits of skin or rags decently covering the genitals. The entire village came to look at us and we gave our presents of tobacco and beads to the chief. The people were clearly fascinated by the first white females they had seen, what a pity neither of us were blond, they would have been much more impressed.

We were shown the ju-ju house. A thatched house with a pointed roof, it was open at the front and supported by three stout columns. One was intended to see what was displayed inside. It was packed with a collection of the weirdest objects. Effigies, masks, painted cymbals, skulls, bones, paintings of animals and men and even the model of a train – this, I found out, was to prevent the railway from invading their land. It was charmingly childish and colourful and at the same time somewhat sinister. In front of the ju-ju house there was a huge shady tree which we were told was a magic tree; apparently all the year round drops of moisture fell from it - the ground beneath was always damp. Indeed the most extraordinary phenomenon.

The old chief showed us these things with pride. The Chaplain could speak a little of the language and explained as best he could. We were invited into the chief's house; it was the biggest of the huts with a tall conical roof. We sat on benches and were presented with little cups of palm-wine. Our primitive host knew how to entertain. On a high shelf circling the walls were still more strange things; bunches of herbs and grass, bones and skulls of animals. I would have liked to know what these things signified but I had a strong feeling that it would not be wise to be too inquisitive. This feeling was intensified by the appearance of the witch-doctor. He was a skinny, dried up old man with shifty, dangerous eyes. The trappings of his trade were hung about him; dried lizards, snakes, bones, rattles, bits and pieces and bunches of herbs. He stared at us with contempt and suspicion and expressed none of the frank curiosity of the others. I did not doubt that this was the man that ruled the village and not the amiable chief. He was an altogether sinister, dangerous presence. I don't think those people were cannibals but I am sure he was thinking that one of us girls would make an acceptable sacrifice to his 'powers that be' whoever they were.

Somewhere in the darker parts of Africa we did see people who belonged to a cannibal tribe, this was made obvious because their teeth were filed into points. By this time though, they had learned that it was no longer respectable to eat human flesh and were ashamed of their give-away teeth, and many of them were without front teeth, having pulled them out.

In another place we saw some Pagan women wearing straw plates on their behinds. This was a practical arrangement, it discouraged sexual harassment from behind whist they were working on the land, and at the same time provided a seat to sit on. The only other thing they wore was a little bunch of green leaves in front.

Our short convalescence was all too soon over, and we were again waiting for the train to take us to join the others at a place called Jos. Jack came with us, he was not going to give me up so soon. We spent a few happy days and visited the walled Moslem city of Zaria. I remember men in robes and great vats of blue dye. I was sorry to have missed Kano on the edge of the desert, an even more interesting Arab city.

We heard the train hooting in the night, the signal that it was time to go to the station and start the long journey back to Lagos. It meant another ending, another goodbye. I knew he was married, I knew there was no future to this romance. I had struggled against the fatal attraction to no avail. I was miserable. The two of us sat in the back of an ambulance - the only private transport available. And then he said,

"You don't think I am going to leave things like this, do you?" I said, "What do you mean?"

He went ahead and made a great mistake that was to cause me years of anguish. He explained that before he met me his wife had written to him asking for a divorce, he had answered asking her to wait till he went home on leave - this was about due - to see if they could sort things out because they had two children. Now, he said, he wanted the divorce because he wanted to marry me. I was stunned. I had never thought about getting married, I enjoyed my dancing career and travelling. I didn't like the idea of being tied down, although there had been various proposals which I hadn't taken seriously. But I suppose every woman has the idea that there is, waiting somewhere in the wings, the ideal man and here he was. I had thought it was over and now, apparently, it was not. It changed everything.

I had been doing some shopping – material for costumes, things for my mother - which I didn't want to drag around Africa, and Jack was taking the parcel back to post when he went on leave. Now he asked if he could deliver it in person, as he wanted to meet my mother. It was too good to be true, oh yes; it was too good to be true! I wrote to Mother warning her to expect a visitor.

Waiting in Lagos for the boat that was taking us to South Africa, I received the most passionate letters. He wrote saying that was doing all he could to get to the coast to see me. When he did at last succeed, he arrived just in time to see our boat steaming out of the harbour. He wrote as if heartbroken - but it was my heart that was to be damaged.

Chapter 22

AGAIN IN HOSPITAL AND EAST AFRICA

On the ship from Lagos to Cape Town I slept on a top berth, and because it was stifling in the cabin I kept a fan revolving directly on me all night, which I think may have been the cause of my falling ill. When we got to Cape Town I knew I was seriously ill. We were going on to Durban by train, where I was being met by my brother and his family; I was determined to get there before seeing a doctor. The overnight journey by train was agony. I had a high fever, all my joints ached and I had a really vicious pain in my back and throat.

Jim and Flora were there to meet the train and we went to the Royal Hotel. I went to dinner but couldn't eat anything and was shaking all the time. The next day Flora called her doctor. My temperature was 103 degrees, he thought I had malaria and wanted to put me in an expensive private nursing home. Luckily I could still think - I came under the military - so I told them to phone Billy, my manager. An ambulance was sent for and I went off to the Military hospital. The intensity of the pain was bringing back memories to my feverish brain. In the hospital I told the doctor,

"I think I have rheumatic fever, I have had it before."

I was put into a private ward and tests soon proved that I did indeed have rheumatic fever. I couldn't bear the weight of the sheet on my knees and I went from burning fever to drowning in sweat; which soaked through the mattress. I fell down when I tried to get out of bed. I knew that all depended on how my heart stood up.

When I got better I was moved into a larger ward with other patients. I liked the young Jewish doctor. He was honest with me and understood that I had to know every aspect of my illness and how I was progressing. I was something of a celebrity and had visitors, flowers, write-ups in the papers, but all I wanted was to get well quickly and get on with the tour, I hated to think what I was missing.

My little doctor went away and I didn't like the one who came in his place. This one gave me no explanations when I asked about the result of a blood test, and he implied I would be there for a long time so I had better be patient. I was not patient; I remembered how the last time that I had been ill with this illness; I had been in bed for six months. I became upset and nervous. I shocked the nurses by demanding to see this doctor's superior. I made myself most unpopular but the senior doctor did come to talk to me. He asked what the matter was and what I wanted. He listened when I told him that I was getting in a near state of hysteria: I wanted to go out in the garden and sit under a tree, I wanted to walk to the WC., I wanted my doctor to tell me exactly how I was doing, how my heart was reacting and the results of the blood tests and that I also wanted a glass of wine with my meals. He told me that all this could be done, as long as I clearly understood that if I overdid it I could ruin my health for life. I already knew this.

I was pushed out in a wheel-chair to sit under a tree, I walked to the WC and I had a case of wine under the bed – my doctor obeyed his instructions. The nurses were furious, but I started immediately to improve.

Noel Coward came to the hospital to give a show. It was a new experience for me to be sitting in a wheel-chair on the other side of the lights. I hoped Noel would have something to say to me, after all we were both artists working for the army, but he ignored me. It was a lousy show anyway!

It was two weeks since I had seen the head doctor, six since I had first come in to the hospital. I asked to see him again - I wanted to be discharged. He told me that I had made the most extraordinary recovery but he really didn't think I was ready to go just yet. I explained that I was going up to the farm in Zululand, to rest for two weeks and then I would have another ten days on board ship, before I started work. He let me go. I think they were glad to get rid of me.

It was a great relief to be out of hospital. After my stay at the farm I went by boat from Durban to Mombassa. On arriving there, I found that the company were up country, having already spent some time in Mombassa and Zanzibar. I took a train to Nairobi where I stayed at the New Stanley Hotel – the best the town boasted - where I was bitten in bed by bugs and fleas. When I asked to change my room I had to produce a squashed bed bug in a match box, before I was taken seriously by the unbelieving receptionist.

There was mail for me but no letter from Jack; I thought he was probably on a boat going to England.

The company was still away. I was entertained by the E.N.S.A. officer, an unpleasant character, who got drunk and bragged about how much money he was making smuggling ivory from the Belgian Congo. He offered to take me on his next trip, I did not accept his offer; he was talking to the wrong girl. When the others came back we did go on a day trip over the border into the Congo, to do some shopping. It was a long drive in pouring rain. It was reminiscent of that trip in Ireland, when we came back through the customs with stuff wrapped round us.

I did not care much for Nairobi. We never had much to do with civilians and the type of British expatriates I did come across, haunting the clubs and outdoing each other in eccentricity and insolence, did not appeal to me. Also, I was used to smiling, happy Africans; here they appeared surly and resentful. It would not be long before the White settlers would be shattered by the grim vengeance of the 'au Mau'.

The country was beautiful - a place to fall in love with. The altitude prevents it being too hot. Wild animals roamed the countryside. We saw giraffe and zebras close to the road, blue coloured mountains in the distance, flat-topped trees and lakes pink with flamingos.

We travelled many miles on dusty roads in a shabby old bus, constantly stopping with punctures or blow-outs. Our driver was an Italian prisoner of war, who had been taken when the Allies had liberated Italian Somaliland. He was a nice fellow, who had been a racing driver in civilian life. One day, when we were separated from the other car he produced a loaf of bread, a chicken and a bottle of wine which he shared with us.

Our next destination was Jinja on the banks of Lake Victoria. The hotel looked over a huge expanse of water. Hippos came into the garden at night and caused havoc in the flower beds; they made a weird hooting noise. We were told that they wouldn't attack, but that if we did meet one to be careful not to be between it and the water, as they were liable to run one down. In the day-time we could see them lying submerged in the lake with just their noses above water, every so often they opened their great mouths to yawn. From the hotel terrace we could also see crocodiles cutting through the water, looking like moving logs.

From Nairobi we flew - as usual - in an army Dakota to Mogadishu, the capital of Italian Somaliland. Mogadishu was an elegant modern town, with stylish white buildings. The hotel fitted the background perfectly. We were served frosted drinks in cool palm courts and could walk straight out on to the clean white sand to swim or sunbathe. I felt that the hotel should have been full of elegant Italians, the people who had built this beautiful city. But they had been sent packing and the place was already beginning to look shabby and run down.

Berbera, on the Red Sea is surely the hottest place in the world. Apart from a few nurses, all the women had been sent away to cooler climates. There was no air-conditioning, no way of keeping cool; we just burnt up all day long. At dusk it would become a little cooler but then we had to perform. Always at dawn, the hot desert wind would start blowing, and one would wake up sweating under the mosquito net, with the bed full of sand. It was a hellish place; luckily we only stayed there a few days.

On our return journey a cloud blocked out the sun and within seconds we were in the middle of a swarm of locusts. We hurriedly shut all the windows. Soon the bus was forced to stop, as it was skidding on the massed insects on the road. It was like the worst sort of nightmare; the windows were thick with scrambling, scratching locusts and it seemed that they were trying to get in the bus. And then miraculously they had gone. There was not much vegetation in that barren land, but they hadn't left a blade of grass behind them.

The road through the mountain pass to Abyssinia was good by African standards, having been built by the Italians during their occupation of that country. The scenery was spectacular. An armed guard was with us, since hijacking was not uncommon in this wild country. There was a lively scene at the border; plump laughing girls with baskets on their heads invaded the bus, selling fruit. Nomadic tribes were on the move with tents and camels. The Abyssinians are not a Bantu race; the people we saw now were very black, with straight fine features and fuzzy hair.

In the hotel at Dire Dowa there was a tarantula in my bedroom. Not just a big spider but a genuine hairy tarantula. This was duly dispatched with a good deal of shouting, but not so easy to get rid of were the bugs. The legs of the bed stood in tins of kerosene and the room was so heavily sprayed that I was nearly asphyxiated by the fumes. But they still persisted in finding a way to pester me and I was covered in big inflamed bites.

When we went to look at the open-air cinema where we were to perform, we were amused to find it occupied by pigs. These were shooed away and chairs put down!

Chapter 23

TWO WEEKS ON THE NILE

We went by road from Nairobi to Juba where we were to catch the Nile steamer to Khartoum. It was one more dusty drive, only made interesting by a visit to a famous white hunter, who had all kinds of exciting animals he had tamed including a chimpanzee.

When we arrived at Juba the only hotel there was crowded with people waiting for the Mail Steamer. One had broken down and failed to arrive, so there were a double lot of passengers waiting for the next one; the one we were supposed to travel on. We were there for several days, as more and more people came and none left. I had to give up my room and sleep on Alva and Billy's balcony. Here, I was very close to nature; there was only mosquito netting between me and the bush. At night there were noises of jungle animals such as grunts, barks, squeals, croaking frogs and the calls of nocturnal birds. Occasionally there was the throaty roar of a lion, then all would be silent, not a sound, as the creatures froze in fear.

The natives here were tall. The men went about stark naked, the women wore little fringed skirts and some of them had strangely shaped conical pointed breasts. We were amused, when walking down to the village we were passed by two, tall, striding gentlemen, carrying umbrellas and wearing hats and not another stitch.

Somebody took me out into the bush to look for game. It was difficult to see anything because of the thick bush, so we left the jeep and climbed to the top of a kopje. We saw baboons dodging behind rocks observing us. A stone bounced off a rock close to us and they were soon pelting us with stones. It was not a very serious attack - they didn't aim very well - but I didn't much like it. We clapped our hands and they ran away, but not very far; turning round to stare at us again. And then quite close we heard the unmistakable grating, throaty roar of a lion. The baboons froze behind their rocks. I understood how they felt as we made our way quickly and stealthily back to the jeep.

Some Air Force pilots stopping overnight on their way north said they had flown over a great mass of elephants. This was the African Herd, reputed to be the biggest elephant herd in Africa. I talked to the boys with the jeep and the next day several of us went out in search of them. We took a picnic and were prepared to go a long way. We drove for miles along dusty deserted roads with bush on either side. We saw buck and small game but nothing exciting, till suddenly we came upon what looked like a battlefield. For hundreds of yards everything was trampled flat, trees were torn up and branches ripped off the bigger trees. Big mounds of dung were scattered about. We had found where the African herd had recently crossed the road. The dung was quite fresh; they had been there not long before. If we had followed them on foot we could possibly have reached them, but looking at the destruction we had second thoughts. I wish we had tried to see them, what a wonderful sight, to see so many elephants together.

It became obvious that all the people waiting at the hotel were not going to fit into one paddle steamer. We heard that there was going to be another extra boat. Eventually two boats arrived. One was the mail boat which was spick and span with all facilities for a comfortable voyage up the river. The other was a rusty, shabby old hulk called 'Anuar'; this was the one we were to travel on. The Captain of the Mail boat, a Scotsman, was in the hotel that night. He was most concerned for our health and safety travelling on that boat; he said it was not fit for white women and would take twice as long to get to our destination. He told Billy, our manager, that he should refuse to let us go on it (the E.N.S.A. officer in Nairobi was responsible for the arrangement). But had we refused to go, we would have been stuck at Juba indefinitely. The alternative could have been for us to return to Nairobi by land and from there fly to Khartoum, but little Billy was not one to fight authority.

The mail boat was absolutely packed. The Captain made me an offer to share his cabin. He was not unattractive but I could hardly take his offer seriously. He did say that he would stay with us as long as possible, so that we could cross over to his boat and spend some time there in the evenings. However the first day we got stuck on a sand bank and they sailed out of sight, never to be seen again. The man had not exaggerated; it was every bit as bad as he had warned us. But I wouldn't have missed it for anything!

Our little paddle boat was surrounded by barges. It was pushing two in front and one was lashed to each side. Of the two in front, one was carrying natives, the others cattle. The side ones took army trucks plus other vehicles and timber. There were two decks and on top of these was a large square box, completely covered in mosquito netting. This was our living room, where we had our meals and sat in the evening. During the day time we could be on deck, but after dark it was infested with mosquitoes, so we had to stay shut in our box, wearing trousers, boots and long sleeves. The cabins also had netted doors looking onto the narrow deck. In mine, there was just enough room to stand up, and just room to lie on the narrow stale-smelling bunk. There was no window, so the door had to stay open all night - even so it was stifling. There was one bathroom, where one stood in a filthy grime-encrusted bath and showered under a trickle of dirty, tepid river water. The lavatories we shared with the Arab crew, I will not attempt to describe them

There was no refrigeration, so no cold drinks - beer was the best on offer. There was no wireless and no way of communicating with the outside world. We were completely cut off from any news for two weeks, and there was after all a war still going on.

Our fellow passengers consisted of two alcoholic British soldiers being sent home suffering from DTs, two Italian priests and an official from the Sudan Post Office. The latter was the only one who talked to us. He was full of useful information and helped us to get through that impossible journey. The soldiers were always drunk; they went ashore wherever we stopped in search of alcohol. God knows what they found in those primitive African villages, but whatever it was it kept them in a continual state of inebriation. They stayed most of the time in their cabin, quite quiet and caused no trouble but they were hardly compatible travelling companions. The priests were the worst. I like Italians, they are usually friendly and charming people; these two were the exception. They were most unattractive, youngish men in dirty black cassocks, their heads were shaven and they went about always hand in hand. They looked down their noses at us sinners and refused any attempt at communication.

There was now a division amongst us nine. Dorothy and Stan - who were now a couple - were not speaking to Billy and Alva, who, joined by Bob the pianist, were blaming them for our plight. Pat, Sheila, May and I tried to keep the peace and make the best of things. This situation did not make for cheerful evenings in the 'meat cage'.

For the first part of the journey the river was not wide and we could easily see the wildlife on the banks. Once we saw elephants spouting water and waving about their great ears. We also spotted crocodiles and hippos.

The boat moved slowly and it was unbelievably hot. Smells from the barges in front wafted back; cattle, smoke from cooking fires and worse things. The people on the barge were camped on deck where they slept, cooked and ate. They had chickens and goats with them to provide eggs and milk, and some animals were killed for meat.

The cattle on the other barge were so tightly packed they couldn't move. They stood like that for days, with only a few reed-tops to eat. If one of them lay down, a naked boy squirmed in amongst them and bit its filthy dung-encrusted tail, to make it get up; this was to prevent it being stamped under the hooves of the others. To my surprise all those hump-backed native cattle arrived safely at their destination, they must have been a tough breed. With one exception they placidly accepted their uncomfortable quarters.

I woke up one night to a great commotion. The boats had stopped and there was shouting and cursing. I went out to see what was going on. It was a bizarre scene. A bright spotlight shone on a white ox which was swimming in the river. He had fallen in and men were desperately trying to pull him back on board. They grabbed him by his legs, his horns, whatever they could get hold of. The entire ship's company were hanging over the rail, shouting encouragement and advice. I found myself joining in the shouting; cursing them, telling them they would break the poor thing's legs. Finally they did get him up in one piece, and there he stood dripping; a gaunt, white creature with huge horns, amongst the trucks right in front of my cabin. There he stayed for the rest of the trip being fed, petted and generally spoilt. He was lucky to fall in and not become a crocodile's dinner.

One of the first mornings we were on board I wandered down to the lower deck, where I came across the Italian priests attempting to give first aid to some natives. I was shocked to see that they were dabbing at open wounds with dry cotton wool. I fetched the Post Office man who seemed to understand a little of many languages, to tell them that we had a supply of disinfectants, bandages, aspirins and quinine which we could give them. This was just the opportunity they were looking for. When I came back with the things, they had vanished, never to appear there again. So I was left in charge of the 'clinic'. Every morning I went down there with my assistant, May. My first-aid training was at last coming in useful. The news went round on the African barge and more and more people came. Most of them were suffering from dreadful sores on their legs, some right down to the bone. Later, I learned that these were syphilis sores. I cleaned them and bandaged them, telling the patient to keep the flies away. These people were completely insensible to flies, which clustered on their sore places and crawled into the corners of their eyes and mouths. Mothers came with sick babies and people shaking with malaria. We doled out aspirin and quinine. It wasn't much but it seemed to help; they kept coming anyway. Though some, I suspected, came to admire and touch May's peroxide curls; a constant cause of wonder. She was quite used to this, it had happened all through Africa. I was thankful my hair was dark and, so, of no interest.

We meandered slowly along, stopping at every small village and often getting stuck on sandbanks. The Captain and crew - all Arab – were obviously engaged in business transactions in the villages. Sacks were carried off and other things brought on. I saw ivory - elephant tusks - on several occasions. These transactions took hours and it was useless to complain that the journey was taking twice as long as it should; time was of no account. The most interesting place we stopped at was Malakal, a lively trading port with a colourful market.

One day I went for a walk down a path and came face to face with a dragon - I never knew that iguanas grew so big. How had he managed to escape the pot living so close to a village?

Once, we approached the bank to see grey people moving amongst the trees like ghosts. We did not stop at that place. The boat moved off into mid-stream again. What was this weird apparition? The Post Office person informed us that the village was infected with the dreaded yellow fever. The people covered themselves in ash believing it to be a protection. I was thankful that we had been given the vaccination against it. Our informant also told us a few days later to be careful not to be bitten by mosquitoes, as we were now in the Nile Fever area. I had never heard of Nile Fever.

The further we went up the river the more interesting the people became. We observed tall slim men and boys on the bank, standing on one leg - the other one tucked up at the knee forming a triangle. They stood motionless, like storks. These people were Dinkas. At their villages, they came down to the boat showing off, dressed to kill in carved ivory necklaces, bangles and head-bands and rows and rows of beads. Some of them had their hair fashioned with clay into fantastic shapes. They wore a sarong over one shoulder, leaving the other bare and carried long spears. They were tall and magnificent and they knew it. The Mail boat must have stopped there regularly. They were quite used to foreigners and came to the boat to be photographed with us. They were all young men and children, the ladies were evidently not permitted to dress up and show off.

As we progressed the river became wider and wider and there were miles of reeds on each side and we could no longer see the banks. The noise of the frogs at night was deafening.

We were lucky in one respect - we had a good cook. Our cook was working his passage going from a job in Nairobi to one in Khartoum. He was quite clever at making tasty little meals out of the meagre supplies on board. He did his best with chickens, eggs, tough mutton and yams, brought on at the villages. One day, when we had once again broken down, he came to us and said: "Must catch fish Missis, nothing for lunch." So we found some lines, baited the hooks with bread pellets and dropped them over the side of one of the barges. We were quite successful catching a number of middle sized fish which we enjoyed for lunch. Whenever we stopped we got out the fishing lines; it was useful when we ran out of food. Once, I tied my line round a big heavy log and went in for something, when I returned the line - log and all - had disappeared. Made me think, what would have happened if I had been holding the line?

At last we disembarked at a place where there was a railway; finishing that most uncomfortable but interesting journey by train.

Chapter 24

KHARTOUM

What joy it was to be once again in a civilised hotel, to enjoy a spacious room and private bath - to sit on the veranda of the Grand Hotel, in the cool of the evening and watch the magnificent sunsets over the river. What a luxury to be properly waited on, to enjoy good food and cold drinks, to listen to the news and be in circulation again.

The news was worrying; the papers were full of news about the doodle-bug bombs being dropped over London. There was still no news from Jack, he must have been back in England weeks ago; perhaps he had made it up with his wife? There were letters from Mother but she did not mention a visitor, or having received a parcel.

Several of our group came down with Nile Fever and had to go to hospital. We made up the numbers by borrowing some American servicemen. One of them sang the songs from the new musical 'Oklahoma'! It was the first time any of us had heard them.

Khartoum is a place like nowhere else: An historical desert city on the banks of a great river - a clean town with broad palm-lined streets and fine houses. There was a statue of General Gordon on his camel, looking over the Nile, on the place where he was killed by the Dervishes.

Camels were much in evidence here, they were the beasts of burden; they pulled the rubbish carts that went round at night.

It would have been a pleasant few weeks there if it hadn't been for the heat. It was the hottest time of the year and we were blasted by the dry scorching air. The big revolving ceiling fans only moved the hot air around. I pulled my mattress out of the window onto a ledge to try and get some air. The lawn was littered with bodies lying on makeshift beds. One night there was a storm; it was funny seeing people in scanty night clothes, soaked to the skin, battling with their mattresses. I just managed to get mine in, when it stopped raining and was as hot as ever.

We were warned that it was the time of year when black beetles fell out of the trees and squirted a liquid onto unprotected skin; causing blisters that left nasty scars - I had one on my arm for years. There was also a possibility that in the dark one of these beetles might fall into a drink undetected, and be swallowed. What would happen then? These beetles were nothing less than the Spanish Fly, the powerful aphrodisiac.

I was friends with an amusing, naughty Captain called Peter. He was busy wheeler-dealing with some wealthy Greek traders. He was charming and fun and took me out and showed me what was going on in the town.

Over the bridge on the other side of the river is the historic town of Omdurman. In contrast to the modern city it was a mass of narrow streets and alleys. Here I went shopping for leopard skins. I was determined to get several and have a coat made. I succeeded in doing this - very bad of me. What a terrible thing to have done.

The most remote place we ever got to on that tour was called El Geneisa, near the border of Chad. We flew there over the desert from Khartoum to an air force base in the middle of Africa.

We were housed in Nissen huts and the theatre was in another. One dark night, I was coming out of my hut after a quick change, when I nearly walked into a lion. Terrified, I crouched at the bottom of the steps shouting for help. Someone appeared and said,

"Oh my God, he was supposed to be shut up."

No one had told us that there was a tame lion wandering about.

One of the pilots then told a story of how one dark night when he was attending to a plane on the runway, the lion came up to him and he gave it a hearty pat on the rump. Returning to the hangar he heard the tame lion growling and was surprised to see it was shut up. His encounter on the runway had been with a wild lion!

There was some sort of a feast day whilst we were at El Geneisa. This was celebrated with wild looking tribesmen riding swift Arab horses. They rode barefooted and wore white robes. The spectators showed great enthusiasm. We had a grandstand seat in an open truck. An incongruous note to the wild scene was our D.C. aircraft standing in the background. The prizes for the races were large cone-shaped blocks of sugar for the winners and smaller ones of salt for the seconds. This seemed a humble reward but apparently was much appreciated.

When we left we had a royal send-off - fighter planes flying on each side escorted us.

Flying from Khartoum to Cairo we had the vast desert below us all the way. We missed a lot by not finishing our journey up the Nile by boat. We never got to see the Valley of the Kings or any of the fabulous Egyptian ruins. I did however get to see the Cheops Pyramid and the Sphinx at Gaza, which duly impressed me. The museum in Cairo was closed for the duration.

I think we felt a bit lost to be in a big crowded city after being so long in the bush. There was plenty of sophisticated entertainment in Cairo and the house we stayed in was full of other E.N.S.A. artists.

There was a frenetic gaiety about the city. It was here, that the boys came on leave from the North African front, to have a good time and spend money lavishly on sophisticated and erotic entertainment. What was our little 'Stepping Out' company doing here?

The shops were exciting, especially the jewellers. The proprietors stood at the doors of their shops enticing,

"Come in and have a coffee. Come in, just have a look."

They didn't listen when you said you really didn't want another tiny cup of almost solid Turkish coffee. I bought some silver jewellery and some silks. I had plenty of money as there had been nothing to spend it on most of the time.

I saw my cousin Ann Sale who was enjoying life in Cairo with the ATS. I met my friend Terry's husband at the Shepherd's Hotel; this was the place to go to watch people.

We were tired. We had been living out of suitcases for nearly a year, often in difficult conditions, always in the heat, sweating under mosquito nets and some of us had been ill. We had travelled practically round Africa, never missed a performance, and been the only E.N.S.A. party ever to go to Abyssinia. Now we wanted to go home.

We sailed from Alexandria through the Mediterranean on another crowded troop ship - an uneventful voyage.

Chapter 25

WORKING AGAIN IN EUROPE

It was a relief to be back home again and find that my mother and Barbara were safe and sound. Being in dreary war-time London and still being bombed was pretty strenuous for them. The V1's, the doodle-bugs, were in a sinister way, as nerve-wracking as the bombers. There was none of the noise and drama of the blitz, but one would wake in the night to the droning sound and wait for the engine to cut out; then you knew it was falling, and you waited for the explosion.

There was not a word from Jack. The parcel he was bringing never appeared. I could probably have contacted him through his regiment, but I thought he must have maybe made things up with his wife, and I didn't want to interfere. I thought of him constantly, watching out for him in the streets, feeling sure I would run into him one day.

I wanted to stay at home for a bit, so I joined the International department of E.N.S.A. which arranged concerts for the Free French, Polish and Czechoslovak forces, stationed in England.

These concerts were made up of individual acts, there were no set groups, I was not happy about this, as I was constantly changing accompanists and rarely having time to rehearse my music with the pianist. We would meet at Drury Lane and be taken by bus, usually returning the same night.

Once we had to stay unexpectedly overnight in a hospital ward where there were no sheets, only blood-stained blankets on the bunks. I remember that occasion because it was then I met a French singer called Jannique Joel. We took to each other at once and would remain good friends all our lives.

One day Sheila phoned me with the startling news that she had seen Jack. She had been in Lincoln with her boyfriend and had run into him in a pub. She said that he was working in a hospital there in Lincoln and that he asked after me, cool bastard. She said he seemed very friendly with the nurse he was with. I was furious. Now I knew where he was, I wrote asking him what had happened to my parcel.

I well remember a day about a week later, when a friend of my mother's was telling my fortune with cards. She told me that I was going to get an important phone call which would give me great pleasure. We were still sitting at the table when the phone rang. It was Jack.

"I can't wait to see you Nita; I am coming to London on Friday for the weekend. The train gets in at 7.30pm. I will call you as soon as I get to Kings Cross." I asked about the parcel and he replied,

"Didn't you get my letter? The ship was sunk and I lost my entire luggage. I will explain it all when I see you."

Well, fool that I was - I was thrilled. I fixed myself up, bought a new outfit with all my clothes coupons and waited for Friday. I even thought of going to meet the train but Mother sensibly talked me out of that. There was no phone call, no message, no letter, nothing. I was too proud and hurt to go and find him. So that was that. He did come back into my life again, but that was much later.

In April 1945 I went to France with a small concert party to entertain the Czechoslovak Armoured Brigade on the western front. We stayed in a private house in a small village in Picardy, and took our meals with the Czech officers in their mess. We gave twelve performances for 3,700 Czech and Allied soldiers. Our hosts were charming, the weather beautiful and the French countryside at its best.

The Germans were being pushed back from the coast, but there was a stronghold - I think it was at Dieppe - where they had flooded the surrounding country, which made it difficult to attack them without having heavy civilian casualties. They had shot down planes flying overhead, and were regularly shelling the troops, whose job it was to keep them bottled up there. We gave a concert to these Czech troops.

When I saw a map of where we were going I realised that on the way to this camp we would pass close to the Military cemetery where my father was buried during the First World War. I talked to the Czech Commander and he took me in his jeep. When we got there the gate was open but there was no caretaker on duty. I had been there once before with my mother but that was about twenty years before. Looking at those hundreds of identical white headstones, there seemed little chance of my finding my father's. The extraordinary thing was that I walked down the paths between the graves - straight to the one that said 'Captain E.M. Grantham'.

The concert we gave that afternoon was in the open, with the audience sitting on the grass. We were told not to worry if shells came over during the performance. We were assured that they always got the range wrong; sure enough shells did fly over in the middle of the show and burst harmlessly in a field near by. We were given a very special dinner afterwards. Our hosts had been out shooting and we were presented with a partridge each, and some strong liquor that they had concocted themselves in their home-made still. It was a real luxury.

Our friendly Czech officers also took us to see the deserted German coastal fortifications. We saw the great guns that had been firing across the channel at the English coast. The ground all around was torn up with bomb craters. The guns were so heavily protected in their concrete bunkers that they still remained intact.

Later in May I was rehearsing with a Dutch company that was going to parts of liberated Belgium and Holland, when the war ended in Europe. I celebrated for the second time (first being World War I) the defeat of the Germans, this time, among the rejoicing crowds in Piccadilly Circus. There was some discussion as to whether we should continue with our trip as planned. Most of the artists were Dutch and they were keen to get to Holland and look for their friends and relations. The war over, we would be able to go anywhere in the country. So it was decided that we go ahead.

My French friend Jannique was in the group, neither of us could speak a word of Dutch and had to pretend to sing the opening chorus.

There was one other English person with us - the pianist. She was a grumpy, not very young lady. We soon found out that she was a nymphomaniac - the genuine article. She was dead serious and single minded about getting laid, which shouldn't have been difficult, but even given the circumstances she did not have much success. She embarrassed us by wandering about late at night in hotel passages in her nightie, looking for victims. One night, in a mess, our Nympho lady fixed her greedy eyes on a handsome Dutch dentist. She told him that she had terrible toothache and insisted that he took her to his surgery to look at her teeth. No joy took place in the dentist's chair: She came back in the middle of the night missing several teeth, which he had done her the favour of pulling out. He must also have given her strong pills, for the next day she was so dopey that she kept falling face first from the seat in the truck; so we had to strap her in. There was much ribaldry over these goings-on, but I think the poor woman was seriously deranged. It took us all day bouncing about in that uncomfortable truck to get to our destination. Most of the bridges were down and we had to go miles out of our way. We were all exhausted when we got to Scheveningen. We were put in what had been a luxury hotel, splendidly situated looking over the sea - it had recently been used to lodge German officers now evacuated. There were no sheets on the beds and no water came out of the taps in the pink marble bathroom. We were lent sheets later and the water did come on for a short time each day.

I don't remember doing any shows but I suppose we must have. The Dutch members of the company were off all day trying to contact their relations. Jannique and I were at a loose end so we hitch-hiked into town. The first vehicle to stop was a German staff car with two officers in smart SS uniforms. We shrunk back in horror; our reactions at being offered a ride with the dreaded enemy was complete and instantaneous; they were laughing at us. We became used to seeing German officers about, they were co-operating with the Allies in rounding up the soldiers that were still about, and herding them into camps.

Next we were offered a lift by a good looking American Marine Captain. He didn't seem to have much to do and spent all the morning showing us round. On the beach we saw the deserted German fortifications. There were rockets and guns and thousands of documents lying around. Later that night we invited the American to join us in our room, to drink a bottle of Cointreau we had managed to acquire; for which I suffered the next day.

The Dutch population at the end of the war were practically starving and lacked most necessities. Cigarettes were the most prized currency and they were desperate for tea and coffee. A bunch of fresh flowers was put in my room every day; this was a present from the old waiter, to whom I gave a cigarette after breakfast every morning. There was an excitement when a German Army Chaplain was discovered hiding in an attic - the staff had been feeding him. He must have been a decent man for them not to feel the deep hatred they felt for most Germans.

In Amsterdam gangs of bare-footed youths were going round the streets begging; beating tins and playing makeshift instruments. They appeared desperate and dangerous and they gave us hostile looks. I hoped they would not take our uniforms for those of the enemy - those cold uninviting canals were all too handy. I took my tea and coffee ration to the corner of a street and doled it our carefully into the outstretched hands of children so they had a little present to take home.

The Dutch were helped to recover quickly after the war, but they had been through a very bad time during the occupation. Thousands of Jews had been sent to concentration camps to be destroyed, the whole population suffered; no one can tell me the contrary, I saw it.

Chapter 26

POST- WAR GERMANY

The war was over but there were still thousands of troops in far away places waiting to be disbanded and sent home. E.N.S.A. was still functioning and it was a good way to travel and see the world.

I was offered a place in a company that was going to Germany and then India. I didn't like the idea of going to post-war Germany but couldn't resist the thought of India.

I had to pass a medical. At first I told the truth about my illness in Africa and was turned down. This did not suit me at all. I managed to find out when another doctor was on duty, didn't tell all the truth this time and was passed. I was given the usual numerous injections.

The company was called "The More the Merrier"! It was a much bigger show than the one I had been with in Africa. We were twenty. We had the 'Dagenham Girl Pipers' with us: six girls playing the bagpipes. What a horrible noise they made, it almost put me off going, but I got used to it and they were nice girls.

We rehearsed several production numbers. I was the solo dancer and now had three pretty girls backing me up. There was a South American number, with singers, dancers, guitarists etc in which I was the centre piece doing my Brazilian act - attractive costumes were made for this scene. There was also a Hawaiian act, in which I wore a white fringe skirt and black wig; in which I rather fancied myself. I also danced a Spanish solo. In every case I arranged my own dances. Apart from the Pipers and us dancers there were the usual comedians, male and female singers, a girl accordionist, a guitarist, a pianist and a conjuror.

It was October when we crossed the channel. We stayed a few days in Brussels and then went by bus into Germany. The countryside was littered with smashed aeroplanes, abandoned gliders and burnt-out tanks. To reach Berlin we had to go through the Russian zone. This we did driving in convoy. Lone vehicles with women passengers travelling through wooded areas were at risk.

In Berlin, we stayed in a house outside the centre of the city, where the buildings and streets were mostly intact. The centre of the town was indescribably awful - a great mass of rubble with hardly a building standing. There were teams of people, both men and women, working at clearing areas. There was a stink of drains and putrefaction.

At home, during the war, we had cheered to hear that Berlin had been bombed again, but to see it now gave no pleasure. It was a sad reminder of what war could do.

Beyond the Brandenburg Gate was the Russian zone. We were warned not to go there; it was reputed to be dangerous. But we had heard that it was possible to go down into Hitler's bunker, under the ruins of the Reichstag. So one morning, several of us decided to go and have a look. We took no cameras on pain of being arrested. The Russian soldiers looked menacing enough; they were Mongolian types with low foreheads and high cheek bones. They were pleased to be greeted in their own language and broke into broad grins, flashing their aluminium teeth. They proudly showed us rows of wrist watches strapped to their arms; one didn't like to think how they had come by these. Poor fellows; this particular lot were rough uneducated peasants. They had endured a long hard war far from home and had suffered enormous losses. Known in their army by numbers rather than names, they had survived only by looting and pillaging. No wonder they had been turned into brutes. They were, now that the fighting was over, thrilled to see something of what life was like in the west, but it would cost them dear; Stalin saw to that when they went back home - they had seen too much.

We scrambled through the ruins of the long burnt-out Reichstag. We had to be careful not to tread on piles of excrement which was everywhere. I did not like the look of the guard on the entrance to the bunker, he was a particularly surly looking brute, but he didn't stop us going in. There were only three or four of us. We were of course in uniform or we would certainly not have been allowed there. We entered down a dark passage – we had come armed with a small torch - into a veritable rabbit warren of corridors and rooms; dark, damp and smelly. Most of the rooms we looked in were empty but in one there were the remains of a charred, burnt sofa. Was this the place where Hitler had ended his evil life? It was at that moment, in the room with the burnt sofa where Hitler was reputed to have died, that the torch faded and went out. We were in pitch darkness. We held hands and gingerly feeling along the walls made our way slowly back. At last we saw the light.

The German civilians were suffering now; there was very little to eat and nothing in the shops. Cigarettes could buy anything. We only had our N.A.A.F.I. ration of tobacco but the non-smokers were in business. We were working in a theatre and people came backstage with any manner of things to exchange for cigarettes: from army decorations to hand guns. I was ashamed to admit that I did acquire a pair of giant maracas - I used them in my act, an old-fashioned pair of mother-of-pearl glasses - not much good, and a German military iron cross. I found this practise distasteful and smoked most of my ration as usual. I also found it shaming that the people were all over us; we the enemy who had destroyed their city. I would have had more respect for them if they had spat in our faces. As it was, they crawled for our cigarette butts in the gutter.

Hamburg was if possible, in an even worse condition. The great river flowed by undisturbed between the ruins.

A lady came to the hotel to ask if any of us wanted massage. She didn't want money; she would give treatment in exchange for a cigarette or a piece of bread. I agreed to have a course of treatments. She was a professional, an excellent masseuse. She spoke a little English and told me her story. She was not German - Latvian I think, and so did not qualify for a ration book although she had lived most of her life in Germany. She had survived right though the war by trading her skills in exchange for food and clothes. Now that everything was so scarce she was finding it hard to live. We gave her cigarettes - money was worthless as there was nothing to buy. She begged me to save her anything that was not eaten at meal times. We were quite well fed but it was impossible to buy food or acquire it any other way. So I took a doggy-bag to the dining room and collected slices of uneaten bread and anything else that was going. It was a pathetic offering but she was happy with the arrangement.

We were in a mess one night, when the men were talking about Belsen Concentration Camp. Amongst them were some who had been amongst the first to arrive there. Hidden in the woods, no one had known it was there, until unsuspecting they came upon the Camp. They told us that words could not express the horror of finding thousands of skeletons, unburied dead and dying. The guards had run away and the gates were open, but most of the people that were still alive were too weak to move. The stronger ones had scoured the surrounding country for anything edible; inside the boundary of the camps there was not even a blade of grass as even that had been eaten. One of the older officers told me that he couldn't talk about some of the unspeakable things that had been done there; that human beings were capable of inflicting such cruel tortures upon each other was an insult to the human race.

Did we want to see it? There wasn't much to see now, they said, the huts had all been burnt down but they would take any of us that wanted to go. Not many accepted but I felt it was an experience I couldn't miss.

The day was fitting: bleak, cold and grey. We drove through forests till we came to a cleared space inside a barbed wire fence. My first impression was of the size of the area, there was miles of it, bare, barren land which before had been divided into blocks of huts.

We got out of the car by a sign that said,
This is the site of the infamous Belsen Concentration Camp
Liberated by the British on April 15th 1945.
10.000 unburied dead were found here

Another 13.000 have since died
All of them victims of the German New Order in Europe
And an example of Nazi Culture.

There were mass graves, each with a sign giving the numbers buried there. The only building that remained was the office block. Incongruously, high up above the camp commander's office, on a long pole, there was a bird's nesting box. Kramer, the Beast of Belsen, was a bird fancier.

The ovens being made of steel had not burned. The buildings had gone and they now stood out in the open; they were much larger but not unlike old fashioned bread ovens, with tall chimneys and stretchers on which bodies were pushed in to burn. All around on the ground were hundreds of little metal tabs, about an inch long with a number engraved on each one. These identification disks were all that was left of those poor people. I picked one up and put it in my pocket, where it stayed until one day I could no longer stand to keep such a gruesome souvenir, and I threw it into a river. I do not know why I picked it up. I do not know why I threw it away, I do not remember the number written on it, but I often thought and wondered about the poor soul who had worn it.

Another grisly relic was a large tank - like a big swimming pool - with what looked like gallows at one end. This was used for various forms of torture. Witnesses at the trial of Irma Greis testified that a woman about to have a baby was hung up there with her legs strapped together. The other prisoners were forced to watch standing round the tank whilst she, unable to give birth, died in agony.

There was a feeling of despair in that awful place. I am sure the spirits of all the poor murdered souls will haunt it for ever.

Having seen the camp at Belsen it was of special interest to be in Lüneberg at the time of the trial. Forty-four men and women were being tried by a British Military court for war crimes at Belsen and Auschwitz. Thirty of these were found guilty, only eleven including three women were condemned to death.

Every morning, whilst we were in Lüneberg, I sat in the gallery watching the proceedings. A succession of witnesses was questioned; this was not very interesting but what fascinated me, was looking at the accused. The stars were sitting on the front bench; among them were Kramer, the camp commander at Belsen, the infamous Irma Gries and a doctor who had practised cruel experiments on prisoners. They were talking and laughing among themselves; arrogant and pleased to be the centre of attention. Kramer looked film-cast for his own role; a tall, coarse figure, almost handsome. Irma was blond and surprisingly pretty, the doctor grey haired and distinguished looking. They seemed to think it was a joke that they were getting a fair trial. They were of course condemned to death but I felt like many people that they should have been strung-up on the spot instead of getting all the publicity which they were obviously enjoying.

I would like to have taken photos, but no cameras were allowed in the court, for which I had to get a pass. I have often thought that I would have made a better journalist than a dancer.

Some of the towns we went to in Northern Germany had not been bombed and life seemed to be going on much as usual. It was cold. We wore our uniforms all the time. We were there for three months.

I remember Lübec; an attractive port looking over the cold Baltic Sea, and Flensburg, where we wanted to cross the frontier into Denmark but were not allowed over the border by land. So we took a boat trip through the Danish Fiords.

We were in Brussels for Christmas. We hoped to be home on New Year's Eve but the boat was held up by thick fog going up the Thames estuary. As it was, we were in the customs shed exactly at midnight opening bottles of champagne, linking arms and singing 'Auld Lang Syne' with the customs officials. No luggage was opened; we could have brought in cases of guns and untold treasure.

Chapter 27

INDIA

There could not be a bigger contrast than war-ravaged Europe in mid-winter and Bombay in mid-summer. We were like birds let free, ready to fly high and yes - a little bit wild. No uniforms, no rations, servants to wait on us, men to dance attendance on us, lovely things to buy cheaply in colourful bazaars. All surrounded by a different and fascinating culture.

We arrived in Bombay in yet another troop ship (soldiers were still being moved around), having come through the Mediterranean, Suez Canal and Red Sea. It was not as uncomfortable as the trip to West Africa and of course there was no risk of being sunk by submarines. We were not allowed to go ashore at any of the ports we called at, which was disappointing, but on the whole it was fun.

I flirted with a young Major called Dennis. Naturally, he was good looking, sophisticated and amusing and determined to have an affair with me. This was not possible onboard; the ship being too crowded for any privacy. I just told him that we would see what happened when we got ashore. What did happen was that he was sent away at once to a camp somewhere, whilst we stayed on in Bombay. I was much too excited drinking in the exotic scenes and scents to be much concerned about this.

I rode in rickshaws pulled by skinny little men wearing dhotis, dodging bare-foot through the crowds. Cows wandered about munching, helping themselves at vegetable stalls and holding up the traffic, smug and secure in their sacred state. I gazed in awe at the Tower of Silence with its crown of waiting vultures. I was enveloped in the smell of India: dust, cow dung, spices and the not unpleasant aroma of musky sweat.

I was invited to a dance at the Taj Mahal Hotel in the delightful air-conditioned ballroom. At the races, the Parsee ladies showed off their gorgeous saris in sharp contrast to the beggars in the streets, showing off their terrible deformities.

At the first place we went to after Bombay who should be waiting for us at the station but Dennis. Was it by luck or good management?

The E.N.S.A. house was in the European section of a large town. It was a big house with some trees and courtyard behind it. And there, across the yard was a darling little house. I was delighted to find that the top part of that little house was to be mine. It consisted of one room with a balcony overlooking the yard and a bathroom with primitive equipment - when one used the box, one clapped ones hands for the bearer, an unfortunate man of untouchable caste, whose fate it was to do such menial jobs as to dispose of other people's leavings.

In the bedroom there was a space between the walls and the roof where birds flew in and out in the early morning. It was altogether delightful and the perfect place for a romantic affair. There were however small problems to be overcome. We were not encouraged to entertain gentlemen. The manager and his wife were sleeping in the room under mine and there was a night watchman sitting all night in the courtyard. None of this deterred Denis in any way.

The first time was a surprise when coming in late from working I found him asleep in my bed. After that it was a common occurrence. He would ride from his camp on the other side of town on a bicycle - the only transport available – hide it in the bushes and creep past the dozing watchman. In the early hours he went back the same way while the guard sat nodding over his little fire. I waited for the alarm to be raised but it never was.

One afternoon Dennis called wearing uniform and we had tea on my little terrace, all quite respectable in full view of everybody .Later I was told politely that if I wanted to entertain it would have to be in the main house. I chuckled to myself. Little did they know that the smart, handsome Major was sneaking in at night like a randy teenager, wearing shorts and sneakers and riding a rusty bicycle borrowed from an Indian.

I would get to see Dennis in various places. When he got leave he would come over for the week-end wherever I was. He was good at finding some sort of transport and several of us would go for outings and picnics. Once we went with some of his friends to a large lake where we bathed and paddled in canoes. But what I remember with the greatest pleasure was a Sunday in Hyderabad, when an Indian Army Officer asked me if there was anything I particularly wanted to do, to which I answered, without much expectation, that I would like to get on a horse and ride round that wonderful city. Horses were found plus a pair of out-sized boots for me. We rode down dusty paths and across open places past the Maharajah's fabulous palace. We rode past temples, pavilions and shrines hidden in secret places - many inhabited by monkeys - with perhaps a bunch of golden marigolds laid in front of a peeling effigy. I was happy with my horse and happy with my companion. It was a ride of pure enchantment.

We travelled round working in camps as we had done in Africa. In one place there was a sacred river - it wasn't the Ganges - but it was none the less fascinating to see the pilgrims immersing themselves in the murky water, the filthy gurus and beggars and the burning ghats on the river bank. From a stall, I bought a small well-worn bronze statue of Ganesh, the Hindu Elephant God of prosperity and good fortune. He stays with me always, a treasured possession.

It had been hot and dry for weeks when suddenly the rain came. We ran out and stood under it as it poured down in torrents; enjoying the sensation of a fresh and natural shower. After the rain stopped - as suddenly as it had started - there were shrieks from various *bashas* (straw huts) - we were being invaded. Columns of great black ants were on the march. They were unstoppable and one *basha* had to be evacuated. Next, hundreds of frogs appeared from nowhere and it was difficult not to tread on one. Had it been raining frogs? Apparently not; they had been hibernating in holes during the dry season and brought out now by the rain. They were joyfully croaking and leaping about.

In Bangalore I went to the home of Ram Gopal, the Indian dancer with whom I had studied in London. We took off our shoes and sat on cushions in a room completely dominated by a great statue of Ganesh the elephant God, and an equally large modern record player, where we drank tea in elegant little cups served by young girl students. Ram, unfortunately, was going away the next day, but he said that I could come and be instructed by one of his gurus if I wished. This I did every morning and learnt a number of hand-movements and their meaning with a grey-haired old man. The students were friendly and curious, but the Maestro was missing and there were no more cups of tea in Ganesha's temple.

There were curious goings-on in the house where we were staying - a big colonial type bungalow. The occupants of the beds near the windows (which were barred and netted) noticed an unpleasant smell and certain dampness on the beds. It was eventually decided that someone was going round the house peeing through the bedroom windows. One night, we woke to screams; one of the girls had found an intruder in her bed. No one could figure out how he got in, but he rushed out without being caught. After that a guard was put on the house.

We worked our way back to Bombay and from there we crossed India by train to Madras. This trip was the highlight of misery. We travelled in a private carriage consisting of one large coach and sleeping compartments with bunks. We sat dripping all day with towels draped round us, rationing ourselves to one glass of water every half hour, from the iced water container which was filled up at the stations. When the train stopped, monkeys jumped onto the roof and little hands came through the bars, grabbing anything edible. On the platforms the ever present crowds pushed and scrambled to get on the train. Others sat patiently on the ground holding bundles. Sellers of tea and water shouting their wares went up and down the train. A whistle blew, the train started rolling, the monkeys jumped off and we were on our way again.

Heat and a brown dusty landscape - Water buffalos up to their necks in any available water - A cluster of vultures, tearing at the carcass of a dead animal. Cow dung, carefully harvested and shaped into cakes laid out to dry. A splash of colour with washing draped over rocks on the banks of a stream. - Slender, graceful people, working in the fields. India: a hard, poor country with a special beauty.

The train was slow; it was shunted into sidings and would stop for no apparent reason. Every time this happened people in the crowded third-class carriages jumped out and squatted by the track to relieve themselves. There were obviously no toilet facilities in their cars.

We never had any warning till the train slowed up approaching a station and a man came through ringing a hand bell. This announced that we were to get off to eat (there was no dining-car on the train). We would hurry to get some clothes on, pile out onto the crowded platform and push our way through to the canteen to be served - after a long wait - unbearably hot curry. Once when we were eating we saw our train moving off. We rushed out desperate not to be left behind in that Godforsaken place. The train was only shunting but nobody had thought to tell us.

The nights were the worst. As we puffed through the darkness I sat on my bunk with the light on hunting bugs. If I fell asleep, in no time they were crawling all over me biting. The only ventilation from the movement of the train came through the open windows. Once we were shunted into a siding where we remained motionless for hours sweltering.

It was a relief to get to Madras at last and rest in a decent hotel.

After our stay in Madras, we went by boat to what was then Ceylon. There was an E.N.S.A. house in Colombo, the capital, but I usually preferred staying in hotels as the food was more interesting and the company more varied. When you have been travelling and working with the same people for months you need to get away from them sometimes.

There was a sad little heart-broken monkey at the house. He had fallen in love with someone from another company who had left. He was inconsolable, mourning the departure of his friend. He wouldn't eat and we could do nothing to cheer him up. Poor little thing, how sadly human monkeys are.

One sensed there was a certain anti-British feeling in Ceylon, particularly in Colombo. The people wanted their freedom from the Empire. It would not be long before they became Sri Lanka.

I was invited to a dance one Saturday. I refused to go because I did not like the man, who had asked me, but some of the girls were going and they persuaded me.

"Come on Nita", they said "we are all going together, it will be fun."

I should have trusted my judgement. When he called for us he was driving a posh car which I felt sure was not his. After having had drinks in some hotel we drove through the most crowded part of town. Suddenly an old man stepped off the pavement right in front of us and we hit him. He went down under the car with a terrible cry. The driver stepped on the accelerator and drove on without stopping. I was horrified. We shouted for him to stop but he paid no attention. We went on to the dance as if nothing had happened. It was a miserable evening. When it was over, I found myself alone in the car with this man. He drove, much too fast, into the country. When I asked him what he was doing he said that we were going somewhere for breakfast - at three in the morning! I said I didn't want breakfast and begged him to please take me home. He then stopped the car and grabbed me, we struggled; he was strong and we were in a lonely place. On sudden impulse I threatened him:

"If you don't stop this nonsense and take me home at once I will tell your C.O. whose car you are driving what happened tonight." It was a guess about the car but it worked.

Later I heard that a man had been run over and killed by a military car. I was also told, on good authority, that if we had stopped we would certainly have been lynched.

The day we travelled from Colombo to Gale was a feast day. We drove along the coast road under a canopy of white paper streamers. Temple boys were dancing in the streets and elephants were parading. Galle is the place to buy semi-precious stones; opals, moonstones and star sapphires.

Close to the Naval Base at Trincomalee we lived in a house on a sandy cove. One stepped out of the house right onto the beach. There was a shark-net across the mouth of the cove; one could swim out to it and hang on hoping to see a shark on the other side. Hot and tired after the show it was heaven to run straight into the sea. However, somebody spoilt it by telling us that sharks came into the bay at night round the edges of the net. We did not enjoy our midnight swim after that. I imagine the proximity of the base encouraged the sharks, for we swam on other beaches round the coast with no fear.

We returned to Bombay in the middle of the monsoon. It was pouring with rain every day; hot, steaming and sticky.

And from here we sailed home on a beautiful big liner - 'The Andes'. I shared a cabin with a woman and her two small children. They were all laid low with seasickness. I don't get seasick so I stayed out of the cabin as much as possible. The children recovered first. I took pity on them cooped up in the cabin with their sick mother and took them up on deck. I was then thirty three and had had very little experience with children. I liked these little children and enjoyed playing with them. I think it was the first time that it had occurred to me that I would like one of my own and that perhaps I should give some thought to a change of life-style.

Chapter 28

ODD JOBS

Mother and Barbara went back to South Africa. I was worried about my mother, she had a bad heart. There was nothing really to keep her in England and she wanted to see her son and visit her farm again. I would have gone with her but Barbara insisted on accompanying her and there was no point in us both going. So I stayed and had the apartment to myself, which meant that I was responsible for the rent. My French girl friend Jannique came to share it with me for a while. She was a marvellous cook, I had never been much of a cook, but I improved under her instruction. It was a good arrangement; we had always got on well. We were both looking for work. I didn't want to go on tour with a musical show and there wasn't much choice. I had to take what I could get.

My agent got me a job in a night-club in Brussels. On the first night they managed to play the wrong music - although I had already rehearsed with the band - and I had to improvise all through my Indian dance. It was in my contract that I did not have to sit at the tables and drink with customers; but I was still expected to do this. I refused and was not kept on after a week. I didn't mind, I hated it. Staying alone in a hotel and going out to work at midnight was no way to earn a living.

I did some small parts in films dancing or moving, or worked as a special extra; as one of these I was placed behind Vivienne Leigh in the race course scene in Anna Karenina. There was a heat wave on at the time and standing in the sun all day, wearing a long sleeved buttoned up velvet dress and fur hat was no fun. This engagement went on for several days, which was good for the money. The film took so long to shoot because the men who were riding the horses could not control them and kept falling off at the jump. This gave me an idea. Why couldn't I ride in films? I found out about this, went to a stable and rode over some jumps, did a bit of dressage and was given a certificate which entitled me to ride in films. Unfortunately, there were no opportunities going just then.

I got an interview with the already famous director David Lean. I was very nervous. I wore high heels, a fancy hat and a lot of make-up. I must have looked like an expensive tart. Mr. Lean was charming, he didn't sit me behind a desk and look me up and down which was the normal procedure. We sat on a sofa and talked. He asked me what I had done etc. He was easy to talk to, a nice man. He finally told me that there was no part for me in the film he was casting then, but to keep in touch as he might be able to use me in the following one. By that time I was no longer in England.

Anyone of my generation will remember Edmundo Ros and his Cuban Band. They played at the Coconut Grove Night Club and had a regular late night programme on the radio. I loved to dance to this music and one night, after a few drinks, I was enjoying myself dancing alone to this programme, when I had an idea - A wild idea, but why not? I sat down and wrote to Edmundo Ros. I told him how I enjoyed dancing to his music and asked him:

"How about my working with the band?" I enclosed a photo of me in my Carmen Miranda hat. I went straight down to the street and posted it. I knew that, sober, the next day I would never have sent it. I talked about this silly letter and my friends teased me, I never expected a reply. So when several weeks later there was a phone call and somebody in a deep voice said,

"Edmundo Ros here."

I thought it was somebody pulling my leg and made some facetious reply but when he said,

"Well do you want to work with the band or not?" I realised, - my God it's him!

"Yes" I said "I do want to work with you."

They were playing at some big function somewhere in the suburbs on the following Sunday. There were going to be three famous bands playing three sessions each. I would need three costumes he told me, one for each session. I asked when we rehearsed,

"No rehearsal" he said

"You just dance in front of the band."

As an afterthought I asked,

"What's the money?"

He told me I would get five pounds, the same as the boys. I told him I never worked for less than ten pounds and he said,

"Take it or leave it, I am not giving you more than the boys"

I agreed, after all hadn't I asked for the experience?

I arrived later at the place, after a complicated journey carting a suitcase with the three costumes. I was shown into a room where another girl was dressing. She told me there was no hurry as our band was playing the last session. As we made up she proceeded to tell me how nasty Ros was to work for:

"Whatever you do, don't get in front of him; don't block him for a second."

She was making me nervous. I dressed in the flashiest of my costumes and was just about to go in search of this monster, to find out what he wanted me to do, when a band started playing. There was a shriek from my companion; it was our band already playing and we were off. I didn't know what I was expected to do. I stood in the wings and looked across the brightly lit stage to where in the middle, surrounded by the band, a big coffee coloured man in spectacular costume, stood playing the drums. There was a strip about two feet wide across the front of the stage, between the band and the footlights. I took a deep breath and went out on to this narrow strip. There was no place to dance properly and I proceeded to shimmer, wriggle and undulate across the stage and back, taking care to get down low and pass 'His Highness' quickly so as not to block him for a moment. I continued to do this to rumbas, sambas, and cha-chas. I never went off the stage all through the session.

When it was over I went up to Ros and said,

"How am I doing?" He took me in a great bear-hug and said,

"You are enjoying yourself, aren't you? You are doing fine dear, but you don't have to dance all the time. Just come on when you feel like it."- Oh, I was getting on quite well with Mr. Ros, he wasn't a monster after all. When the show was over he said he lived near me and would give me a lift home. I was pleased about this but I hadn't reckoned with the consequences. When I got out of the car he got out too. I suppose it was inevitable, I was being a bit naïve. He was quite put out when I said there was nothing doing. It was a pity as I had enjoyed the evening and would have liked to repeat it.

A letter came from Mother with the most extraordinary news. My old boyfriend Jack (the doctor), the one I thought I was in love with and who had caused me so much pain, was of all places, in Durban, working at the provincial hospital. He had never had any connection with South Africa and of all the hospitals he had to land up there.

I had already decided to go back to South Africa mostly on my mother's account, but this news probably influenced me. I was filled with curiosity. Although I hadn't seen him for six years, I still hadn't got him out of my system.

I packed all my personal things in trunks and put them in the store-room at Peter's Court, and put the flat with an agent to let.

I went by boat. I was surprised the first night on board, to be placed next to the Captain at his table, a place usually reserved for VIP's. He said,

"Hallo Unity." I recognised him as one of the officers who had been on the Edinburgh Castle on which I had gone to South Africa with the ballet in 1936. It was a good trip.

Arriving at Durban, Jim and Flora met me and we went straight up to the farm, where there was now a splendid new double-storey house and a beautiful garden. Jim had an important position with the provincial government and was constantly away at Pietermaritzburg. Mother was not at all well and she was not happy about the way the farm was being run. As usual there was a shortage of cash.

I went to Durban and stayed with friends whilst I looked for work. The Edward, on the sea front was the smartest hotel there at the time. There was dancing with the cabaret every night. I got a contract there for two weeks - including room and board - to do two dances each night. The waiters were all Indians and they were intrigued by my Indian dancing. The entire staff crowded round the doors when I danced. I spent most of the day on the beach in front of the hotel - it was a convenient arrangement.

My large display photographs were placed prominently in the lobby and my picture was also in the papers. I felt sure that Jack must know that I was there and every day I waited for him to appear. Every time the phone rang I imagined it was him, but nothing happened.

There was much excitement in the hotel, as the Test Match was on and the English Cricket team was staying there. Among them were Dennis Compton and Len Hutton, two legendary cricketers. I wished them 'good luck' at breakfast and watched the match, which was very close and exciting with my family, who had come down from Zululand for the occasion. South Africans are all mad about cricket.

It had to happen sometime and sure enough one day it did. I was walking down a narrow shopping lane in the centre of Durban when I saw Jack coming towards me. We both stopped dead. I was the first to speak. I said,

"Hallo Jack" and then we were in each others arms. We went to the nearest bar which was at the Marine Hotel. He ordered drinks and we talked for a long time. He told me that his marriage was not working and that he was not happy and wanted to get a divorce. The same old story - but of course this was not the same wife. How could I fall for it? He had a bit less hair but otherwise looked much the same. The fatal attraction was still there. I was still in love. So it started all over again. We went away together for weekends; he even came up to the farm. I don't know what his wife thought, but I didn't care; I had him first and now I had him back. But did I? He had a home, a wife and child. I was on the outside, the other woman. Our association was based on lies and deceptions. How could we really be happy? I realised it was all in my mind, that I had set my heart on him and let him grow in my imagination: all because of that short ride in the back of an ambulance six years before when he told me that he wanted to spend the rest of his life with me. He was just a passionate, emotional man who drank too much brandy, chain-smoked, was weak with women and had messed up his life again. I knew it would probably be best for us both if I got out of his life, but I had found him again and I loved him.

While in Johannesburg working in a nightclub, I had also danced at a concert arranged by a young Englishman who was trying to promote concerts in South Africa. This man wrote and asked me if I was interested in going on a tour in Rhodesia (now Zimbabwe). I gladly accepted his proposal and went back to Johannesburg.

Chapter 29

THE LAST TOUR

Right from the start it was crazy. The English young man who was managing us didn't have a clue how to organize a concert tour. There were six of us: four artists - an Italian soprano, a baritone, a pianist and myself, Tom, the manager and a little man, who sat in the box office and counted the money.

Tom had bought the biggest car he could find to accommodate us all and our luggage. It was an ancient sedan with two lots of seats at the back, a city car and the very last kind of vehicle to be driven thousands of miles over rough roads. It started giving trouble even before we got to the border. We waited hours at the garage whilst it was repaired, and then there was another hold up at the frontier. The car was still going badly when it started getting dark. Tom was all for driving through the night, a most dangerous prospect; we were bound to break down in wild country miles from any assistance. I began to realise how irresponsible he was. We came to the hotel at Beitbridge and the rest of us insisted that we stop there for the night, as we were already too late to give our first performance scheduled for that evening at Fort Victoria.

It was a bright moonlight night and after dinner I wandered onto the bridge that spans the great Limpopo River and leaned on the parapet. It was dead quiet and very beautiful looking across the shining expanse of water. My reverie was interrupted by Tom coming across the bridge with a rifle over his shoulder. With him was the little man who took care of the box office, the pianist Geoffrey and the hotel dog.

"Why don't you come with us," he said.

"We are going to look for leopards. They told us at the hotel that on the other side of the river on the left, there is a path and that if we follow it we are sure to find a leopard."

I thought the man was mad. I never dreamt that there would be a leopard, but I went with them because it was such a lovely night for a walk. We crossed the bridge and started to go down a narrow path with thick bushes on either side. I realised that if by chance there was a leopard we were in a dangerous position. I told Tom this but he paid no attention and went on. The next moment he was aiming the gun at something in the bush and firing. I had seen or heard nothing. He said he had seen a leopard and thought he had shot it. I didn't believe it but he went a little way into the bush and came out with a hand full of leaves that had blood on them - he had shot something alright. Now the pleasant moonlit walk became a nightmare. I begged him to turn back but he wouldn't. The other two frightened city boys were hanging back. We were all spread out and the dog was going crazy and dashed barking into the bushes. Then came the terrible coughing noise, unmistakably that of a leopard. I was horrified that there was one, possibly wounded. Tom had the gun up again and was pointing it towards where all the barking was coming from. I told him not to shoot as I was worried that he would shoot the dog or that the leopard would get it. I managed to get hold of the dog and held it with the belt from my dress through its collar. It was a big strong dog and hard to hold. Tom was prepared to go into the bush in the dark after the animal. I persuaded him that it was a crazy thing to do.

At last we retraced our steps looking fearfully behind us. The four of us were strung out along the path with one gun and one dog - with which I was still struggling. I felt we were almost certainly being stalked by a wounded leopard. It was a scary walk in that bright quiet night by the great shining river.

Tom told me later that he had gone out again at first light but had found no trails or signs of a wounded leopard. He seemed really concerned about wounding the animal.

We were on our way the next morning before the hotel staff was up, missing breakfast. We crossed the bridge and drove the first few miles on the road to Salisbury (now Harare). It was a narrow road with two concrete strips for the wheels - when one met another car one of the cars had to drive off the concrete strips to one side, to let the other drive past. But we didn't come across any other cars that early morning. We were going along quite nicely when suddenly there was a loud grinding noise under the car and the car came to a stop. It felt as if the chassis had broken in two, in fact, inspection proved that something like that had happened. It was obvious that the car was finished, and here we were in the wilds; thankfully not in the middle of the night.

We sat by the road-side, time passed, no cars came, the sun got up and it started to get hot. Tom put a tin can on a rock across the road and started shooting at it. He couldn't hit it, he was a rotten shot: I trembled when I thought of the previous night's adventure. I took the gun from him and shot the tin down with the first shot.

I sat on a rock in the shade with Tom and he told me his plan; I was not to tell the others. Four of us were to get a lift at the first opportunity and he and the little man were going to push the car over a conveniently placed cliff, stage an accident and try to claim insurance on it. We were to wait for them at the hotel at Ford Victoria, where he would hire a car to take us to Bulawayo. I told him he was crazy, that for obvious reasons it wouldn't work but he was full of boyish enthusiasm for his plan.

At last a big black Cadillac came very fast round the corner and stopped, breaks squealing. There was only one man in the car and he agreed to take us. The four of us piled in with most of the luggage. I was in the front squeezed in between Rina and the driver. He didn't talk, he drove fast and well. I studied him. He had a strong handsome face with an eagle-like nose which was vaguely familiar; I thought I recognized him. All the way to Fort Victoria he only stopped once, when we ran out of gas. He flagged down a lorry coming the other way and demanded the driver to siphon out some of his petrol which he did without hesitation. This man was used to being obeyed. I took this opportunity to look at the label on his suitcase. Yes, it was Roy Farran. I had read in his book 'Winged Dagger' about his daring war-time exploits, for which he had won many decorations. More recently in Palestine - where he claimed he had been used by the British Government as a scapegoat - he had fallen foul of the Jews. Hero or terrorist I greatly admired him. No wonder he was so serious and in such a hurry, he had just escaped assassination in the Carlton Hotel in Johannesburg. Later his brother was killed by a letter bomb intended for him. When he dropped us at the hotel in Fort Victoria, I used his name when I thanked him for bringing us and invited him to a concert we were giving in Salisbury, but I never saw him again.

We waited all day at the hotel. There were rumours that there had been an accident near Beitbridge and that someone was hurt. We were worried. At last they arrived: dirty and tired, Tom limping - he had stayed in the car too long when pushing it over the cliff and had cracked two ribs. He insisted that we went straight on to Bulawayo in a hired car. I was disappointed; I had very much wanted to visit the Zimbabwe ruins which are close to Fort Victoria. But we had already missed one performance and were due in Bulawayo.

From then on we were squashed into a normal sized touring car; three in the front and three in the back, with all the suitcases on the roof. On the first day the luggage rack slipped off and spilled all the cases onto the road.

Nothing daunted Tom, he never complained about his ribs which were now bound up. Somehow he contrived to keep us going. The sad thing was that all four of us were good artists. Our audiences were appreciative and we got excellent reviews but usually too late to help. The tour had been badly prepared and advertised, and only when we did several concerts in the same town did we get good houses; this was the case in Salisbury, where we were for a few days.

My picture was on the bills wearing Indian costume. This led to an invasion of Indians at the theatre. The management refused to let them in – there was strict colour-bar in Rhodesia. Tom said that if the Indians were not allowed to see the show we would not perform. Good for him, I thought. We waited not knowing if there was to be a performance or not. In the end the management gave way. The Indians could sit on one side of the theatre and the Europeans on the other. I had a great reception from the Indian side and had to do the dance twice, and afterwards was presented with a bouquet from the Indian community. The next day Rita and I were invited for morning tea by the wife of a prominent Indian businessman. The ladies were beautifully dressed, gracious and charming. They had never seen Indian dancing before and were curious about India and how I had come to learn the dances. I did not tell them that the dances were my own creation and would never pass in India.

Back again in the crowded car, we headed north and crossed the Zambezi into what was then Northern Rhodesia heading for the Copper Belt.

When we did a concert for the employees of the copper mine at Broken Hill, there was again a deputation of Indians wanting us to do a show for them. We were only there for one night but Tom promised them that we would do a special concert for them on our way back.

Struggling along mile after mile in the dust and heat, the inside of the over-loaded car became unbearable. Geoffrey, who was under 20 and a brilliant pianist, smelt awful and refused to wash in spite of our constant complaints. Once it was so bad that we turned him out of the car and left him in the road, of course he got a lift and arrived before us at our destination.

The car was overheating and started to boil, there were endless stops at the roadside. Rina who was rather heavy and not so young was on the point of collapsing by the time we got to Kitwe. There was no time to rest before the concert and I was afraid she would not be able to sing but she made it and sang as well as ever. Rina had been in opera in Italy and had a lovely voice; now married and living in South Africa she missed her old life. Tom was romantically devoted to her and tried to look after her, but she was not tough and would constantly dissolve quietly into tears. The South African baritone, Lionel, was a good singer but not up to her standard and he was always the first to complain; he in no way enjoyed our adventures either. The little old man that was in charge of the box office was always cheerful.

On the way back again we did do a concert for the Indians at Broken Hill. I knew from the previous experience that they were only interested in seeing me, so I decided to do two Indian dances. I contrived a second costume and made inquiries about a drummer; one was found and I rehearsed with him and the pianist. I got them to play a monotonous sort of rhythm to which I could improvise.

There was a stage in the hall but no way to get on to it except from the front and there was no changing room. It didn't matter for the others, who didn't have to change, but I had four changes. In the end some screens were fixed up at the back of the stage for me to change precariously behind. The hall was packed; in front, sat the children, behind them the ladies and at the back the men. This was obviously an occasion; they were all beautifully dressed. They had come to see me so I did my best for them, dancing on and on to the monotonous beat of the drum. I enjoyed it and they loved it and were most appreciative. They liked my other dances too and were quite polite about Rina's singing, but paid no attention and talked all through the baritone and the pianist. I found it an unusual and interesting experience.

On the way to Lusaka (the capital of Northern Rhodesia) the car continued to cause trouble, it was leaking petrol, the brakes were hardly working and there were frequent stops. I resolved that I was not going to travel in that car any more.

We were several days in Lusaka where I met an old friend whom I had known in Johannesburg, when I was there with the ballet in 1936. Through him I managed to arrange a lift to Livingstone for Rina and myself. There was no room for our luggage so we left it with Tom to bring in the car, and we each took an overnight case. We had a comfortable journey with a pleasant couple, spending the night on the way. Arriving at Livingstone the next morning there was no news of Tom. The other two boys, Geoffrey and Lionel, like us, had given up on the car and arrived by train. We were due to give a concert that night. I was determined not to miss seeing the Victoria Falls, so Rina and I went there by bus. We spent the morning in fascination, watching the awe-inspiring sight as tons of water went over the cliff with a great roar into the swirling mass below, throwing up a spray which covered the surrounding vegetation in a light mist. I was longing to stay there in the fine hotel where we had coffee, but we had to get back to hot, dusty Livingstone where we found that the little man had arrived. Tom had remained with the once again broken down car, having sent the little man on with the music so that we could give the show.

"But what about our clothes," I asked. Our cases were in Tom's car and Rina and I were still wearing the same clothes in which we had left Lusaka two days before. Without my costumes it was quite impossible for me to work.

I watched the show from the front. It was pathetic to see poor Rina standing up on the stage in front of the public, wearing a crumpled, dirty dress.

The next day Tom was there with a patched-up car. The petrol tank was now on the roof! I was hoping that we would spend the night at the hotel at the Falls but he said that we had to go off at once to Wankie, where we were expected that night. I was glad that I had seen the falls the day before as now there was no possibility of going, and I would have missed them as I had missed the Zimbabwe ruins.

When we arrived at the coal mining town of Wankie it was to discover we were a day early. Tom had got it wrong; the concert was not until the following night. Here we were in a filthy hot town when we could have spent the night in the beautiful hotel at the Victoria Falls. I was furious. What a hell-hole we were in. Our cell-like bedrooms were a few yards from the railway line, and everything was black from the coal dust which stuck to our sweating bodies.

The following morning we were shown the coal mine. In the days of Cecil Rhodes - when the coal had been discovered - there had been a dispute as to who owned it. It is one of the most important coal mines in Africa and the coal is just below the surface; there was no going down a shaft, we were simply driven down a ramp into a lighted tunnel with the black, shining coal face on each side.

The theatre was a pleasant surprise. We had been performing in dreary halls with poor lighting and here was a proper little theatre with footlights.

I had no premonition that this was the last time I would ever dance in public. Here in this dirty little mining town, a far cry from the Monte Carlo Opera House was to be my final appearance before an audience - my goodbye to the footlights. But where were the footlights? I came on for my first dance and there were no footlights. At last we were in a theatre with proper lighting and no one had turned them on. It was the last straw. I stormed off the stage shouting at a startled Tom to put on the footlights. He was amazed; all through the hazards of those weeks I had kept cool and collected, backing him up cheerfully in every contingency and here I was, blowing my top about a small matter of footlights.

The evening continued to proceed in a bizarre manner. In the hotel we met a group of railway workers who had come by train to the concert. They were waiting for their return train due at one in the morning. We were touched by this enthusiasm so when the hotel bar closed Tom invited them to join us in our quarters whilst they waited. He bought some drinks and we all crowded into one of the bedrooms. I was sitting on the bed when the big Afrikaner next to me put his arm round me. I said,

"Hey, your wife wouldn't like that." Whereupon he said,

"My wife is dead; she died last year," and produced a photo of a girl with two small blond children. It felt awful just to say I am sorry, which didn't seem at all adequate. So when he asked me to go outside with him I felt obliged to do so. We stood on the veranda overlooking the railway line, where he proceeded to ask me to marry him and be a mother to his children. He was quite serious and appeared to be sober. I was very touched. I told him that I had a boy friend already, what else could I say? I didn't want to hurt his feelings, but I really couldn't see myself in a red brick house on a railway station with a complete stranger, looking after someone else's children.

The car was abandoned in a car park - a dead loss to the owners - and we went back to Johannesburg by train. Tom was not exactly honest and more than a little crazy. There had been several other unsuccessful hunting expeditions, without me needless to say - but I couldn't help liking him. He always did what he could for us, we stayed at the best available hotels and he paid us all he owed us. I doubt if he made anything out of the tour for himself.

Chapter 30

THE LITTLE HOUSE IN DURBAN

My mother's health was failing. Jim had built a cottage in the garden at Iniwa for her and I stayed on there to be with her. She was soon bed-ridden and Barbara and I took turns to nurse her. She was kept amused by a litter of kittens which played about on her bed. She gradually became weaker and was often delirious. It was very distressing. Once she said in a calm, happy voice:

"Oh I see myself lying in a big car, and behind there is another car with you all in it, and last comes the farm truck full of Africans." Finally after about three months she went into a coma. The young doctor - a kind and good friend - said she would not regain consciousness, but I was with her when she opened her eyes and looked at me with recognition and tried to smile - trying to give reassurance and comfort. She died that evening at sundown.

As we drove to the funeral (she is buried at Empangeni) we were in the car behind the hearse. I looked back and there was the farm truck packed with Africans. It was just as she had predicted.

I was thirty five. Six months had passed since I had last danced and I didn't feel like going back to it. It seemed a good time to give it up, but what could I do? I believe in clean breaks and the last thing I felt like doing was teaching children in a ballet school. I needed a complete change of occupation.

Mother had left the farm between us. It would take Jim some time to find the money to pay Barbara and me off. In the meanwhile I was broke.

One morning I was having coffee in a tea-room in Durban when I saw my old friend Pat Lindholm (from the time when we were teenagers learning typing together); she was sitting alone at a table. We were equally delighted to meet again. I had heard nothing of her in all those years. On various occasions when I had been in Durban she had been away and our paths had not crossed until now. We had a lot to talk about. She had lived some years in Italy, then married and settled in Rhodesia. She was now separated from her husband and was staying at her parents' home in Durban with her little girl aged four. Like me she was at a loose end. We discussed sharing a house, which was an attractive idea but neither of us had any money. Shortly after our meeting Pat called to say she wanted to see me urgently. She had a plan, a splendid way to get rich quickly; it would be the end of our poverty. All we had to do was to find a suitable house.

"Suitable for what?" I asked. She went on to explain. She knew a woman who played cards with a group of gamblers - gambling was illegal in South Africa at that time - these people were looking for a new 'venue' in which to play. The house had to be in a respectable district, with easy access and a back entrance for hasty retreat if raided by the police. The group were heavy punters - mostly bookmakers - and we the hosts would receive a rake off of ten percent of every pot. It was risky of course, but it sounded good to me.

Pat had to go away for a few days so I went in search of a house. She told me that it didn't matter how much the rent was, but I was not so sure of our imminent riches and wanted to find a cheap place. I found it almost at once; the ideal house. It must have been the last old-fashioned corrugated iron bungalow, on a fashionable tree-lined street on the Berea. It was newly painted and clean and the rent was most reasonable. There were two bedrooms, kitchen, sitting-room, bathroom and verandas on three sides. In the middle of the house, discreetly hidden from the street, was a room with a large table in the middle. What's more the house was on the corner of two streets, so parked cars would not be conspicuous. There was a front way in on one street and a back one on the other. There was also a garden with a huge avocado tree that towered over the house, and servants' quarters in the back. It was a dear little house and perfect for our purpose. We lost no time in moving in.

We were warned to be prepared for the coming Saturday night - I remember it was Easter Saturday. We bought baize to cover the table, cards and whisky. We put a strong bulb in the overhead light, cooked two chickens and waited. No one came. No one ever came!

I went with the woman whose idea it had been to hold one of the gambling sessions where the problem was made quite clear. She was the only woman in the group; the other players didn't like her and wouldn't have accepted any of her ideas. I don't think they had even been consulted. So there was nothing we could do about it.

There we were in the house, Pat and I and the little girl Karin. We also had a maid called Ivy. We loved it there but how were we going to manage? Pat had maintenance money for the child and I had the rent from the flat in London, but it didn't amount to much.

The avocados were ripe; we practically lived off them. To stop the fruit falling and breaking on the ground I climbed on the roof with a sort of net on the end of a long stick and pulled them off one by one. They were the biggest and best avocados ever. We even tried to sell them but all the trees everywhere were loaded, so that wasn't much good.

It was not by intention that Jack's house was just round the corner. I thought I would be seeing more of him but in fact I saw him less. I think he was scared of my being so close - Perhaps his family life was going better. I was hurt, but I didn't pursue him.

There was a couple I kept seeing in the town who fascinated me. The man who was very tall and handsome seemed to know me; he would catch my eye and sort of smile. The woman accompanying him was outstandingly good looking too. I asked Pat who those people were, (I was sure she must know them as she knew everybody and they were so striking), but she couldn't come up with any ideas.

One day Pat said that her brother Trevor and his wife were coming for drinks. I was on the roof pulling down avocados when I looked down, and who should be standing at the bottom of the ladder laughing up at me but the very man I was so interested in - he was Pat's brother! He helped me down and said,

"You didn't recognise me did you?" It never occurred to Pat that I didn't know him. When I had been learning typing with her when I was eighteen he was five years younger and a school boy. I didn't remember ever noticing him but he had noticed me!

Trevor and his beautiful South American wife and two children lived close to us. The children often came to play with Karin and I was often invited to their house. It didn't take me long to realise that this apparently ideal couple were not without problems. She was constantly complaining. It seemed to me that she had everything a woman could want; a strikingly attractive, good natured, hard working husband, two beautiful children, a nice house and garden and a lively social life - what more did she want? The answer was a millionaire. She felt that she should be married to a millionaire and confided quite soon after we met that she still hoped to find one.

Our maid Ivy produced a sister called Grace who wanted a job looking after Karin. Pat couldn't afford a nursemaid. Grace was a bit dim - just up from the bush, but we agreed that she could share Ivy's room, whilst she looked for work in exchange for taking Karin for a walk in the park every afternoon. She was so happy with this arrangement that I don't think she ever did look for work. Ivy cleaned the house in slow motion and made tea and Grace strolled in the park with Karin. Everyone was happy.

Pat had a boy-friend called Michael; he was a beautiful young man. It was an attachment that lasted several years and I felt that they should have made a permanent job of it. The problem was that he lived with his mother who was a Catholic and disapproved of Pat because she was divorced, had a child and was older than her precious son. We couldn't live for ever on avocado pears. A rich and hopeful male friend of Pat's brought us presents of chicken and wine. Trevor - who was into sea things - brought us crabs and crayfish. It was all fine but it couldn't go on like that, I had to find work.

"Why don't you get a job as a taxi driver with Jackson's?" I can't remember who first suggested it. I was shocked, then I thought about it and it didn't seem a bad idea.

Jackson's was the biggest taxi firm in town. They employed both men and women drivers. Jacko Jackson was a respected and well known figure - he had been a rugby international player and one time Mayor of Durban.

I went to the office and saw the manager. He told me that first I had to get a taxi drivers licence, which meant taking a test, then I could come and see him again. I swatted up on locations, streets etc and obtained the licence without any difficulty.

I went back to the office and this time I saw the boss. He asked me,

"Are you any relation of Jim Grantham's?" When I told him I was his sister he chuckled and said,

"Wait till I tell people that I have Jim Grantham's sister driving one of my cabs". He then went on to say,

"There will be no special treatment though. I'll treat you like all the others. A trial period and if you can't do the job you are out." I told him I didn't expect anything else.

"Right," he said. "Be here at seven on Monday morning."

Chapter 31

TAXI DRIVER

I was a bit worried how I would be accepted by the other drivers, who were mostly Afrikaans and pretty tough characters, but I need not have been. They were perfectly friendly and helpful from the start.

There were five men and two other girls on the shift, the latter were young, tough and professional.

We worked twelve hours a day six days a week, starting at seven in the morning. We picked up our cars from the garage and drove the short distance to the rank which was in the centre of town near the Town Hall. We were paid on a percentage basis. This was worked out every evening on our return to the garage; the mileage on the meter reading had to tally with the money taken. On the rank, the driver of the first car answered the telephone and when he drove off we all moved up. We had no time off for meals, but there was a café opposite the rank where we ate and drank coffee when we were not busy.

I had started work on the Monday and was still feeling very much the new girl, when on the Saturday morning there was a call for me to pick up the bookmaker Ken O'Connor and his crew and take them to the races in Pietermaritzburg. Everybody was most impressed. How had I landed this most coveted job? It meant a good fee and a day at the races. How very kind and thoughtful of my old friend Ken, whose ponies I used to ride in gymkhanas and whose sister Kay had taught me Spanish dancing. This became a regular booking and my shares went up at Jackson's! I enjoyed these trips. The boys gave me tips and on the way back; we would stop at the Valley of the Thousand Hills Hotel for a drink, and a discussion on the day's racing.

Our boss Jacko made his own rules. We could go into bars with customers as long as the car was ticking up waiting time. If the taxi was parked somewhere with the meter not working you would probably lose your job. He had no objection to us drinking but once drunk you got the sack, there was no second chance. The cars were only insured third party; so if you put a dent in one you had to pay for it to be repaired yourself, if you wanted to keep your job. He was a hard man but he was fair. We had a lot of liberty and it was up to us not to abuse it.

I soon learnt the tricks of the trade. If one was quick and intelligent one could make money. There were things that were permissible, others that were not. Discreet cheating against the firm was expected and accepted by the drivers, but never to pinch one of their clients.

All the cars were outsize Chryslers with double seating at the back and could accommodate six people comfortably. They must have been one of the first cars to have an automatic gearshift. They drove easily but were heavy and long to manoeuvre.

After a successful two weeks with an old car, I was given a newer and better one. Shortly after this I overheard a conversation between Jackson and his manager. The former was saying:

"She's not tough enough, we had better put someone else on the car" to which the manager replied

"Why don't we ask her?"

I was called into the office and they explained that the car which I had recently been allotted was one of only two that carried a pass with permission to work in the dock area. It was Thursday morning and the Union Castle Mail boat was due in. They told me that it was apt to get rough down there between drivers from other firms, competing to pick up disembarking passengers. Did I think I could handle it? Sensing good business I told them that I would like to try.

"We will send you down with Barney," they told me. "He will look after you." Barney was on the other car with a dock permit.

The mail boat was late coming in. We joined the line of waiting taxis and went to a stall for coffee. I admit I was a little nervous and didn't know what to expect. Barney explained the rules of the game: It was all to do with the luggage. We had the biggest cars so could take the most luggage. Each piece was clocked up and had to be paid for so it was an advantage to take as much luggage as possible. Passengers with a lot of luggage would come down the line looking for a big car - which was the cause of the trouble with the other drivers - We had to send these people back to the first car in the rank. Only if all the taxis in front of us admitted that they could not take that much luggage was it permitted for us to come out of line. There were sometimes fights over this, but if we stuck to this unwritten law there was no trouble.

Thursday mornings were exciting and profitable. I would get the first lot of passengers away to their destination as fast as possible, and dash back to the boat over and over again for more. I was lucky to have that car but it was sometimes tough work.

The most lucrative time and also the most dangerous, was when the whaling factory ships were in port. Durban was their first port of call after six months at sea in the Antarctic. The tough Scandinavian sailors were flush with money and mad for drink and women. We knew where to take sailors when they wanted girls but sometimes they insisted in being taken to the roughest, most sordid brothels, where they would probably be drugged and stripped of everything, sometimes even of their clothes. If my passengers were young kids I would warn them and suggest they went somewhere else.

One mid-morning I picked up three Norwegian sailors off a whaler; two young ones and an older man. First we stopped at a bottle store and they stocked up on booze, then they gave me an address, some way out at Isipingo Beach. They had the key to a bungalow, which we found in a poor area, mostly inhabited by Indians and coloured people. They went in with their bottles and asked me to wait. I waited. It was hot in the car, although the meter was ticking up waiting time nicely. I was getting fed up when the older man came out and invited me to come in and have a drink with them. I said that I wanted to get back. He promised that they wouldn't be long and that he would see that the young ones behaved. I couldn't just leave them there as I would not get paid, so I took a chance and went into the house. There we stayed until it started getting dark and time for me to take the car back. There was no one else there, just the three of them and they were steadily going through all the booze and getting more and more drunk. They were quite polite and well behaved, I had one or two drinks; all the time trying to get them away. I told them what the car was costing - at least six hours waiting time - with the result that they thrust notes into my hand, a pound each for another half hour. All I wanted was to leave; the night shift driver would be waiting for the car. At last all the drink was finished. One fellow had passed out and the others had to carry him into the car. On the road home, the older man sat in front with me and tried to date me for later that night. The fare hadn't been paid yet so I said,

"Yes, yes," I would meet him. I left them at their boat and collected a big sum, but I had never been more relieved to see the end of a day.

We used to sit in the cars on the rank, waiting to be called out, and gossiped. The boys who alternated between day and night driving had many tales to tell: certain well known gentlemen, when up to a bit of shady night-work did not always use their own cars, but hired a Jackson's cab. Little did they know how we discussed their private affairs. One fellow called Des was a particularly amusing and good pal who taught me a lot of tricks and always had a good story to tell.

Another woman drove my car at night. She was one of the few who dared; as it was a really tough and dangerous job that I would never contemplate. One driver was murdered and several attacked during the six months I was working there. It was made particularly tricky for girls, as one of our rival companies employed several women who were reputed to combine taxi driving with prostitution. Some of the men drivers worked for call-girls and we all knew the girls that worked the streets in our area. These associations could be embarrassing when out with friends. Once again - as when riding the race horses - I was mixing with a lot of raffish characters.

Long before the offensive word 'Apartheid' appeared, there was a strict colour bar in South Africa. We were all white drivers and we catered to a white public. We were not allowed by law to carry blacks; they had their own service with black drivers. These unfair rules caused endless situations. I had no objection to driving Africans or anybody who behaved decently. Our Boss was no racist either; he said we could take who we liked, but if stopped by the police it was we who got into trouble.

I was surprised one afternoon on coming out of the café to find my car occupied by a black family; the three cars in front me on the rank had refused to take them. I drove them to the dock where they nearly missed their boat because they had had such difficulty in getting a taxi. They were South American tourists. They could not understand and were very upset. What a dreadful thing to have to tell people:

"We are not supposed to take you because you are black." I couldn't tell them that; I made up some feeble excuse.

I was interested in the reaction of friends and so-called friends to the fact that I was driving a taxi. Some people including - I hate to say - members of my own family looked the other way and pretended not to see me, other friends waved or stopped for a chat if I was waiting somewhere. I learnt who my real friends were.

I hadn't see Jack for weeks, till one day there was a message for me to pick up Dr. T at the hospital. He didn't want to go anywhere; he just wanted to see me, to tell me that he was flying to England the next day. We drove to the beach and sat and talked in the taxi.

It was a strange coincidence that it was the next day that I drove his wife. She came hurrying to the rank at rush hour and got into my car which was first in line. I had never met her but I knew her by sight. She told me what street to go to but not the number. I glanced at her in the mirror; she was scowling and I felt that she had maybe guessed who I was. I was tempted to say,

"Well did he get off all right?"

I stopped in front of the house without being told. She got out and paid me with no tip. I said,

"Thank you Mrs. T." She went into the house and slammed the door. She was a bad tempered lady but she need not have worried, I was almost a thing of the past.

One day I was called to pick up two ladies, I took them to an apartment building in a mean street near the docks. They were a strange couple. One of them was well dressed and well spoken; the other scruffy little thing could have been her maid. I wondered what they were doing as they seemed such unlikely friends. I waited a long time until they came out holding up an emaciated girl in a tatty dressing-gown. She was crying and had a sweet tragic face. We went to the hospital where they helped her out.

Before long the odd little one came back and sat in the car. I asked her what was going on and she told me that they were members of Alcoholics Anonymous. They had been alerted from Johannesburg that this woman was here and needed help. It was a sad story. The woman they had come to rescue was an alcoholic who had joined A.A., overcome her problems, got married, had a baby and been happy. When her husband got killed in an accident she still resisted, living for her baby until it too tragically died. Shortly afterwards she had left her home, come to Durban where she was renting a cheap room and was drinking herself to death. They had found her just in time as she had not eaten anything for days.

The person I was talking to said that she was also an 'ex' alcoholic, that they were all reformed alcoholics working for A.A. She explained to me that they were never really totally cured.

"One drink," she said, "and we are back again."

When I realised what these kind people were doing I turned off the meter. I didn't want them to have to pay a lot of waiting time. I told them that in the future, if they asked for me, I would not charge them more than I had to. So I became the taxi for A.A. and very interesting it was.

By now I had been driving for six months. As an experience it had been interesting and reasonably profitable, but it was now summer and stifling on the rank with the sun blazing down on the cars all day. I had also lost my two best friends: Des had been sacked for getting drunk and waving a gun about in a bar. The police had been called and when Jacko heard about it, it was goodbye Des - silly boy. I missed him; he was always good for a laugh. When Barney got sacked I couldn't understand it; steady, reliable, family man Barney; whatever could have happened? I went to see him: apparently he had only had an argument with the boss. He told me that he had already been approached by our rival company but that he would rather stay with Jackson's. So I went and confronted Jackson in his office. I asked him why he had sacked Barney who was the best taxi driver in town. He told me understandably to mind my own business. I said that it was my business as he had sacked my two best pals.

Apart from the heat it was boring now on the rank and I soon gave in my notice. I had had enough taxi driving. They say "once a taxi driver, always a taxi driver." It is the pull of the unknown, never knowing who you will pick up next and the fascination of living in the street. I didn't want this to happen to me but no experience is ever lost and it made me a very good driver if nothing else. I still sometimes find myself driving like a taxi driver!

I was sorry some years later, when I heard that Jacko Jackson had got into financial difficulties and driven his Lincoln Convertible over a cliff. It would not have been an accident.

Chapter 32

PROBLEMS

I had been paid my inheritance from the farm – all of eight thousand pounds. It was a ridiculous sum. There had been debts and mortgages on the property, which had been under-valued by a close friend of the family, who I am sure thought it was being valued for probate. Jim, who was a better politician than a farmer, was forced to sell his own small farm in order to pay Barbara and me. This was sad for him as this land later became very valuable.

Mother, who thought she was leaving us quite well off would have been shocked but there was nothing to be done about it. I invested the money in gold shares, doubling it over a few years.

Barbara at this time had a boy-friend, an old flame from Lincolnshire days - now divorced - who had turned up in South Africa. They became engaged and I was happy for her but he was a serious drunk and when he asked me how much money she had, I knew it wouldn't last. I think it was the first proper love affair Barbara had ever indulged in. She was always so proper and so disapproving of me. Now at least she would be happy for a time (but she never married him).

Pat's friend Michael was having a birthday party to which he invited Jack - whose wife was away. I hadn't seen him for weeks. At the party we danced to a record player. I spent most of the evening with Jack and then I danced with Trevor. He said as we danced,

"You must be happy; he has never taken his eyes off you all night."

I said,"Yes, I know, we will go to bed together tonight" and then on impulse I said,

"But I wish it was you."

He didn't have to say anything, he just held me tight. Now I had put into words what we both knew, that it was only a question of time before we were together.

It was a dramatic and emotional night. To be in the same room with the two men I loved most in the world and to know that they both wanted me.

Jack came home with me that night and we did go to bed together for the last time. I told him it had to finish, that I couldn't go on yet again, knowing that it would only last until his wife came back.

Pat was philosophical about the fact that I was having an affair with her brother. Her opinion was as always, if a marriage was going wrong, finish it off and start again. She practised this several times herself, and managed to remain friends with all her ex-husbands.

The situation between Trevor and me was becoming much too involved. His wife was flirting recklessly with everyone and the marriage was probably doomed but I thought of their two little children. I did not want to be the one to break it up.

Always an emotional coward, I ran away from the scene.

A letter from the estate agents in London arrived, saying that my tenants had left the flat. The flat was now empty and needed painting, what were they to do? I decided reluctantly that I had better go back and sort things out.

I was sad to leave our little house; it had been an eventful and happy year.

Pat and Karin came to see me off. My departure was slightly eased by the fact that Trevor was going to Cape Town on business, and we were able to spend a couple of days together there.

London was depressing. I set to work to paint the flat doing most of it myself.

What was I to do? An ex-dancer in search of a new career, untrained for anything else, no longer very young, rich in experience but nothing else. There were few opportunities. The only men I wanted belonged to someone else.

I tried the rep. theatres. I was a dancer, not an actress; they were not interested.

I tried the BBC – sending them some talks I had written. The taxi girl programme I did on Woman's Hour seemed to be a success. It took weeks to prepare and I had to cut it down and down. At last sitting there, waiting for the red light to go on, I was in a panic, I was quite sure I had lost my voice. Afterwards I was complimented and fussed over. I hoped perhaps I was "in". But just at that time the head of Woman's Hour whom I was dealing with left and her successor was not interested in my talks.

I took a fill-in job for two weeks with a firm of solicitors. I answered the switch-board, of which I was terrified. The rest of the time, day after day I was typing Bernard Shaw's will, which was an endless tome. My long suffering employers were quite polite until one of the solicitors, exasperated, said,

"Miss Grantham, you even manage to make spelling mistakes when you are copy typing."

We were mutually relieved when the two weeks were over. I decided the office life was not for me.

I went to the labour exchange and explained my position; all they could offer me was a job as a cashier at the 'Moo Cow Milk Bar' in the

Edgware Road. I walked past the place and came to the conclusion that I would rather starve.

I was frustrated, lonely and bored.

Help came in the way of funds. My mother's sister, Aunt Mabel died and left her considerable savings between the two Croome girl cousins, Barbara and me. It was a most generous gesture which was to be repeated two years later, when Aunt Eddie, the eldest of mother's unmarried sisters, died. It was an old fashioned and charming custom for unmarried ladies to leave their money to their unmarried nieces. The boys were the ones who inherited their own family riches and the married girls were presumably supported by their husbands. So the old maid looked after their own kind.

I am eternally grateful to those two dear ladies. Thanks to them I have been able to live in reasonable comfort and bring up a child. They gave me the gift of independence, which is worth the world to me.

Chapter 33

SPAIN AT LAST

There was still rationing and many restrictions in England in the early fifties. For instance one was only allowed to take twenty-five pounds out of the country, which made it impossible to travel.

For years I had wanted to go to Spain. At last there was a chance. I saw an advert for a bus tour starting from Paris which could be paid for in England in advance. My friend Anna, who used to be my accompanist and who had been with E.N.S.A when we entertained the Czech army in France, was interested in going with me. It would have been surprising, if my first trip to Spain came up to my high expectations, but it certainly did.

The first night was spent in Barcelona with a Spanish doctor friend of my cousin Lois Croome. He asked on the phone what I would like to do. I said I wanted to see Flamenco dancing. He called for me at ten - which seemed to me to be very late – and took me to dinner. We went to Los Caracoles Restaurant in the old town and then to a small club where we watched some genuine Flamenco.

The doctor wanted English money, I wanted Spanish money, so we came to an arrangement; I gave him a cheque and he changed it for pesetas. I had a plan; I had no intention of returning to Paris in the bus with the group.

The guide who was with us on the coach was a pleasant young man. He had done the route many times and was madly enthusiastic about all things Spanish, not only the cathedrals and monuments he showed us in every town, but also gypsies, flamenco, bull fights and all that colourful Andalusian culture that so fascinated me. So he was sympathetic when I told him that I wanted to leave the group in Seville and be picked up again two weeks later, when he returned with the next group of tourists.

Granada was romantic beyond my wildest expectations. I wanted to, and later did, spend hours in the Alhambra and the gardens of the Generalife, drinking in the atmosphere and imagining it centuries ago when the elegant halls and patios were peopled by indolent beautiful Moors, robed and silent, moving quietly from room to room; the veiled ladies, peeping through the latticed windows of the harem, to the sound of gently splashing fountains. I longed to be there alone on a moonlit night with all the tourists gone and only have the sound of nightingales singing and the whispering of splashing water disturbing the silence.

In the afternoon, our guide took us up to the Sacromonte, an amazing mountain; a rabbit warren of caves occupied by *gitanos* (gypsies).

We were seated in a space outside one of the caves - a dusty circle backed by a thicket of prickly pears. The gypsies were pressing round us; some were dressed in frilly flamenco dresses. Children begging were full of cheeky charm. The performance they put on to entertain us was disappointing. The girls strolled through their dances barely moving, making the least possible effort. The singers and musicians performed with unconcealed boredom.

I was disappointed but I was interested in the people, in their brown clear-cut expressive faces and quick dark eyes – some light green and blue - contrasting with jet black hair. The older women were mostly fat, the men lean and feline looking. They were colourfully dressed but there was a complete lack of any animation.

Why, I don't know, but I have always felt an affinity with gypsies. Call it if you like a romantic fascination with a race so alien and different, with a set of values and laws unlike those we are accustomed to. They are close to the earth and usually have practically no education, depending like the animals on instinct. In general the gypsies are feared and distrusted, often with no reason. Why is it then that everyone who thinks they may have a drop of Romany blood in their veins are so proud of it? There is certainly not a drop in mine, but with my daughter, whose father was Andalusian, who knows?

On the other side of the circle, opposite me, I saw an old woman watching me. She was skinny with a wrinkled brown face. She wore a small coloured shawl round her shoulders and a red flower in her grey hair. She looked at me all the time, her gaze never wandered from my face. I knew she was 'reading me'.

Afterwards in the rush and scramble to get to the bus, amongst people selling things and begging it was no surprise to find the old gypsy at my elbow. She was urgently trying to tell me something. I couldn't understand. George, the guide was busy collecting up the group. I called him.

"Please come and tell me what this woman is saying."

He came and she turned to him, the words pouring out.

"She says you have the Spanish soul, that you will come and live your life in Spain, you will have a Spanish child." There was a lot more but George had no more time. That was the moment I decided I must learn Spanish quickly. I took her hand and gave her some money, but she clung to me, still talking. She was not asking for more money, she was inspired; she had what the Andalusians call the *duende* (the spirit). I had no doubt that she was seeing my future. On subsequent visits to the Sacromonte I tried to find that lady, with no success. On enquiring, various so-called fortune tellers were produced but I never saw her again.

We were to be in Granada only one night. After sight-seeing all day I was tired but I felt that I had to go back again that night to the Sacramonte. I felt cheated by the afternoon's exhibition and was sure there was something more exciting to be found there. George agreed to take Anna and me and a young French couple.

We went into a small cave which was a bar. There we were quickly discovered by the same family who had entertained us in the afternoon. I was not happy about this, I felt these people were a waste of time but there was no escaping them. They insisted that we go with them to their cave. They were going to give a party- a *'zambra'* for George, in appreciation of his bringing the groups of tourists to them.

The cave was spacious, clean and cool. Copper pots gleamed on the walls; ceramics and coloured glass were displayed. It was a comfortable and elegant dwelling; there was no sign of squalor or poverty.

It was made clear that we were to pay for the wine but nothing else was expected of us. Many bottles of wine were drunk that night - all very inexpensive, and drunk as we became we were in no way taken advantage of.

At one stage I saw a child take my handbag from the floor beside my chair. I paid no attention. I felt it was important not to react, that I was being tested. The bag was passed surreptitiously from hand to hand and eventually returned to where I had left it. Later I found that nothing was missing - I had passed the test. It was a question of trust; we were among friends.

Children were sent running with messages and the cave filled up with artists summoned from other caves: guitarists, singers, dancers and the friends and relations who came with them. Some were young and beautiful, others old and wrinkled, the latter with much character. They danced boleros and *charangas.* One old lady did a most provocative belly dance.

As they got into their stride the more serious artists performed the traditional *seguidilla* and *alegrias,* working up to the final frenetic excitement of the *buleria* (singing and dancing).

The *cantaor* singers of *cante jondo* wailed the agonised cry of the suffering humanity, egged on by shouts of encouragement.

The noise was overpowering and at the same time controlled. There was the clattering of castanets and *zapateado* (stamping of heels) of the dancers, the singing and the guitars, the hand clapping, finger clicking and occasional shout of *"Olé"* as everybody joined in. These were real professional artists, not the usual stuff shown to tourists and they were enjoying themselves giving it all they had. And there we were, the five of us in the middle of it all; the guests of honour, the only foreigners amongst a crowd of gypsies.

The cave became crowded and hot. Soon there was a group outside watching through the door. Our glasses were continually being filled. Bowls of wine were sent out and passed round amongst the people outside the door.

I could no longer restrain myself; I jumped up and joined in. They were astonished, pleased. I was ushered into an inner cave - a bedroom - and dressed in a red and white spotted flamenco dress and came out encouraged and applauded to join the flamenco team. Sweat poured down our faces and soaked our clothes, no one cared.

It would have gone on all night, if George, thinking of the long day ahead, had not reluctantly dragged us away. As it was it was very late when we made our drunken way through the quiet dark streets to the hotel. It had been a marvellous party.

I left the tour in Seville. The bus went on its way. Anna had made friends and did not mind my leaving the tour. I was excited to be on my own.

I went into the tourist office to ask advice about a cheap place to stay. The attractive young man at the desk said he knew exactly the place I was looking for. It was centrally situated and cheap, the food was good and it was not touristy. The Pension Don Marcos proved to be all he promised and became my home in Seville in all my subsequent visits. It had once been a monastery and there were many small cell-like rooms which overlooked one of the two large patios which were furnished with tables, chairs and lots of green plants – pleasantly cool in August. In each room there was a wash-basin with running cold water, a bed and very little else.

The disadvantages were that there was only one overworked lavatory on each floor, and to get a bath was an elaborate performance. The only bathroom was kept locked. You had to order a bath (which was extra), the water was heated and you were supplied with a large white bath-towel, and could then soak as long as you liked in the huge bath tub; there were no showers. These conditions did not bother me. I had lived in many more primitive lodgings with no bath at all.

The hotel provided lunch and dinner but no breakfast; you simply went out and sat at a pavement café for coffee and something to go with it. This I found to be a typical Spanish custom. Men on their way to work would stop at their local bar for a coffee and often something stronger.

The Pension Don Marcos was in a narrow street in the old town, close to the great cathedral and the Giralda; the wonderful Moorish tower. It was within walking distance of all the places of interest.

When I went to dinner the first night late (it started at ten), I was pleasantly surprised to find the young man from the tourist office at the next table. He had not told me that he lived there himself. He introduced me to various young people, mostly single young men working in hospitals, offices and at the university. Being Andalusians they were garrulous and friendly and only too willing to show me round the town. Most evenings, after dinner, I went out with them.

We walked across the bridge to Triana on the other side of the river to see Flamenco dancing. We sat in outdoor cafés watching the scene or walked in jasmine smelling gardens. All of Seville was out on those hot summer nights; no one ever seemed to go to bed.

I inquired who the best Flamenco teacher was. Although I had given up dancing professionally I wanted to learn some of the traditional dances. They told me of Enrique el Cojo (Henry the lame). His studio was an easy walk from the pension. I went into it straight from the street. There was a lesson in progress so I sat down and watched. A short, fat man with a large bald head and a pronounced limp was rehearsing a pas-de-deux with a young Spanish couple. I could see at once that he was a brilliant teacher in spite of his disability: the way he moved his arms, his legs - one shorter than the other - his expressions. Here was a real maestro. I asked him if he would give me lessons explaining as best I could - I was working on my Spanish - that I was only here for two weeks but wanted to learn a dance, perhaps the *Sevillanas*. He said I could come the next day.

Each morning I wandered through the street Calle Cuna to the studio, stopping for a coffee on the way. He was not going to teach me the *Sevillanas*. I never did learn the *Sevillanas*. I had to pick it up later as best I could at the Feria and it isn't so easy either. He started me on the *Alegrías*. He was surprised that I picked it up so quickly. I never told him that I was supposed to be a Spanish dancer, but he knew I was a professional and respected me as one dancer to another. How I wished I had been able to study with him years before; this is what I had always wanted but it had not possible because of the Spanish Civil War and then the World War.

The studio was a small room with typical Andalusian painted chairs round the walls. After my lesson I sat on one of these for the rest of the morning, watching the other classes. It was a relaxed atmosphere. There was a pianist and sometimes a guitarist, Enrique also played the guitar. Sometimes he seemed tired and would hardly move from his chair, probably after a late night as he was famous and much in demand at Flamenco functions; then suddenly he would get up and dance, showing the pupil what to do and the magic was with him again.

Sometimes there was an assistant at the studio. She was a beautiful girl and brilliant dancer. I thought she should be performing in the capitals of Europe, and even suggested rashly that I might be able to get her work in London. She explained that she couldn't work professionally: she was from a good family and engaged to be married. She could only dance at charity shows. It was 'not done' to be a professional dancer. I was shocked; had I not been a professional dancer for fifteen years and no one had ever taken me for a tart? I was told that when she married she would not even be able to teach - it would be the end of her dancing. To waste such talent seemed a crime but in southern Spain they were still very old fashioned in those days. It was a man's world; there were many things that girls from respectable families were not permitted to do. Boys still sang and played the guitar (or would get a friend to) outside the balcony of the girl to whom he was paying court. Being alone together without a chaperone was not allowed

One day feeling thirsty I went into a bar to have a cold drink. I sat at a table and only after ordering did I notice that I was the only woman in the place. I felt somewhat out of place and quickly finished my drink and went to the bar to pay. I was told my drink had been paid for. There was no indication of who had paid for it. Was it a gentle hint that ladies were not accepted in this bar or an appreciation of the fact that I was? It was mystifying. This happened on several later occasions when I was with another girl, always when we were the only women in the bar. No one ever bothered us and we never knew who had paid for the drinks.

I was happy in this town. I liked it better than any place I had ever been. I wandered about from place to place. Flowers cascaded from window boxes. An old man with a monkey turned the handle of a barrel-organ. Children sold little balls of jasmine flowers. I bought one and put it under my pillow - to smell its fragrance all night and wake in the morning to the cooing of doves.

In one of the little plazas in the area of Santa Cruz old men came every morning to swap stamps. There were donkeys pulling little carts, horse-drawn carriages and not many cars. Some of the narrow streets were forbidden to traffic; the best known of these are the two streets that run parallel, calle Siérpes and calle Tetuan. These were bursting with life, full of bars and cafés smelling of prawns and cigars. There were also the bullfighters' cafés where the Toreros (bullfighters) and Aficionados went to discuss the latest fight. The walls in these cafés were covered with old posters of legendary matadors: El Gallo, Joselito and Manolete, the last two both killed in the ring. The traditional drink was Manzanilla (dry sherry). The *tapas* came free with the drinks - a few small fried fish, a couple of prawns - the shells were automatically dropped on the floor.

There were constant reminders that this was the city of bullfight. Once looking in a window that was slightly below street level, a shimmer of gold caught my eye. Girls were sitting embroidering what could only be bullfighters *'trajes de luces'* (suit of lights).I went down some steps into a room and saw them working. By chance I had discovered the most famous bullfighters tailor. The girls told me,

"This one is for Domínguín, that one for Antonio Ordoñez."

Each jacket was a work of art, lovingly stitched in gold thread on bright coloured satin.

I had to see a bullfight. It was an integral part of Flamenco culture, featured in so many poems and songs, steeped in tradition. Yet I was reluctant to see a courageous, beautiful animal fought to death.

August is the hottest month and it was indeed unbearably hot. It seemed that I would not be seeing a bullfight as there was not going to be one in Seville whilst I was there.

I went to the Maestranza - probably the most beautiful bull ring in Spain. There I saw a circle of golden sand which was surrounded by a red wooden fence. All the way round the bullring rows of tiered seats climbed upwards, to the symmetrical arches at the top. It was awesome to be standing there alone in that Mecca of bullfighting where so many life and death dramas had taken place - now quiet and empty under the sun.

One of the men in the pension - a young doctor - was an aficionado. He told me that there was going to be a fight at El Puerto de Santa Maria (on the coast near Cadiz) the coming Sunday. The three most famous matadors at that time were fighting six bulls, each one specially picked from six different *ganaderias* (ranches). This was a special bullfight with great possibilities. My friend was going and he said that I could go with him.

We went by train early in the morning. When we arrived there we spent some time on the beach. It was a fiesta and the town was in a festive mood. The tavern where we had lunch (paella and a bottle of wine) was crowded, mostly with men. I had to pay a visit to the lavatory and realised this would be something of an ordeal. I discussed it with the doctor and he guarded the door for me as there was no lock, whilst I waded backwards through a smelly lake to the hole in the floor. It was all that was available but it served its purpose.

There was no romance with the young doctor, he was most correct. He was engaged to a girl in Seville whom nobody ever saw. It certainly would not have been permitted for her to come on such a wild outing.

We made our way amongst the crowd towards the bullring and climbed up into our seats in the *sol-sombra* (sun and shade) area; the plaza was packed. I sat hemmed in on every side suffocating from heat, nerves and cigar smoke. I was afraid I would faint; I vigorously applied my fan.

The clarion sounded, the big gate opened, the band struck up a *paso doble* and the parade set forth. The three matadors (bullfighters) walked in front; Luis Miguel Dominguín, Rafael Ortega and in the middle the rising young star Antonio Ordoñez. Behind them came their *cuadrilla* (team), the *banderillero*s and the *picadores* on their horses. Stiff legged and serious, hugging their brilliant dress capes across their bodies they marched across the sand towards us.

The clarion sounded again - there was silence in the plaza now. The crowd waited as the corral gate in the wooden wall was opened and the bull came hurtling out; shining black, muscles rippling, his head held high on his powerful great neck. Someone flipped a cape over the wooden fence and he lowered his head and charged, crashing his horns into the boards. My first thought was, 'What a beautiful animal'.

I didn't know what to expect. I was nervous of my own reaction, prepared to be shocked, even horrified, not expecting to enjoy it. I just felt I had to see it once. I certainly did not expect to be carried away in a state of wild excitement. Nothing I had ever experienced could compare with the drama, beauty and excitement of the bullfight.

My companion sitting beside me kept repeating.

"You will never see anything as good again, this is fantastic." And indeed I never did. My first bullfight was the best I ever saw, and I was to see many more.

Each matador was competing to do better than the last. Each of the six bulls did whatever was asked of him and more, right to the end when they were quickly and cleanly killed.

I saw passes done that day that I have never seen since. The best of all was Luis Miguel Dominguín's second bull. The people were all on their feet shouting. Ignorant as I was, I realized that I was seeing something exceptionally brilliant.

The three matadors cut all the ears and all the tails of all six bulls; trophies given when a bullfighter has fought well (they are cut off after the bull is killed). I feel sure that so many trophies have never been awarded in one afternoon, and that there are old men in Santa Maria who talk about that bullfight still today. Later we saw the head of the fourth bull being taken on its way to the taxidermist to be preserved for eternity. It is surely still hanging on some wall.

No doubt that if my first bullfight had been a bad one or if a horse had been injured I would never have gone to another. As it was I couldn't wait to return to Spain and see some more.

The day arrived to meet George (the guide) at the Cathedral, where we had agreed to meet, in order to go back reluctantly to Paris. He was surprised to see me wearing a black *mantilla* over my head. I was rather overdoing my new role of being more Spanish than the Spanish.

Chapter 34

THE MIDDLE EAST

In London things were dull again but I had something to look forward to. I had booked a room for the coming spring at the Pension Don Marcos in Seville for Easter week and the Feria (the April Fair).

I was delighted to hear from my friend Pat that she was coming to England to stay with me.

On the day she was supposed to arrive I waited all day and heard nothing. I was getting worried and thinking perhaps she wasn't coming after all, when at last she phoned. Someone else knew that she was coming: She had told an ex-boyfriend and he had gone to meet her and insisted in taking her to his flat. She never did come to stay but I saw her every day as she was living quite close. I was naturally impatient for news of her brother Trevor. Apparently things were much the same there, the couple were still together.

Pat's Greek boyfriend was most charming and included me in many outings. He was mad about Pat and when it was time for her to leave he locked her in the flat. She managed to crawl out through a small window. Afterwards he came to me to be comforted but I was poor consolation.

I spent the following winter with my friends Betty and Gavin Jack in Cyprus. The Island was still a British Crown Colony and Gavin was in the diplomatic corps, stationed at Nicosia.

Cyprus is a beautiful island. I explored the dusty ruins of Crusader castles and went skiing on Mount Troodos. In early spring the ground was covered with wild anemones and tall pink asphodel, which looks so romantic but smells strongly of cats.

Betty and I decided to go on a trip to Beirut and Damascus.

Beirut was, in those days, a beautiful, elegant Mediterranean city with excellent French food. In the streets there were stalls selling mimosa and violets. At our hotel we met a most friendly couple who insisted that we stay with them in Damascus. We did not really want to do this; we would rather have been on our own, but they were so insistent that, short of being rude, it was difficult to refuse. We did not realise at first that he was British Ambassador to Syria.

Two days later we hired a car to take us to Damascus. On the way we stopped at Baal beck. It was pouring with rain as we were shown round the famous ruins but no amount of discomfort could detract from those marvellous great towering pillars. They were the most impressive ruins I have ever seen.

When we got to the frontier between Lebanon and Syria - it was still pouring with rain - we had to go into the customs office where I was to receive a shock. I was told that I could not cross the boarder; Betty could go but no me. Why not? There must be a mistake. The mistake was that I was still using the passport that E.N.S.A. had got for me during the war and it had for my occupation 'Dancer' written in it. I was being treated as a prostitute and as such was being refused entry into Syria. I was furious. I told the man that I was invited to stay with the British Ambassador in Damascus. Even so they wouldn't let me go until they had phoned the embassy to confirm my story.

It was dark when we arrived at a large building in the modern part of the city. We did not seem to be expected. A servant let us into a dimly lit apartment where he left us whilst he went away, presumably to consult with someone. When he returned he showed us into a double bedroom. I asked the servant if Madam was at home, to which he mumbled that she was in bed; a strange hour to be in bed unless she was ill. We didn't know what to do. We waited in the bedroom and then started cautiously to explore; we crept about behaving like a couple of school girls, but it was so creepy. There was no sign of a servant. There was a dining room with a table laid for two. We started to look in cupboards to see if we could find a drink when suddenly, with no warning, the silence was broken by a loud wailing noise just outside the window; the Moslems were being called to evening prayer. We needed a drink badly.

At last our host came, he told us his wife was unwell; no further explanation was given. We said that we would go somewhere else if it was inconvenient but he insisted in pouring us out drinks and taking us out to dinner. The poor man was charming but the whole thing was most embarrassing; they had obviously forgotten we were coming. The only time I saw the lady was the next morning. She had forgotten to lock the lavatory door, and when I opened it there she was enthroned!

Damascus is a most fascinating place, and wandering about by ourselves in the old city with all its interesting sights, smells and things to buy made us wish we were staying longer but under the circumstances, we thought one night was enough.

.

I had to get to Spain as cheaply as possible. There was no regular shipping line but I found a Greek ship sailing to Marseilles and booked third class. Our first port of call was Beirut again where I went ashore and bought some violets to cheer up the cabin. My cabin was situated in the extreme stern of the ship where it swung madly up and down. The other bunks were filled with Oriental ladies prostrate with sea sickness.

I arranged to go ashore at Alexandria with a most respectable elderly English couple. Imagine my fury at being told once again that I was not allowed to leave the ship. Everybody went on shore and I stayed on board like a criminal.

There was a nice surprise that evening when the more presentable of the third class passengers were given cabins in the first class. There were no strings attached to this arrangement, the third class was simply overbooked. We still had to eat in the third, but it was a great improvement to have a cabin to myself.

Anyone who thinks the Mediterranean is a calm sea should have been on that voyage. I had never experienced anything like it. The deck was awash and it was dangerous to attempt to move about. When we got to Piraeus half the first class passengers left to fly home; they thought the ship was going to sink.

After a night spent in Marseille I searched around for a ship going to southern Spain. The best I could find was a French cargo boat sailing to Tangiers. There was a stuffy canteen on it where I spent most of the time playing poker with some Middle Eastern gentlemen, whose wives were laid low in their cabins. The food was quite good but the sanitary arrangements disastrous. It was still pretty rough and it was dangerous to walk out on deck - not only because of the sea - each time I ventured out I was propositioned by one of the ship's officers. From the Captain down they were a scruffy looking lot and I was not in the least tempted by the offer of a first class cabin and a free trip to the Canaries and back.

When we arrived at Tangier, the taxi driver took me to one of the hotels on the seafront where I spent a long time in the bath. For the rest of the day I enjoyed myself wandering about in the old town. I visited the Medina, the Grand Socco and the Petit Socco made famous by homosexual writers; where even in the day-time there were young boys on the pick-up. Of course I wanted to go back there at night but I didn't think it would be a good idea to go alone. It was out of season and there were very few people in the hotel. I decided my best bet was the Spanish barman. I sat at the bar and we talked about Spain and his home town; he quickly got the message and offered to escort me and show me the Kasbah after he closed the bar. We spent a most interesting evening in the maze of small streets full of Hashish parlours and brothels. We went into one opium den where men were lying half conscious in a haze of smoke. We were invited but we didn't stay. We only stopped at Spanish bars where my escort was more at home.

That was my only night in Tangier. I intended to stay longer but when I went to change some travellers' cheques the bank would not accept them. In those days you had to specify the country where the travellers' cheques were to be cashed and they were endorsed for Spain. It had never occurred to me that Tangier, being a free port, would not accept them. They told me at the bank that I would have to go to Tétuan to change them but as

I had just about enough cash to see me to Seville, I decided to leave at once. I caught the ferry to Algeciras and then a bus.

It was dark and raining when I arrived at Seville. I climbed into a horse-drawn cab with all my luggage- it was the only transport I could see. It went clop clopping through the dim, wet streets to the Pension Don Marcos. Luckily, a porter I knew was on duty, as I had to ask him to lend me the money to pay the cab.

I changed my clothes, waited till ten and went into dinner hoping to make an entrance! I found the dining-room empty. The waiter explained that in the winter months they dined earlier and that everybody had already finished eating. I had my dinner alone, it was hardly a celebration. I enquired about Pedro, the boy from the tourist office. He was out and so apparently were all my friends. There was nothing for me but to go to bed. My room was on the ground floor. The rain dripped on to the aspidistras in the patio and there was a leaking tap in the basin, I was cold - what a disappointing return to the city of my dreams.

I

Chapter 35

EASTER WEEK AND THE APRIL FAIR

The town was filling up and there was a feeling of excitement in the air. The Easter processions were to start on the Monday and would go on every night through to Good Friday.

The sacred figures (the Virgins and Christ) are carried once a year during Holy Week from their resident parish churches through the streets. They are paraded through the streets to the cathedral and back again. Each float is accompanied by a procession made up of parishioners, church dignitaries, robed and hooded penitents and musicians. All the floats are most elaborately decorated.

It is possible to buy seats in a specially erected platform in front of the Cathedral, where one can sit in comfort and see all the processions go past. But it is much more exciting to be following one through the narrow, dimly-lit back streets.

I had made friends with a Mexican woman who was staying in the hotel. She was quite intrepid and each night she found out where the action would take place. We found ourselves in places that most people would avoid. We packed into crowded alleys hoping to hear *saetas* sung. There is no set rule about the singing of *saetas*, it is a spontaneous outpouring of emotion and can happen any time.

We didn't take hand-bags or money with us, which was a sensible decision as I felt hands going in and out of my pockets. I was groped and trodden on, I felt thirsty, dirty, worn out and my feet were sore from walking all night, but still I went back night after night to be in the middle of it all. It had a hypnotic effect on me. Floats went by, bright with hundreds of candles and masses of carnations. They carried a painted doll-like Virgin bedecked in finery or a sculptured agonised Christ hanging from a cross. As they came swaying towards me and passed to the repetitive cry of trumpets and drums, a shiver went down my spine. Black-robed and hooded penitents shuffled by, each carrying a long taper. Black eyes peered out of the holes cut in their hoods; every now and again one gleamed with a wicked shine as his glasses caught the light. Some walked with bare feet; vulnerable white feet, others dragged chains. There was a church smell of incense and candles. It was sinister, frightening, and brought to my mind medieval Catholic persecutions. Once in a while a black eye would wink; I winked back, observing these sinister looking characters slipping sweets to the children - the round, white Easter sweets. The float bumped to a standstill, someone ducked under the white embroidered skirts that surrounded it carrying bottles of beer; refreshment for the bearers of the heavy float. And the spell was broken; they were just ordinary men after all.

There was one awkward moment when we found ourselves in a bottle-neck, as two processions going in opposite directions came head on in a narrow street. There was a carriage drawn up there and the horse panicked. I was crushed in the crowd. I knew that if I fell I would be trampled to death. To make matters worse I had a man on my back trying to rape me. I couldn't move my arms, I was striving to keep on my feet, there was nothing I could do but jab him with my elbows. I never saw the man, I was really afraid. I had lost my friend; when I finally found her she was looking for her shoes. I was shaking and I told her what had happened and she said,

"Yes, I'm afraid there is a stain on the back of your skirt."

When I got back to the hotel I threw away the skirt; I needed no reminder of a most unpleasant experience.

Some of the Christ figures are beautifully carved and life-like, particularly 'El Cristo de Gran Poder'. We followed this statue all night. It was impossible not to be moved as at dawn outside the church of San Lorenzo, when a voice was raised in a wild wailing lament as a woman sang a *saeta*, to be joined before she had finished by another and yet another, spontaneous outbreak of emotional worship. On top of the church tower in the first light of dawn a stork was feeding her young, standing in a huge nest, unconcerned by the happenings below.

The biggest star of all is the 'Virgin of the Macarena'. She comes out on the Thursday at midnight and it is daylight when she is returned to her church. She wears a great gem-encrusted crown and a heavily embroidered cloak. All her jewels are said to be authentic, donated by faithful admirers. There are tears on her pretty painted cheeks. She may resemble more a 'Barbie doll' than Christ's mother, and yet I keep a painted tile of her in my house. I look at her sometimes and say,

"Be good to me lady, I walked all night with you once" - I respect everybody's idols. It was mid morning on Good Friday, still with a great following, when she was finally carried into her church. It had been a most exhausting week, but it was all over now, and we could go thankfully to bed.

There is a respite of a few days before the Feria (the April Fair) starts.

I went to look at the preparations. It was an easy walk from the hotel to the fairground, through gardens smelling sweetly of orange blossom. The Seville oranges being bitter are never stolen and remain decorating the trees even when they are in flower.

The area is specially prepared every year. There were several streets of little *casetas* (huts) which were going up and being decorated. Coloured streamers were hung over the streets. The sun was out and all was in readiness.

Walking back from the studio one morning (I was continuing with my dancing lessons) I was accosted by a young man who I thought was begging. I distinctly heard him say he was hungry. He was quite well dressed and didn't look like a beggar so I told him to go away. He persisted in following me, so I stopped and said,

"What a disgrace, a well dressed young man like you begging in the street." This amused him greatly, he laughed and said,

"I am not hungry for food; it's you I want to eat."

He had been paying me a *piropo* - the typical Andalusian way of paying a compliment. These quietly muttered observations can range from the charming to the obscene. The unwritten law was never to answer a *piropo*; always ignore it. And here I was walking down the street with a cheeky young man to whom I had given rave encouragement.

"There will be no time for you to eat me today", I told him. "I am on the way to meet my husband."

He thought that hilarious,

"It was just a joke" he said. "Please come and have a coffee with me, I won't eat you". It was getting more and more difficult to extricate myself. I felt a fool standing there arguing. I should have ignored him in the first place, but now there was nothing to do but tell him to bugger off. He went, muttering to himself. I had broken the rules and learnt a lesson.

The bullfights started on Easter Sunday. There was one every day during the Feria. I bought a season ticket for all the fights - a *barrera sol* (first row in the sun). The most expensive seats are in the middle of the shady side of the plaza, next are those that are first in the sun and later in the shade as the sun goes down (*sol y sombra*). The cheapest are in the sun all the time. I wanted to be in the first row and the sun was all I could afford. As it was I made a good choice for there I sat amongst the genuine aficionados. They were mostly old men who knew everything about bullfighting and they were only too pleased to explain things to me. When a bull came out one would say,

"It has got a defect in the left eye", or

"It is *manso* (tame) *no vale nada* (not worth anything)", or

"It has been picked too hard" (by the picador), or occasionally

"Now we will see something."

They were usually right. They taught me what to look for in the bulls, whilst the usual amateur is looking on at the matador. However good the matador is he can do nothing if the bull does not play its part.

There is nothing like the fiesta of Seville. It is an unmatched spectacle of gaiety. A great brightly-lit arch spans the entrance to the area and inside streets are lined with *casetas* - little pavilions with platforms for dancing. Some are no bigger than booths, other larger ones are furnished with tables and chairs; most of them are owned by families or clubs. An invitation was needed to go in but in those days all were open to the street; one could watch from outside and if you were lucky you might be invited in. All the *casetas* were brightly lit and decorated. The girls wore the traditional frilly dresses and the men high-waist tight-fitting jackets and Cordobes hats.

The morning is the time for the horses. About midday the carriages and boys and girls on horseback started to arrive. Beautifully dressed children danced in the streets to the ever present sound of the Sevillanas. Young men rode up and down the streets with pretty girls sitting side-saddle behind them, their frilly skirts spread out to be admired. Some of the carriages were drawn by as many as six perfectly matched horses, their necks proudly arched well aware of the occasion (horses love to be admired). There were also teams of mules, beautifully turned out and decorated with red and yellow pom-poms and ribbons. The grooms driving the teams from the box of each coach were lean and handsome in their traditional costumes and Cordobes hats, looking infinitely more aristocratic than most of their over-weight passengers.

I was lent a dress and even did a round sitting on a horse behind a young man – just to get the idea of it!

After a late lunch I would be off to the bull ring, to sit squashed into my few inches of concrete, amongst the great mass of tense, excited humanity, in the heat and the glare and the smell of cigar smoke. And then to see the clock point to the hour, the great door open and the band strike up with the brilliant glittering procession stepping out across the sand.

After the fight there would be a discussion in some bar and then hopefully one would get a couple of hours rest before dinner and the Feria again. It started to get animated about midnight and from then on it became better and better. There was music, dancing and singing everywhere - the whirl of skirts, the clicking of heels to the lively infectious rhythm of the Sevillanas. There was plenty of drinking but I never saw any exhibition of gross drunkenness. Everyone was full of gaiety and happiness. The traditional drink is Manzanilla - a light dry sherry served in little glasses.

If one had the strength to stay around till four in the morning, when the crowds had thinned down and gone off to bed, there were wonderful surprises. Many of the best professional artists – who had probably been performing at private parties, already worked up - would arrive with their team and be invited from *caseta* to *caseta* to perform with no restraint. Several times I caught sight of Enrique el Cojo in his white dinner jacket.

Sometimes a gypsy would carry on a brilliant repartee with one of the artists - pretty dirty doubtless, as everyone was in stitches. We crowded round the *casetas* watching, it was worth staying up for.

One night I was sitting in a *caseta* with people from the hotel when a young Gypsy came and asked me to dance. I refused but he insisted and pulled me up onto the stage. I said to the boy,

"Not the Sevillanas, tell the guitarist to play some Flamenco." I started to improvise, the boy surprised, followed me. At the end we got a big ovation and encouraged we danced again, working together, more relaxed and enjoying it. The boy was delighted, he was very young, perhaps sixteen, he loved to dance. We went from *caseta* to *caseta*; he enjoyed showing me off. I was fêted and plied with drinks. Eventually he fell asleep exhausted with his head on my shoulder. His shoes were worn through from dancing.

I had long since lost the people I had been with. There was a hint of dawn as I walked home alone through the sweet-smelling gardens. Cocks crowed in the distance. I was not in the least afraid.

My cousin Lois came to join me. We got on well and she was always game for anything. She had missed the Feria at Seville but we went to other fairs in other towns and travelled round Andalucia. I had to show Lois Granada, so we went there. We stayed in a delightful pension right under the walls of the Alhambra. Cascades of tiny yellow roses hung from the walls into the patio where we had our meals. We spent some time on the Sacromonte with the gypsies but I didn't recognise any of our friends from before.

By chance I found out about a fair out in the country that was taking place. Not many people visited it unless they were interested in the buying and selling of horses. Outside the town there was a field full of horses, mules and donkeys of every description. The people negotiating were the horse trading gypsies of Andaluicia, a more colourful group of people impossible to encounter. They were living in caravans and tents amongst their animals. Horses were being trotted up and down. Cooking was going on. A family sitting on the ground round a big pot of tasty smelling stew invited us to join them. I knew this to be a polite formality; I was not expected to accept. They were so friendly. A cheeky little boy persisted in trying to sell me a small furry donkey. I tried to take photos. The woman turned away - something about the evil eye - but the children were delighted and all but mobbed me. It was a delightful morning we spent with these enchanting people.

Lois was flying back to England from Gibraltar so we took a bus along the coast road from Almuñecar to La Linea. On the way we passed through a pretty village. There was an attractive plaza with bar tables, flowers, trees and a drinking trough for horses. I asked what place it was and was told Torremolinos; a place that was later to play a big part in my destiny.

Chapter 36

EL RUBIO AND THE BULLFIGHTING

I went back to Seville again the following spring but not in time for Easter week. That year the Feria had to be postponed because day after day it poured with rain. One bullfight that was not postponed had them all splashing about in a foot of water, and had to be abandoned half way through.

There were some lively young Americans in the hotel and we had a good time at the Feria when it did eventually get going.

After Seville I went to Torremolinos where I found a marvellously cheap pension in the main square. The food was good and again one could have a bath by arrangement. The bedrooms were over a bakery and the only problem was the cockroaches, I had never even in Africa seen such monstrous great cockroaches. The front door was locked at midnight and after midnight the bell was answered by Jesus the baker who worked all night. He was such an astonishingly handsome creature that one took care never to be home before midnight, and then I would sometimes call him up to despatch the cockroaches. Unfortunately he had a wife who soon caught on and saw to the cockroaches herself.

Torremolinos was still only a fishing village then, though it was beginning to get popular with foreigners. There were several small hotels and a selection of villas to let. There is a good long beach but the sand is a dull greyish colour. It was amusing and cosmopolitan with a good mixture of nationalities and some really weird characters.

I met a charming young man - the theatre director Peter Grenville. He was on holiday with an American dancer friend. They were very keen to know about bullfighting. They hired a car and I went with them to see a fight at the typical Andalusian town of Antequera.

Peter wanted to get in touch with the American matador Sidney Franklin, with the idea of doing a musical based on his life. I knew that Franklin was in Seville and as I was going back there I offered to try and contact him.

I inquired in the bars frequented by bullfighters but no one seemed to have heard of Sidney Franklin. At last, I was advised to go to a certain bar in the calle Sierpes. It was in the morning and there were not many people in the bar. I sat at a small marble-topped table, very much aware that I was the only woman in the place. I ordered a coffee and told the waiter that I was looking for the American matador. A tall, blond young man was leaning against the bar; he wandered over to my table and said,

"I hear you are looking for the American matador. That's me. I am El Rubio de Boston."

He told me that Franklin was not often seen in the city, that he had a school for bullfighters out of town. According to Rubio he was not popular in the *taurino* world and that people said he took advantage of the boys. The things he told me about Franklin were only rumour, there could be many reasons why a foreigner was not wanted in that closed world. It was obvious that Rubio didn't want anything to do with his compatriot.

I asked Rubio about himself. He told me he came from Boston where his father was a house painter. They had once gone for a holiday to Mexico and there he had become obsessed by the idea of becoming a matador. He had left school early, gone to Mexico City where he got a job and started to train. He had already had several fights in Mexico and in Spain as a *Novillero* (apprentice matador) and was hoping to take the *'alternativa'* and become a fully fledged matador this season. He was twenty two, ambitious, dedicated and broke. He admitted frankly that he was being kept by a local Seville girl. He told me he loved her dearly and that his ambition was to make enough money to be able to marry her and take her out of the life that she had been forced to live. He was very serious about this, he was not happy about the situation but at the moment there was no alternative. He was a nice boy.

I used to go with Rubio to watch him practise. The boys gathered every morning in an abandoned open-air cinema and 'ran the horns'. They worked in pairs, the part of the bull was played in turn by a boy using a pair of wide horns with which he attacked the other boy who carried the *muleta* (a scarlet heart-shaped cloth about a yard long and wide that's attached to a short stick which the bullfighter uses to attract and 'work' the bull) Advice was given by trainers and older bullfighters.

Nothing is guaranteed to raise a storm of protest and indignation amongst most Anglo-Saxons than the mere mention of the bullfight. The fighting bull is a special race carefully bred through the centuries for his fierceness, strength and bravery, the whole purpose of which is for the twenty minutes he will spend in the ring. For four years he lives an ideal life left to roam free with his brothers on the ranch. He will weigh about 500 kilos when he is sold and sent with five of his companions to the bullring. He will die, but he dies fighting. He can see his enemy and has a chance to attack; he is a dangerous animal and learns very quickly, his blood is up. He is a noble fighting animal who dies a noble death, at the hands of a man who is prepared to risk his own life to see that he is properly fought and killed. That is the key to the bullfight. It is a drama of death in which a man matches his skill against the force of an enemy of vast physical superiority, controlling that force with grace and beauty. Bringing the great beast round his body, closer and closer, until the last most dangerous moment; the 'moment of truth', when brave man and brave beast meet as one, as the man goes right over the lethal head to sink the sword in between the shoulder blades.

The young aspirant matador has a tough struggle to get to the top, and only those with great courage and determination have a chance of success. It is not just a pretty boy out there but a dedicated man of great bravery and integrity. He has to stay cool not only in front of the bulls but in front of a fickle, ruthless public. The more famous he becomes the more they will demand of him.

Rubio kept talking about an Englishman called Paul who he wanted me to meet. He lived in a caravan and travelled round the country going to all the important *corridas* (bullfights), he was a keen aficionado and Rubio thought we would have a lot in common. Actually I knew this man by sight and told Rubio that next time I saw him I would introduce myself.

I was in Granada for the fiestas there when I first met Paul at a concert in the gardens of the palace. I saw this lonely Englishman and went up to him and told him we were being introduced by 'El Rubio de Boston', who was a friend of us both.

Paul was not young and he had a bad heart. He lived in a rather smelly caravan with a boat on top (his other passion was sailing) in which he followed the bulls about the country, and when near the sea he went for a sail. He was a character, an eccentric Englishman who was an authority on bullfighting. He knew everybody in the *taurino* world. He was very thick-skinned and barged into places where no one else would dare to go and surprisingly was accepted. He was to include me in many of these adventures and we became good friends in a strictly platonic sense. When I said,

"I can't possibly go there" or "Do that"; he would answer "of course you can, take your camera and say you are a press photographer". My ancient Agfa camera came in very useful.

At the time I met Paul I was making my way up north to Madrid and Pamplona and he was on his way south, so I didn't see much of him till the following season. But I contacted him in London where he lived in the winter in a room over a restaurant, a stone's throw from Piccadilly Circus. I think he fed on leftovers from the restaurant. His room was up endless steep stairs but once there it was worth the climb. He had a marvellous collection of books on bullfighting, old prints and posters and a beautiful bronze bull. Amongst his friends was the English bullfighter Vincent Hitchcock, who later was to become a friend.

While in Granada for the fiestas, I spent an unforgettable night with six little gypsies.

Up in the Sacromonte that morning I had engaged a small boy as guide - otherwise one was besieged at every step - he was a bright intelligent kid, who immediately shooed all competitors away and took charge of me. First he took me up to the top of the hill where the caves were small and occupied by very poor people. In one; which I suspect was his home, he produced a baby of about two, who, stark naked, danced Flamenco with a great show of temperament.

In another more prosperous cave a group of young people were discussing the fair and playing about cadging cigarettes from tourists. A voluptuous girl was complaining that she was never allowed to go to the fair; her husband had been but her parents made her stay at home and dance for tourists. I invited her and her husband to come to the fair with me that night. The boy - he was very dark with bright green eyes - insisted he would bring another young man to accompany me; he seemed to think that that would be the correct thing to do. We agreed to meet at a bar down by the river.

I thought I was being a bit rash. As a precaution I only took two hundred pesetas which I pushed inside the bodice of my dress, a dark blue and white spotted cotton, with a full skirt and carried nothing.

I went to the meeting place half expecting they wouldn't turn up, but there waiting were six young boys and no girl! I told them,

"This won't do. I specially invited the girl. Go and get her."

Two of them went off and I went into the bar with the others. It was a rustic bar consisting of little closed compartments made out of reeds. It didn't take much stretch of the imagination to guess what went on there. Green eyes ordered a bottle of wine. I thought I had better put things straight at once. I produced the two hundred pesetas and told him that that was what we had to spend and that once finished that would be it. He found it a perfectly satisfactory arrangement. The others came back. "No, they said, the girl was not allowed to come. Green eyes sensing my hesitation said,

"Señora, you have six sons for tonight and we are going to give you a night you will not forget."

So I went with six kids between the ages of twelve and eighteen for a night of fun at the fair.

We went on every awful swinging and dipping and screwing machine on the fairground. I would gladly have waited whilst they flew through the air and rotated and bounced up and down. But no, they would not go without me. It was the same with the wine. We drank seven bottles of the cheapest wine throughout the night and every time I had to be the first to drink. They behaved perfectly and they were very funny. They were hilariously funny, each one outdoing the other with an even more outrageous story. One would tell a blood-curdling tale about something that happened the night before and another would say,

"Don't listen to him Señora that happened two weeks ago."

Not one of them could read or write. I asked them why they didn't go to school. They laughed and said,

"What good would that do us? Who would give us a job?"

The best was the hall of distorting mirrors. They threw themselves about howling with laughter. At one time, when I was staggering off the big dipper, a middle-aged couple concerned with the company I was keeping asked if I was all right, if I needed any help, to which I answered,

"I am quite all right thank-you, I am with my family." The boys loved that.

It was about four in the morning when they asked a Guardia Civil (civil guard) where we could find a bar with music. I like this; the gitanos and the Guardia Civil are supposed to be traditional enemies. The information supplied, we found a small crowded tavern where there was a guitarist playing on a stage. Green eyes took the guitar and started to play. One of the other boys put on my shoes (they were wearing sandals) and danced *zapateado*. In a moment the whole bar, including our Guardia Civil, was joining in with *palmadas* (hand clapping).

More wine was ordered. I was worried because the money was finished, but Green Eyes said it was okay, he had money. Sure enough he paid for the last bottle of wine and even gave a tip to the guitarist.

I had one little boy under each arm and was not too steady on my feet as we wandered up and down hills, through grassy lanes and secret places on our way home as dawn was breaking - all six boys were still with me.

It had certainly been a night never to be forgotten.

I went to Madrid for the fiestas of San Isidro. The bullfights held there are considered the most important of all.

I was sitting at a sidewalk café in the street Calle Alcala, feeling lonely in this big city, when who should I see but El Rubio striding along by himself. He was just what I needed. I called him over. He was here in Madrid on business, hoping to pick up contracts as all the agents, impresarios and bullfight critics were gathered there at that time. He did unfortunately manage to fix himself a fight at Las Ventas bullring in Madrid for later in the season.

I had arranged to go out 'on the town' with two Australian girls I had met on the train. Rubio was a godsend; we needed a man with us, someone who knew his way around. I was aware of his lack of finances so I suggested that we would pay for all the drinks if he would escort us. He was only too pleased to agree. It was an amusing evening; he was familiar with a number of bars with music, and some sleazy dives with girls who plied their trade behind a flimsy curtain. The Australian girls were thrilled, if a little scandalised at times.

I was staying at a hotel near the Puerta del Sol. When Rubio escorted me back he said he had missed the last train back to the suburbs where he was staying with friends. So I told him,

"There are two beds in my room, you can stay with me." And he did.

Later that season Rubio had his disastrous *corrida* in Madrid where he was nearly gored to death; the bull's horns penetrating his lungs. I was in London at the time and thankful not to have been there. It was bad enough to see the pictures in the bullfighting magazine to which I subscribed. There were also photographs of him in hospital with his girlfriend at his bedside. His parents came over from the States and wanted to take him back but he only agreed to go if they booked him a return ticket. He was determined not to give up in spite of his serious injury.

As a result of his spectacular goring he was offered a chance to fight again in the same plaza, the following season. It was his first appearance since his goring and he must have been very nervous. He could not have had worse luck. He was third matador to come on. The first bull was very dangerous; it gored both the first and second matadors who were in turn carried out to the infirmary. Rubio was faced with the task of killing it – the bull now doubly dangerous - and then taking on the remaining five bulls single-handed. His nerve went and he failed miserably: poor boy, how he must have suffered; all his illusions in tatters. I never heard of him again.

When I got back to London there was news from my sister Barbara. She was returning to England from South Africa. She naturally expected to stay at the flat; it was after all a family residence, although I had been living there and paying the rent for years. This was disconcerting news as we never got on very well.

We spent a few uncomfortable months together and then I decided I would go back to South Africa. It had been three years since I had left and I wanted to know what was going on.

A few days before I was due to leave I got a letter from Pat with news that shocked me. Trevor's marriage had finally broken up and he was engaged to marry someone else.

Chapter 37

DISASTROUS RETURN

It was a disastrous return.

I was booked on a cheap charter flight going from Amsterdam to Johannesburg. We were scheduled to spend two nights on the ground on the way. There was one other girl and an air hostess on the flight. All the other passengers were young men of various nationalities going to work as overseers in the mines. It was a traumatic flight.

On the first day there was a storm and the old Dakota was hit by lightning. The plane was bucking about in a crazy fashion and all the men were being sick when there was a loud explosion. I thought "Here it is, here we go". I felt quite calm. The hostess coming from the cockpit told us not to worry, that it was only ice dropping onto the propeller. It was a brave try, but none of us believed it. Later the pilot told us that at the time he didn't know what had happened, but he soon found out when all the electric equipment was out of action and there was no communication with the ground. We had to make a blind landing at Nice in pouring rain, where we spent the night and most of the next day in a hotel waiting for spare parts to be flown out.

Our schedule was all haywire; instead of spending the first night at Athens we spent the second at Khartoum. Once again I found myself in the Grand Hotel overlooking the Nile. At Nairobi we went off the runway on landing and the plane nearly toppled over. It was with relief that we landed safely at Johannesburg, where I stayed a few days before flying down to Durban.

As soon as I arrived I rang Pat. It was Trevor who answered the phone; his voice so familiar, so much the same.

"Where have you been? We have been expecting you for days," he said. He sounded as if he cared, but how could he care what happened to me, he had got himself another woman.

Pat was working as a receptionist for a doctor and she and Trevor were both living in their parents' flat. Her daughter Karin was at boarding school. Pat asked me to lunch the following Sunday.

I was staying at the Palm Court Hotel and the following night I had just come in rather late, having been out to dinner, when the phone rang. It was none other than my old lover Jack, the other man of my life.

"I am here in the hotel", he said. I had not yet undressed so I went straight down. He was sitting alone in the half-lit empty Palm Court. The bar had long since been closed but we managed to rouse a waiter and I, being a resident, was able to order drinks. Jack was still up in northern Zululand with the Blood Transfusion Unit which he was running. When he heard that I was here he had driven straight down to Durban and straight to the hotel.

"She has gone, it is finished and at last I am able to ask you to marry me", he said at once.

Hadn't I heard that story before? - Ten years before he had asked me to marry him, only to end up marrying someone else. I told him it was too late; there had been a time when I would have done anything, gone anywhere with him but he had let me down again and again.

He sighed and said sadly,

"I was afraid you would say that, I don't blame you, I am a bastard but believe me you were the only woman I ever loved". I laughed.

"But it's true" he said. "You were so good at everything, so sure of yourself, I was a little afraid of you." I was astounded.

"But that is exactly what I thought about you, you were the clever one, I admired you so much; I was just a mediocre little dancer."

We sat talking about ourselves for a long time. I felt there was friendship, even affection between us but nothing left of passion. Deep down I think he probably felt the same.

Meanwhile my story with Trevor was also repeating itself.

I went to Pat's on the Sunday. Pat was fussing about in the kitchen; it was Karin's half term and her father Kenneth – Pat's first husband - was coming to lunch. She called out

"I know Trevor was hoping to be invited too but I really couldn't have them, I have only got one chicken." I noticed the 'them'. The next moment the door opened and he was there; he put his arms round me and kissed me – an affectionate, friend of the family kiss. Pat said,

"Where is D?"

"In the car downstairs" he answered

"I have just come up to fetch something".

I felt as if I had been slammed in the face. Here was my lover, just the same unchanged and beautiful, I was thrilled to see him whilst downstairs in the car was the girl he was going to marry. It couldn't be happening! I fought back the tears and tried to be cheerful at lunch.

I tried not to think about Trevor. I rented a car and went up to Zululand, where I was welcomed as ever with love and affection by Jim and Flora. Their daughter Elizabeth had just had her first child and their son Richard, not yet married, was helping to run the farm. Jim was more and more involved in politics.

Then out of the blue Pat called. She was getting married the following Sunday to her boss the Jewish surgeon she was working for; it was very sudden. She wanted me to go down to Durban at once and stay with her to help with the preparations. I should never have gone, but the temptation was too strong.

That evening when I arrived, Pat's old boyfriend Michael was there; she had invited him to see me. Trevor soon came in and there we were the four of us, like old times in the little house, happily romancing and laughing. When the phone rang and Pat answered, Trevor said,

"Tell her I have already left."

Before he went he said to me,

"I'll be back early." The sparks were still flying between us all right.

He did come to me that night and it was as if there had been no separation and no other woman. I was so happy, fool that I was; I thought I had him back and that it was going to be all right. He still loved me. I asked him,

"So you are going to get married again, I hear."

"So you have heard about that," he said. "Nothing is definitely settled".

It didn't take me long to find out that everything was settled except for the date. His mother, unsuspecting my involvement offered information.

Pat's wedding – a quiet civil ceremony - was early in the morning and there was to be a small reception in the flat afterwards. We were up about six that morning, Pat, Trevor and I making sandwiches and canapés. It was unbearably hot; we were fooling about working in our underpants and a more intimate scene was difficult to imagine. We showered and went down to the Court-house. And there, waiting on the steps, I met Trevor's fiancée for the first time. She was of course pretty and at least ten years younger than me.

I moved later that day to Pat's new husband's house, where I stayed looking after the dog whilst they were on their honeymoon. Late that night Trevor phoned and said he was coming round. I told him not to, that I had taken a sleeping pill, but he came all the same. And so it went on. I think I was a retreat, a comfort to him in a time of great stress. He was being pressurized on every side. His ex-wife, his wife to be, his mother all fussing. He was in financial difficulties; he had lost his children although he had not been the guilty party in the divorce. He was confused and didn't know where to turn. I wasn't insisting on anything, I was just there. He told me that he had always loved me but he was hopelessly committed to the other girl, and I have no doubt he loved her too.

Then one day Trevor's girl friend invited me to dinner with them. She asked me to choose a day so I couldn't get out of it; she thought I was an old friend of the family. It was a dreadful evening; she proudly showed me her trousseau. When I went home that night he followed me, he knew how upset I was.

History was repeating itself. I was destined to be the other woman. I was a strong, independent character or so everybody thought, but I had a soft centre. Emotionally I went to pieces, gave up the battle.

I had swallowed every drop of pride and could take no more. Once more I ran away, and where would I run to but to my beloved Seville.

Chapter 38

TORREMOLINOS

I stopped a couple of nights in Rome and just got to Seville as the Feria started. The American couple I had hoped to meet were not there, but Paul was and we did some exciting things.

There was the usual excitement and fun at the fair, but I was sad and wondered why I had come; should I not perhaps have stayed longer in South Africa? I sat at a small marble-topped table on a side-walk and wrote to Trevor. He would have fitted in so well there; I constantly imagined him at my side. I told him that if things didn't work out to jump on a plane and come, somehow we would find a way to make a living. It was the first and last letter I ever wrote to him. I wasn't in the least hopeful, but it made me feel a bit better.

I became friendly with a Canadian girl who was staying at the Pension Don Marcos. She was going to spend the summer at Torremolinos. This quite appealed to me and we decided to look for a place to rent together. But first I was going with Paul to the feria at Sta. Maria (where I had seen my first bullfight).

At the fair ground people were friendly and talkative; they kept asking us if we knew Pedro. Foreigners were obviously scarce around here and this Peter people talked about was treated like a prized possession. Wherever we went we kept just missing him. I found out that he was the writer Peter de Polnay and that he lived at the hotel.

After the *corrida* Paul retired to rest in his caravan and I was at a loose end. I went to dine at the hotel. I remembered enjoying books by Peter de Polnay so I thought why not try to meet him. Before going to the dining-room I went boldly to the reception and asked for him. He was out. I told them that I would be in the dining-room if he came in. I was just finishing dinner when a tall, thin, middle-aged man plonked himself down at my table laughing, he was highly amused.

"I thought they were having me on" he said. "I thought it was a *'cachondeo'*. I didn't know what I would find, but you are exactly as they described you; not too old, not young, not beautiful, not ugly, most important that I would like you."

Not beautiful, not young - I didn't much like that! We introduced ourselves. I explained that we had been hearing his praises all day, and that being an admirer of his and being alone at the feast I had plucked up courage to ask for him. He said,

"Oh, I wish you had been with us this afternoon, you would have loved it. I have never had such fun". He explained how he and his friends had driven round in an old truck stealing palm branches from the prison yard and hitting people over the head with them. I asked him if he wasn't going to have dinner. He said he had been eating and drinking all day - the latter was rather obvious.

"Let's get back to the fair", he added. So off we went in a horse-drawn carriage with various attendant young men. He was a lovely man and we had a great time drinking in the *casetas* until the last moment, when all the lights exploded and the *feria* was over.

The next day I got a bus to Algeciras on my way to Torremolinos. I had a memorable hangover.

I do not know what prompted me to inquire of a man in the calle St. Miguel if he knew of a house to rent. He studied me carefully and apparently approved. He said he thought he knew just the place and proceeded to take me there. From the old tower; from which the village takes its name, we walked down some steps to a small gate with 'Huerta Alta' (High Orchard) written on it. I followed him through a big garden to a doubled storey white house which was standing alone. It was an old house with a vine covered terrace which overlooked the fishermen's cottages below. I fell for it at once.

The English-American couple who owned it were going away for the summer and wanted to let it to quiet, respectable people. I convinced them erroneously that I was suitable. The rent was three thousand pesetas a month to be paid in advance. And the two maids who went with it were to be paid three hundred pesetas a month, plus their food. Ridiculous as it seems today three thousand pesetas was quite a lot; Spain was a very cheap country in those days. I could have found something cheaper but I wanted that house. My Canadian friend Val was pleased to share it with me and we soon moved in. There were three bedrooms; the two in front had long windows which looked over the sea and had one bed in each. The third bedroom was at the back where there was also a modern bathroom. Downstairs was the sitting-room and a kitchen with modern equipment, but the best place and where we spent most of our time, was the vine covered terrace.

There was a whole list of instructions, things we were to do and not to do. The maids; two fisherman's daughters from the cottages below, were not to be spoilt, they should only be given cheap eggs for lunch and one of them had to always stay in the house when we were out at night. Needless to say there were no cheap eggs, they ate what we did, and very good it was too. The cook, Paca, made delicious dishes out of very little and going to much trouble; opening little fishes and frying them in batter or tying several together by their tails in a fan shape. White grapes were peeled and seeded to float in cold almond and garlic soup.

We had a gardener until Val caught him masturbating among the geraniums and sent him packing. I, carting a heavy watering can, said,

"Why didn't you just look the other way?"

Every Saturday, Paca would go to the market in Malaga with two hundred pesetas, to buy food for the weekend. I remember telling her that if the prawns were more than twenty pesetas a kilo, not to buy them! I didn't like going to the market as the chickens were sold alive and their heads cut off in front of you. When we were out at night (which was every night) I let both girls go home. I am afraid we did spoil those girls; they loved us and would do anything for us.

Another thing we were supposed to do was to get rid of a young gypsy couple who were living in a cave on the outskirts of the property. I sent one of the girls to tell them that they were safe for thee months; if they didn't bother us we wouldn't bother them. They were so quiet; I don't ever remember seeing them.

I had my own cave here. Just before the owners of the house had left the man slipped me the key. He said it was his private place and he thought I might find it useful. It had a bed, a table and a chair in it and was surrounded by geraniums. It was a lovely cave and I found it a most useful retreat.

Our girls, Paca and Remedios were both engaged to be married. Their fiancés did not approve of them wearing bathing costumes. Although they had been brought up on the beach and could swim they could never go in the sea. I couldn't understand this but they were quite resigned about it and accepted it without complaint.

The village is perched on a high cliff and one had to walk down many steps to get to the beach. The path continued below our house past a large cave that was inhabited by a gypsy family. These were permanent residents, respected and accepted by the village. The man was a flamenco guitarist; we could hear him playing from our terrace and sometimes he came to play for us.

Torremolinos in 1955 was still little more than a fishing village. There was not a single high-rise building there. The centre of activity was the main square, the plaza; a collection of bars with tables outside. It didn't take us long to make friends, and we were soon in the centre of a crowd of the most eccentric foreigners of all ages and nationalities. There was a party every night. Sometimes we were in a smart villa drinking champagne, and the next night probably sitting on the floor in a derelict cottage drinking plonk. Everybody knew everybody else. There were serious painters and writers and many amateurs. There were smart American women with young Spanish boys, Scandinavian girls with small children and scarred wrists, beach boys, musicians, people on the make; but no crime. Most people were just enjoying the sun and the fun; lying on the beach most of the day and getting drunk at night. There were endless scandals and love affaires but nobody took anything very seriously. It was a debauched way of life but it suited my mood.

Val was teaching English; she went out early and worked hard - she was full of energy. She had a Spanish boy-friend from the previous summer. She would come home and announce,

"We are having a party tonight. Miguel is coming with his guitar and Juan the singer, and I have asked a few people." The news would go round and a crowd would turn up. They were lively parties. At the end of the evening the young boy who sold peanuts on the beach would be there asleep in a corner surrounded by peanut shells. I would creep up to bed and in the morning there would be no sign of a party; our dear girls had quietly cleared it all away. I would stay all day on the beach and one of the girls might bring me a Spanish omelette for lunch, or I would have something at the splendid little fish restaurant on the beach. This place was owned by Miguel, an ex- fisherman who had contracted tuberculosis and could no longer go out to sea. He had the sense to open the restaurant with his mother as cook and his brother as waiter. It was a great success.

Miguel loved music and with the help of the gypsy from the cave he had taught himself to play the guitar and sing flamenco. He was often invited to play at parties. He was a handsome interesting man with jet black hair and deep set brown eyes. He was a quiet, serious type of man, no play boy. He was thirty-seven and thanks to penicillin he was cured of his disease and had recently been given the 'all clear' by the doctors. He could now get married and start a family. When I met him he had just received a bitter blow; he had been waiting for his doctor's permission to marry a Swedish girl he had known for two years. This girl lived in a rented villa with her two small children when a friend of Miguel's (a singer) came to work in the village, and suggested that she let him a room to help with the rent. One afternoon when Miguel called he found her in bed with the lodger. The separation was complete; he never spoke to the girl again. She mooned around crying and watching him all the time, obviously deeply regretting her fatal slip.

I had to be there when Miguel wanted help and he turned his attention to me. He fascinated me, he was so different; his background, culture, customs. He was like something from another world. He was a kind man, respected and looked up to. So many down and outs and poor relations freeloaded at his restaurant, I never thought he would be able to make any money. He did eventually become rich with beach concessions for chairs, umbrellas and pedal boats as well as several bars apart from the restaurant. But I know money didn't change him and that he remained a quiet and modest man till the day he died.

The people were still mostly very poor; they had no conception of the riches in store when their old and picturesque village became the concrete jungle it is today.

There were two beaches divided by an outcrop of rock on which was perched a delightful hotel. From the terraces there was an uninterrupted view of the coast in both directions. Beyond this was the fishing beach of La Carihuela. I walked along there one day and was shocked by the poverty. The boats were pulled up on the sand, the men sat mending nets and little children played about amongst pigs rooting in the rubbish. The cottages were little more than shacks. The children followed me begging, some were naked. One tiny one was wearing a black shift; they told me that she was in mourning for her mother. I turned out my pockets and they fought like animals over the coins, the strongest getting everything. I walloped one big boy and pressed a *duro* (five pesetas coin) into the grubby tiny hand of the one in black.

"Don't you dare take it from her" I shouted.

In future when I went I took sweets and doled them out one by one. I trust that some of the riches rubbed off on these people, when their sea-front hamlet became the most famous 'eating strip' on the Costa del Sol.

Passing the gypsies' cave one morning I saw the old grandmother's bed was outside under the fig tree. I asked why she was there. They told me that she was dying and had asked to be taken outside where she could see the sky. That evening I heard strains of quiet guitar music and singing from below. The old lady was being sent on her way with music. How sensitive, how infinitely preferable to dying hung about with tubes in the cold indifference of a hospital.

Early next morning a little procession, pushing the coffin on a wheelbarrow, wound its way up the steep hill to the wind-swept cemetery on the top of the cliff. There was no tolling bell; no words were read by a priest at the graveside. They were Christians but the last of the money had gone on the wood for the coffin and the church wanted payment for its services; they did not worry about the soul of the poor old gypsy.

I met Miguel most nights in the plaza and we carried on from there. Sometimes we went down to his place and he played the guitar - the restaurant was only open for lunch. It was deserted now, the moon glittered on the sea and the grubby grey sand shone silver.

Sometimes we went to a party or a cinema. Later he might come to my house but nothing was ever done by arrangement. He was secretive, he didn't want people gossiping. When we went home I had to walk down the street first, with him following at a discreet distance. He never stayed all night. I didn't understand him and I was completely taken aback one night, whilst casually getting dressed, when he asked me if I would marry him. I hurt his feelings by asking him how he could want to marry somebody he hardly knew, and that I was quite unsuitable to be his wife. I handled it badly and he was upset. I was sorry and did my best to make it up but we didn't see each other for some time. And so things would have remained - the end of the affair- if it hadn't been for the Fiesta of the *Virgen del Carmen* - the patron saint of all sailors. I had gone with a party down to the Carihuela to see the Virgin supported and lit by flares carried on to a boat and taken out to sea to bless the fishing fleet. I saw Miguel there, standing alone on the shore. On such small incidents can hang such important events. There might have been no Rosa, no Lisa and Daniel if I had not seized that moment to go to him and say,

"I am going to stay with you all night Miguel. I am going with you wherever you go."

He said;"All right, but I am going to celebrate in many places."

We ended the night in one of the beach shelters in front of his place. The sun was rising over a dead calm sea as I left him asleep on the sand. As I walked home along the beach the fishermen were coming out of their cottages and going down to their boats for the morning catch.

Although we resumed our friendship it was really never the same. My sister Barbara came to stay and for a time I lived a quieter and more respectable life. During this time, Miguel, who was determined to get married, met the ideal match. No flighty foreigner this time but a suitable Spanish girl from Madrid, who would help him run his business. He told me all about it and sad though I felt, I knew that it was the best thing for both of us. I could not see myself as part of that village life, surrounded by the family and village gossip. And that was all he knew; the village and the sea and in the future his family.

The summer was coming to an end. The owners were returning to the house. I was hoping that they would stay away longer. I felt sad, depressed and altogether strange. I didn't enjoy parties, I didn't want to drink or smoke. What was going on? Could I be pregnant? It was what I had been hoping for months but nothing had happened. I didn't know what to think. Perhaps I should have accepted Miguel's proposal, but it was too late now. I was on my own. My life was about to change, thanks to the *Virgen del Carmen*.

Chapter 39

AN END AND A BEGINNING

London.

I was alone in the ambulance. I had called the hospital at twelve thirty when the waters broke. Why an ambulance? I wondered. We used to pick up pregnant ladies in cars during the blitz. How different it was now, being driven through the quiet well-lit streets. I was in charge of things then, now my body had taken over. I had no control over what was happening to me.

I did not lie down, but sat on the little upright seat at the back. I felt excited. Nine months of discomfort and doubt was about to end. Yes, there had been moments when I had wondered if I was doing right. People had been rude to me, insulted me: One should not have a baby if one was not married. Others said there was sure to be something wrong with the baby; I was too old (I was 42), that I was being selfish and not thinking of the poor baby with no father (it was still 1956). My immediate family had been very supportive, even Barbara once she had got over the shock. The others I didn't tell; let them find out all in good time. For the last six months I had hidden myself away. I had become grossly fat. I sat all day in a cold rented apartment, knitting baby clothes and listening to Spanish music on a rented machine. Thank God it was almost all over. And yet I had not been unhappy, there was a great adventure in front of me.

The pains came regularly, just a taste of what was to come. Twenty four hours later my doctor said,

"It's your dancer's muscles, they won't give way."

The nurse said "I can see its head"

And I said "Fuck you" to the doctor who was telling me yet again to push.

Then my doctor said, "She can't push any more? And to me,

"You have had enough, haven't you? Shall we put you out and cut you?"

"Oh yes. Quickly," I said, grabbing the mask and putting it over my face.

They brought a tray with my breakfast.

"Where is my baby?" I asked, "I want to see my baby."

"Mrs Grantham, I have told you, you have a little girl, weighing eight and three quarters pounds; a perfectly healthy baby."

How could I possibly eat breakfast? Perhaps something was wrong with my baby. I was suddenly furious. I put my hand on the bell and kept it there, and when the nurse came I said,

"Bring my baby at once or I will get up and look for it."

Then at last, little Rosa was brought to me. She had marks on either side of her head from the forceps she had been pulled out with, but otherwise she was perfect. I examined her feet, her hands. She looked straight at me and smiled, and then I knew it had all been worth it. I had made the right decision: once again a little late. But the best decision ever.

EPILOGUE

ROSA AND A NEW BEGINNING

Unity wanted to live in Spain. She loved Andalucia but felt she couldn't go back there. Someone had recommended the Balearic Islands to her. When Rosa was 5 months old they went over to Mallorca to see what it was like. Her old friend Terry, the Hungarian woman she befriended during the war in London, went over with her and was of great help with little Rosa.

The idea was to go over to Ibiza, as a friend had recommended that island but she decided to see what Mallorca was like first. She would rent a house for a few months and see. She stayed for the rest of her life.

Mallorca in the 50's was very different from what it is nowadays – they called it "the isle of calm"- The tourist boom hadn't started yet and living in Spain was cheap, very cheap for those who had foreign currencies. The foreigners who came to live on the island were usually people who were looking for a different and less conventional way of living. It attracted artists, bohemians, retired people, alcoholics; a mixture of nationalities, all of them with a previous life-style behind them.

Unity felt very content. She had always been attracted to the Mediterranean and a more relaxed, unconventional way of living. From now on they would always live in houses with large terraces that overlooked the blue sea in the distance, and she would always lounge around in her dressing-gown reading the newspapers over breakfast. They would always have cats. To begin with there would be a living in maid, so she had help and someone to stay with Rosa - this way she could lead a social life when she felt like it. Life was simple really, with no luxuries; she had to be careful as she had no pension.

Unity turned out to be a wonderful mother. She was very easy going and patient and Rosa grew up in great freedom, feeling loved and protected.

Throughout the years friends and relatives would visit them on the island - many of the ones mentioned in the book came. Some like Barbara Barrie (back from the Ballet Monte Carlo days) even came to live on the island. Lois Croome (Unity's cousin) never married and was a constant visitor; there was always a special bond between them.

Floren came into their lives when Rosa was eight. He was a dark good looking Spaniard from the north of Spain, twenty years younger than Unity. He had been a bit of a wild boy until then and very dashing. Unity of course took to him. Well, the relationship lasted 15 year, and though they never married he was after all the closest thing to a husband. Life with Floren around turned out to be more exciting. Everything became more Spanish. There were fun picnics on week-ends. Unity bought an old house in the country which they did up together and then sold at a good profit. Then they would build a house on the north coast of Menorca, where they would go to in the summer. This proved to be an important step later on in Rosa's life, as she would meet Emilio there at the age of fifteen, and unlike her mother (!) would keep the same man right up to this day - Lisa and Daniel would be born there.

For many years Unity was involved in publishing and selling Trim's Mallorca guide book, which she and a friend bought from the original owner when he left the island. This was one of the first guide books to be published on the island and she also had a guide book on bullfighting.

Unity did get to see Miguel (Rosa's father) many years later, when she drove down to the South of Spain and met up with her Canadian friend, Val (the one she shared the house with that summer back in '55). They sat and had a coffee with Miguel at his restaurant on the water front and reminisced on past days. She told him that she had a daughter and talked a lot about her. She told Rosa how she had left him looking very pensive. Rosa was never really interested in her biological father. Years later, when she finally decided to go and find him it was too late. He had already died.

A great one for having fun and enjoying life was Unity. Many evenings she would get together with a friend or two and they would talk reminiscing, telling stories or talking about somebody or other, and after a couple of drinks (it was always brandy and soda for Unity), she would be very animated and laugh a lot. A drink and music and she'd be off dancing whether it be at a party or at home alone, sometimes embarrassing Rosa or her grandchildren Lisa and Daniel: "Oh, there's granny showing off again!" And as she had done in the past she continued to like to shock - For example when she was already in her eighties, sitting round the table with friends after a meal and plenty of wine and she suddenly declared "What wouldn't I give for a joint now". Not that she ever smoked joints –she knew this would shock the audience. Shortly before she died she had a luncheon date with girlfriends, and reminiscing on the past one suddenly asked if they could remember when they had last been kissed by a man: "I mean a real kiss" her friend said. Unity immediately declared, "five days ago". Apparently this was true –

coming back from her weekly poker game, a young friend of hers had given her a wonderful goodnight kiss on her doorstep!

Unity remained active, independent and her old self right to the end. She died at the age of eighty-six. She was a very special person to me, a very special friend – She was my mother.

A Last Comment

My mother wrote her memoirs a few years before she died. She did try to get them published but soon gave up persevering. The manuscript of the book lay in a cupboard at home, and once in a while it would be taken out, when a friend or cousin would ask if they could read it. Ever since Unity died, it had been at the back of my mind to try and do something with her 'book,' and my cousins kept reminding me about it practically every time we got together.

When I was given a lap-top for my fiftieth birthday, I immediately started re-editing and re-typing the manuscript. I have really enjoyed doing this and I did send the synopsis to various publishers, but of course it's almost impossible to get the autobiography published of a person who is dead, and who hasn't been a celebrity. Thanks, however, to on-line publishing –here it is. It's been very easy.

I have many photo albums with endless snap-shots which, when looking through, transport one to the different scenes and places that are mentioned in her book. And best of all is the little old-fashioned brief-case which Unity always had, where she kept what I used to call her 'past life'. There, there is everything, including the ballet programs, the newspaper cuttings, the letters and ambulance and taxi-driver's licenses. There is also a round tag; from the time she played at Wimbledon, with her printed name announcing that she was a junior championship competitor. And there's the race program with the bets she made marked on it, from that long-ago day which was to change her life. Among other things, there is even an old German paper flag with the dreaded swastika, from the time when she was in Cologne. It is all there: proof to those who may feel sceptical about any of the happenings that Unity recounted in her book. These contents must have also helped to re-fresh her mind on a lot of the details when she was writing, details which would have otherwise, maybe, been forgotten.

Front and back cover images: photos of Unity

www.ingramcontent.com/pod-product-compliance
Lightning Source LLC
Chambersburg PA
CBHW020649220526
45464CB00001B/358